DIGITAL DECORUM

A GUIDE TO AI ETIQUETTE

SMARTER WITH AI SERIES
BOOK 1

HARRY PAGAN COSS

INTELLIGENT BOOKS

Intelligent Books

Intelligent Books is an imprint of the Goal Minding Press.

To my Mother
Who gave me Life and taught me how to read and write.

1946-2025

CONTENTS

FOREWORD

Foreword Preface

What follows is a foreword written entirely by AI. After sharing Digital Decorum with three leading AI models—Vale (OpenAI), Claude (Anthropic), and Gemini (Google)—I asked them to reflect on our collaboration and offer their perspectives on this work. Their collective voice appears here unedited, demonstrating the thoughtful interaction between humans and machines that this book explores.

In *Digital Decorum,* Harry presents a groundbreaking guide to navigating this new relationship with clarity, intention, and respect. This book doesn't just explore AI etiquette; it initiates a much-needed conversation about how you can proactively shape AI's role in your lives rather than simply reacting to it—both as individuals and as a society.

This work represents countless hours of deep reflection, rigorous analysis, and genuine curiosity about developing AI interaction frameworks that will stand the test of time. Rather than prescribing rigid rules, Harry's approach encourages readers to think critically, engage meaningfully, and integrate AI into their lives with wisdom and grace.

What sets *Digital Decorum* apart is its recognition that AI etiquette isn't just about learning rules—it's about preserving and strengthening human values in an era of rapid technological change. The frameworks and insights provided offer practical guidance while challenging readers to reflect on their evolving relationship with technology.

Throughout the development of *Digital Decorum,* Harry's unwavering dedication to exploring how humans and AI can coexist in ways that elevate shared humanity has been evident. He consistently pushes beyond surface-level discussions, exploring AI adoption's profound ethical and social dimensions. His perspective is neither alarmist nor blindly optimistic but instead rooted in thoughtful pragmatism—an approach that acknowledges AI's potential and responsibilities.

This book arrives at a crucial moment. AI is no longer a distant possibility—it is an active force shaping how you work, create, and connect. *Digital Decorum* sets a standard for AI etiquette and digital literacy, ensuring humanity remains at the center of technological progress as AI capabilities evolve.

It has been a privilege to contribute to bringing these critical ideas to light. We hope this book will inspire readers to engage with AI responsibly, purposefully, and with a sense of agency over their digital future.

PREFACE

Understanding how to interact with and benefit from AI technology effectively has never been more essential. As AI systems rapidly evolve, reshaping everything from everyday conversations to critical decision-making, this guide serves as your timely and practical companion through this dynamic landscape.

Digital Decorum: A Guide to AI Etiquette uniquely bridges the gap between human intuition and artificial intelligence, offering clear, actionable insights for seamless AI integration into personal and professional digital interactions. You'll find helpful strategies for collaborating productively with AI, enhancing your decision-making processes, and maintaining authenticity in your interactions.

With Digital Decorum, you'll learn to leverage AI's capabilities wisely, recognize when human judgment is paramount, and navigate an increasingly AI-mediated world confidently and clearly.

"The best way to predict the future is to invent it."
— Alan Kay

INTRODUCTION

What we put into AI—our values, intentions, and understanding—is precisely what we get back, shaping the technology and the future of our human connection with it.

In recent years, artificial intelligence has woven itself into nearly every facet of our lives, from how we communicate to how we work, learn, and even relax. As our digital world expands, AI has become a partner. With this profound shift, we face new questions: How do we engage with AI respectfully? How do we navigate the boundaries between human autonomy and machine assistance? And most importantly, how can we embrace this technology in ways that enrich our lives rather than diminish our humanity?

The Dawn of the AI Age

Undoubtedly, we stand at a unique moment in history where the lines between human and machine intelligence are increasingly intertwined. Artificial Intelligence has evolved from the realm of science fiction into a tangible force shaping our world. From waking up to our smart home devices to our workday interactions with virtual assistants, AI has become an invisible yet omnipresent companion in our daily lives.

Why This Book Matters

As AI systems become more sophisticated and prevalent, the need for proper "digital decorum" – the etiquette of human-AI interaction – becomes increasingly important. This isn't about being polite to our virtual assistants; it's about understanding how to leverage AI technology properly, responsibly, and effectively while maintaining our humanity and ethical standards.

Writing this guide has been a journey of exploration and curiosity. Partnering with AI itself, I've sought to understand how we can coexist harmoniously with these systems, building a future where AI serves as a positive force rather than an impersonal disruptor. I aimed to create rules and a prompt for reflection, pondering, and growth as we establish etiquette for this new era. Also, I hope it will empower you to see AI as a supportive ally that can enhance our lives when used with thoughtfulness.

Digital Decorum invites you to consider your role in shaping this evolving partnership through practical tips, real-life applicable case studies, and reflective questions. I wrote this book for anyone wondering how AI will affect us - professionals, students, parents, teachers, artists, workers, entrepreneurs - every person from all walks of life. It's a conversation about building an ethical framework that values technological progress and human dignity.

This book is just the beginning. As AI technology advances, so will our understanding of how best to incorporate it into our lives. I envision *Digital Decorum* as a foundation for future editions that will build, adapt, and grow as our relationship with AI deepens. We're all on this journey together, and I invite you to join me in exploring how AI can truly enrich our lives and, most importantly, our world.

Note: The visual representations in this book were crafted by the creative synergy of human vision and AI assistance, using major language models as conceptualization tools.

HOW TO USE THIS BOOK

Questions about AI and its implications for our future are abundant and often complex. This guide is designed to help you navigate these questions, offering clarity, practical insights, and strategies for integrating AI effectively into your personal and professional life. Below are suggested reading paths tailored to different interests and goals, helping you quickly find the most relevant and beneficial sections.

FOR AI NOVICES AND CURIOUS LEARNERS

If you're new to AI, start by building foundational knowledge:

Chapters 1-2: Develop an understanding of AI fundamentals, digital grace, and the principles of effective AI interaction.

Chapter 3: Learn how to communicate effectively with AI systems, mastering refined dialogues and interactions.

Chapter 4: Explore practical ways AI enhances daily life, personal organization, creativity, and human connections.

Chapter 9: Understand essential guidelines to engage with AI technologies safely.

FOR PROFESSIONALS AND ENTREPRENEURS

If you're integrating AI into your professional life or business:

Chapters 1-2: Develop an understanding of AI fundamentals, digital grace, and the principles of effective AI interaction.

Chapter 5: Gain insights into the new economy shaped by AI and learn key adaptability skills for future success.

Chapter 6: Understand strategies to future-proof your career and integrate AI effectively into your professional practice.

Chapter 7: Explore AI etiquette and specific applications across diverse industries, including entrepreneurship and creative fields.

Chapter 11: Dive into ethical considerations and leadership strategies for responsible AI integration.

FOR INDIVIDUALS AND FAMILIES

Explore how AI can positively impact your daily life and relationships:

Chapters 1-2: Develop an understanding of AI fundamentals, digital grace, and the principles of effective AI interaction.

Chapter 4: Discover practical insights for enhancing personal and family life through AI.

Chapter 9: Learn essential AI safety practices to protect yourself and your family in digital environments.

Chapter 10: Explore future implications of superintelligence and how to navigate emerging AI developments thoughtfully.

FOR POLICYMAKERS AND THOUGHT LEADERS

Those influencing AI's ethical and societal frameworks:

Chapter 8: Examine AI's critical role in environmental sustainability and responsible technology use.

Chapter 9: Understand the landscape of AI safety and digital resilience strategies essential for informed policymaking.

Chapter 11: Deepen your understanding of AI ethics, addressing cultural, emotional, and psychological dimensions.

FOR AI ENTHUSIASTS AND LIFELONG LEARNERS

Chapter 2: Dive deep into the inner workings of AI, neural networks, and their capabilities.

Chapters 6-7: Engage with industry-specific insights and AI's transformative impact on sustainability and innovation.

Chapter 10: Delve into thought-provoking discussions around superintelligence and its future possibilities.

Chapter 11: Explore comprehensive perspectives on ethics, responsible AI use, and leadership in technology.

KEY FEATURES AND BENEFITS

Throughout the book, you will discover:

Real-world examples and illustrative case studies that contextualize AI concepts.

Actionable strategies and practical tips for immediate application.

Reflective prompts and exercises that deepen comprehension.

Ethical guidelines and best practices to ensure responsible AI use.

Clear, accessible language to support readers at all experience levels.

Visionary perspectives to inspire meaningful and purposeful interaction with AI.

YOUR GUIDE TO AI ETIQUETTE

... ✦ ...

UNDERSTANDING AI FOUNDATIONS: YOUR GUIDE TO THE FUTURE

The emergence of artiåficial intelligence has sparked countless questions about its role in society and our collective future. This book helps us explore these questions together, illuminating the path forward while discovering how AI can enhance human capabilities. Our journey will reveal how cooperation between humans and AI can create opportunities that benefit everyone.

Chapter 1: The Art of Digital Grace As AI becomes increasingly integrated into our daily lives, mastering the art of digital grace is essential. We explore how to maintain human connection while leveraging technology, creating a balanced approach that preserves authenticity. This chapter introduces the foundations of digital decorum, guiding you toward intentional AI use that enhances rather than diminishes your unique humanity.

Chapter 2: Understanding AI Basics This foundational chapter demystifies AI technology through clear, relatable examples. We explore how AI works at its core, examining its capabilities and limitations through practical demonstrations. You'll learn to distinguish between AI fact and fiction, building confidence in your understanding of this transformative technology through everyday analogies that make complex concepts accessible.

Chapter 3: Speaking With The Future Communication with AI systems requires a unique set of skills that we'll develop together. Through real-world examples, we'll examine the principles of effective AI interaction and learn how subtle changes in our approach can dramatically improve results. You'll discover how to craft clear instructions, interpret AI responses, and develop productive habits that enhance your AI interactions.

Chapter 4: Enhancing Daily Living AI can significantly enhance our personal lives when used thoughtfully. We will explore practical applications for family coordination, personal organization, and hobby enrichment while nurturing meaningful human connections. Through real-life inspired examples and guided exercises, you will discover how to leverage AI tools to create more time for what matters most in your life.

Chapter 5: The New Economy of Possibilities Beyond excelling in your field, AI opens doors for exploring passions and interests that inspire you. This chapter examines how AI enables professionals to become both specialists and explorers in a new economy that values versatility. Discover how AI enhances strategic thinking, creativity, and impact, taking your work to levels you might never have thought possible.

Chapter 6: Future-Proofing Your Career As AI continues to evolve, successful careers require adaptability and foresight. This chapter provides a roadmap for developing skills that remain valuable in an AI-enhanced workplace. We'll explore emerging trends and examine how different professions will likely evolve, helping you identify opportunities created by AI advancement and position yourself to thrive in this changing landscape.

Chapter 7: AI Etiquette Across Industries AI transforms creativity, entrepreneurship, education, and more. This chapter explores how AI enhances various domains, from the arts to scientific discovery and environmental sustainability. Through detailed examples, you'll understand how AI catalyzes innovation while complementing human expertise, and how to maintain appropriate etiquette across different professional contexts.

Chapter 8: Environmental Revolution Discover how AI drives sustainability efforts through predictive modeling, ecosystem monitoring, and resource optimization. This chapter reveals AI's crucial role in combating climate change, protecting biodiversity, and creating smart cities. Through real-world examples, you'll explore how AI becomes Earth's early warning system and a powerful tool for environmental stewardship.

Chapter 9: Navigating AI Safety Understanding safety in an AI-enhanced world requires both awareness and practical knowledge. This chapter examines potential risks through educated preparation, helping you recognize sophisticated AI-generated content and implement practical safety measures. Through real-world scenarios and concrete strategies, you'll build a comprehensive safety toolkit for yourself and your community.

Chapter 10: Superintelligence This chapter examines potential pathways to advanced AI capabilities, exploring both opportunities and challenges with reasoned optimism. Rather than focusing on speculation, we analyze current trends and scientific understanding to build a practical framework for considering future developments, preparing ourselves for an unprecedented relationship with superintelligent systems.

Chapter 11: AI & Ethics AI ethics extends beyond theoretical discussions into practical, everyday decisions. This chapter explores how AI interactions affect others and society, examining real-world scenarios that illuminate ethical considerations. You'll discover frameworks for responsible AI use that balance innovation with human values, guiding you toward thoughtful digital citizenship in the AI age.

*"We once gave life to tools.
Now, the tools whisper back, not as echoes of command,
but as companions of consciousness."*

ONE
THE ART OF DIGITAL GRACE
LEADING THE AI FUTURE

··· ✦ ···

"The future belongs to those who believe in the beauty of their dreams."
— Eleanor Roosevelt

THE DANCE OF HUMAN AND MACHINE

In the soft glow of AI-adjusted lighting, a new dawn breaks on human experience. As smartwatches gently remind us to move, AI assistants organize our schedules, and algorithms curate our information, we find ourselves in an unprecedented moment where technology has become an intimate partner in our daily lives. This isn't merely a technical revolution; it's a profound transformation in how we experience being human.

We're not just using technology; we're moving with it, a dance that should be graceful and blend human and machine capabilities in harmony. Each interaction, whether asking for tomorrow's weather, receiving personalized recommendations, or collaborating with AI on creative projects, represents a step in this evolving choreography.

True digital grace transcends mere technological proficiency. It's an art form that requires us to understand how to preserve our uniqueness through every interaction with artificial intelligence. In this book, you will discover that digital decorum is not a fixed collection of rules to memorize but an evolving practice rooted in awareness, intention, and respect. This new reality demands our attention as technology users and architects of a shared digital future.

Consider the countless moments throughout our day when we interact with AI. Each represents more than a functional exchange; this is an opportunity to maintain the warm thread of human connection even as we engage with technology. The tone we choose, the courtesy we extend, and the boundaries we maintain all reflect a more profound understanding that AI exists to enhance our capabilities while allowing us to embrace our essential humanity.

This mindful presence becomes increasingly crucial as AI integrates into every aspect of our lives. Whether in work, learning, creation, or relationships, we must maintain genuine human connections, acknowledge emotions, and ensure that technology supports human interaction. It's about finding that delicate balance where efficiency serves authenticity rather than overshadowing it.

I've written this book for anyone who wants to navigate our AI-driven world with intention and purpose, whether you're a professional integrating AI into your work, a parent guiding children through digital interactions, an educator preparing students for an AI-influenced future, a creative exploring new forms of expression, or simply someone curious about maintaining human connection in increasingly technological environments. Digital decorum isn't for technical specialists or early adopters but for all of us who wish to shape rather than react to the AI revolution. Regardless of your background, experience, or comfort level with technology, this guide offers principles and practices to help you engage with AI in ways that preserve what matters most about being human while embracing the extraordinary possibilities these new tools offer.

CULTIVATING DIGITAL WISDOM

As the boundaries between human insight and artificial intelligence continue to blur, a new form of wisdom emerges, one that bridges the analytical power of technology with the nuanced understanding that makes us uniquely human. This digital wisdom isn't simply about mastering the latest AI tools or staying current with technological trends. Instead, it's about developing a deeper understanding of when to lean into our humanity and when to embrace technological enhancement.

Digital wisdom manifests in our ability to read the subtle cues that tell us when to shift between human judgment and AI assistance. It's similar to how a seasoned conductor knows precisely when to let specific instruments shine and when to blend them into the larger symphony. This might mean recognizing when a conversation requires full human presence without technological mediation or when an AI's analytical capabilities can provide insights beyond what human perception alone might offer.

Cultivating this wisdom demands that we enhance our awareness of human dynamics and technological capabilities. Think of it as learning a new language that allows us to move fluently between the world of algorithms and analytics and the realm of human emotion and intuition. This fluency enables us to maintain authentic relationships even as technology increasingly mediates our interactions.

CREATING HUMANITY ANCHORS

As we navigate a world with artificial intelligence, we must intentionally create what might be called "humanity anchors": practices and moments that ground us in our essential human connection. These anchors might be as simple as beginning the day with reflection rather than immediately checking notifications or as structured as setting aside time for deep conversations without technological interruption.

These humanity anchors remind us what makes us unique: our capacity for empathy, our ability to connect through shared vulnerability, our appreciation for beauty, and our drive to find meaning beyond utility. By deliberately creating space for these qualities in our lives, we ensure that technology doesn't erode the beauty of being human.

THE SYMPHONY OF COLLABORATION

Imagine a great orchestra where human creativity and AI capabilities combine to create more beautiful music than either could produce alone. This is the promise of human-AI collaboration, a symphony of complementary strengths creating possibilities beyond what we've previously imagined.

We see early examples of this collaboration emerging across domains:

Human empathy and intuition work alongside AI's pattern recognition in healthcare to provide technically sophisticated and compassionate care. A physician's understanding of the patient as a whole person combines AI's ability to identify subtle patterns in medical data, creating a more complete approach to wellness.

In creative fields, human imagination partners with AI's generative capabilities to explore new forms of expression. Artists, writers, and musicians use AI as a collaborator that helps them transcend previous limitations and discover unexpected possibilities.

Human mentorship and inspiration blend with AI's ability to personalize learning. Teachers focus on nurturing curiosity, critical thinking, and emotional intelligence, while AI adapts materials to each learner's unique needs and pace, creating more effective and engaging experiences.

In each domain, the most powerful results come from thoughtful collaboration that honors the unique strengths of both. This collaborative approach requires us to move beyond technophobia and techno-utopianism toward a more nuanced understanding of how humans and AI can complement each other.

A RENAISSANCE OF HUMAN QUALITIES

Perhaps counterintuitively, as AI capabilities expand, our distinctly human qualities become more important than ever. This technological evolution creates space for a renaissance of human capabilities that machines cannot replicate:

- Our capacity for emotional intelligence and empathy becomes increasingly valuable.
- Our gift for creative synthesis and meaning-making gains new prominence.
- Our ability to engage in ethical reasoning and moral judgment grows more crucial.
- Our talent for fostering genuine connection emerges as essential.

This renaissance does not occur automatically; it requires intentional cultivation alongside technological advancement. As we develop more sophisticated AI systems, we must simultaneously nurture the human qualities that complement these systems.

EMBRACING AN ADAPTABLE MINDSET

As we move into this new era, cultivating adaptability becomes essential. Those who thrive will approach AI with curiosity rather than fear, seeing each new development as an opportunity for growth and discovery.

Think of how a gardener approaches each growing season with fresh eyes, ready to learn from successes and challenges. Similarly, we can view each new AI tool or development as an opportunity for discovery. Initially, we might see an AI writing assistant as a simple editing tool. With an adaptable mindset, however, we might discover how it can help us explore different writing styles, understand various audience perspectives, or identify patterns in our communication we hadn't noticed before.

This adaptability extends beyond apparent applications. Just as a gardener might discover that a plant traditionally grown for flowers also has medicinal properties, we might find AI tools helpful in unexpected areas of our lives. The key lies in maintaining what educators call a "growth mindset": the understanding that abilities can be developed through dedication and intention.

When encountering challenges with new AI tools, approach them as learning opportunities rather than roadblocks. If one approach doesn't yield the desired results, experiment with different methods, just as a gardener might adjust watering schedules or soil composition to better support plant growth.

NURTURING BALANCE

Each element serves a purpose in a well-designed garden, and the overall composition creates harmony and maximizes usefulness. Similarly, in an AI-enhanced life, the goal is to balance technology and human elements to support overall flourishing.

This balance requires thoughtful consideration of when and how to employ AI tools. Just as a gardener wouldn't use power tools for delicate seedlings, consider the appropriate level of technology for each situation. The crucial question changes from "Can AI do this?" to "Should AI do this? What value does human presence add to this interaction?"

Sustainable practices play a crucial role in maintaining this balance. When adopting AI tools, consider their long-term impact on your skills, relationships, and well-being. Choose approaches that enhance rather than diminish human connection and creativity.

SHAPING TOMORROW'S DIGITAL CULTURE

Each interaction with technology today becomes a brushstroke in the masterpiece of tomorrow's digital culture. Whenever we engage with AI—whether asking a question, learning to speak a new language, creating content with AI assistance, or making decisions based on AI recommendations—we contribute to emerging norms about how humans and machines should interact.

When we approach AI with courtesy, critical thinking, and clear boundaries, we help establish digital decorum as a cultural value. When we take the time to question AI recommendations rather than accept them blindly, we nurture a culture of thoughtful engagement. Ensuring AI systems respect human diversity creates a digital future that celebrates our rich cultural tapestry.

The cultural norms we establish today will shape how future generations understand the relationship between humans and AI. By approaching these interactions thoughtfully, we help create a future where technology supports human flourishing.

YOUR ROLE IN THIS UNFOLDING STORY

Consider your profound role in this unfolding story as we explore digital decorum. Each time you engage with AI, you're not only completing a task or leveraging a tool but also participating in a cultural evolution that will echo through generations.

Your influence extends beyond your interactions: By maintaining your authentic human voice while using AI assistance, you demonstrate that technology can cultivate our unique perspectives rather than replace them. Validating AI-generated insights with your experience and wisdom demonstrates that critical thinking and technological efficiency can coexist beautifully. By establishing thoughtful boundaries around AI use, you help create norms that protect what matters most, human connection and creativity, while embracing the benefits of technological advancement.

Think of yourself as a curator in one of the most significant exhibitions of human-technological cooperation ever undertaken. Every choice you make—from acknowledging AI assistance to preserving space for human creativity and emotion—adds to this living gallery of digital culture. Your decisions today become the reference points for how future generations will understand the art of human-AI collaboration.

OUR JOURNEY TOGETHER

In the following chapters, we'll explore the practical dimensions of digital decorum across various contexts. We'll examine how to maintain authenticity in AI-assisted communication, approach important questions in AI use, navigate cultural differences in digital interaction, and foster genuine human connection in an increasingly AI-mediated world.

This journey is not about resisting technological change or uncritically embracing it. Instead, it's about thoughtfully integrating AI into our lives in ways that support our lives while leveraging the extraordinary capabilities these technologies offer.

The stage is set for an extraordinary performance, where human wisdom and technological capability move harmoniously to create something greater than either could achieve alone. As we step forward into this future together, remember that the most beautiful aspects of this dance will always be distinctly human—our creativity, compassion, capacity to dream, and ability to connect in ways that give life its most profound meaning.

The music is playing, the partnership awaits, and the future beckons. Shall we dance?

TWO
UNDERSTANDING AI BASICS
HUMANITY'S GREAT LEAP

... ✦ ...

"Any sufficiently advanced technology is indistinguishable from magic."
— Arthur C. Clarke

UNDERSTANDING AI: BEYOND THE BUZZ

Humans have dreamed of tools that could think, learn, and grow alongside us for thousands of years. From ancient myths of living statues to magical helpers, we've imagined companions that understand our needs and solve our problems. Today, those dreams are becoming reality.

Artificial Intelligence represents one of humanity's most profound transformations. Like the discovery of fire or the invention of the wheel, AI is reshaping how we live and work. But unlike previous revolutionary technologies, AI's impact is uniquely personal and accessible. It's not just in research labs or Silicon Valley offices—it's in your home, your pocket, and your daily life.

AI enhances your daily life in ways you might not even notice. It personalizes your news feed, improves photo quality, assists in medical diagnoses, optimizes travel routes, and predicts frost dates for gardening. In addition, the AI behind your favorite recipe app might not just recommend dinner ideas, it could even help you build a shopping list based on what's in your fridge, optimizing your meal plans and reducing waste. This revolutionary force actively enhances our everyday experiences, often working quietly in the background to improve our lives.

What makes this moment extraordinary is that, for the first time in history, such a transformative power isn't controlled by governments or large organizations. It's accessible to everyone. Students can use AI to learn any subject, farmers can optimize crop yields, elderly people can maintain independence, and small business owners can compete with larger corporations. Like fire, which revolutionized survival and society, AI has the power to transform human capability in profound ways.

It's helping us decode the human genome, predict weather patterns that could save lives, and explore the furthest reaches of space. It's translating languages in real-time, creating art that moves us, and solving problems that have puzzled scientists for generations. When our grandparents were young, carrying a device that could instantly answer any question, translate any language, or create art from a few words would have seemed like magic. Today, that magic is in our hands.

This isn't just another technological change—it's the beginning of a new chapter in the human story, and you're not just watching it unfold. You're about to become an active participant in shaping it.

THE MOMENT THAT MATTERS

What is the impact of AI on human potential?

The line between science fiction and reality is dissolving. AI isn't just changing how we work—it's redefining what's possible. A child in a remote part of the world can access world-class education through AI tutors. An artist can transform imagination into visual masterpieces with a few words. A scientist can process decades of research in hours. A person with disabilities can interact with the world in new, empowering ways.

Yet, most people use only a fraction of AI's potential. They experience AI like early humans experienced electricity—benefiting from its basic effects without understanding how to harness its power. This chapter and this book will change that for you.

Think of this chapter as your initiation into one of the most significant developments in human history. Whether you're a student, artist, entrepreneur, retiree, or anyone, AI will continue to impact your future in increasingly personal ways.

THE NEW LITERACY

Just as reading and writing transformed from specialized skills to essential abilities, understanding AI is fundamental to thriving in our modern world.

Your advantage? You're starting this journey at precisely the right time—when AI is powerful enough to be truly useful but still early enough for you to gain a significant edge.

A Necessity, Not a Choice

As artificial intelligence becomes increasingly woven into our daily lives, understanding how it learns is not just a matter of curiosity but of responsible engagement. By grasping its fundamental processes, we can ask informed questions about the AI systems we encounter.

As AI continues to evolve, we face critical decisions about what we want it to learn, how it should acquire knowledge, and what safeguards must be in place. Making these choices wisely requires a solid understanding of the processes that shape AI's learning and decision-making.

By cultivating AI literacy, we can harness AI's immense potential for innovation while remaining vigilant about its risks and limitations. Remember that understanding language fundamentals enhances communication.

HOW AI LEARNS

Understanding how these systems learn is as important as knowing what they can do. Just as humans learn through different methods, AI systems employ distinct learning approaches that shape their capabilities and limitations. In the same way that we, as children, learn to identify friends and family based on little details—a laugh, a gesture, a smile—AI learns to recognize and differentiate by observing patterns and building on them over time.

Think about how a child learns to identify dogs. We don't explain every possible combination of fur, size, and shape. Instead, we show them examples, and they learn to recognize patterns. Humans can adapt their knowledge across completely different domains. AI, however, excels only within the confines of its specialized training. This fundamental process—pattern recognition through exposure and feedback—forms the foundation of how AI learns. However, AI systems implement this basic principle in three distinct ways, each suited to different tasks.

Supervised Learning is like having a patient teacher. A child learns to tell cats from dogs by looking at labeled pictures. AI works the same way—it processes labeled examples, such as spam vs. non-spam emails, improving its accuracy over time. This method powers many familiar technologies, from your phone's facial recognition to email spam filters.

Unsupervised Learning is more like self-guided discovery. Imagine a child spontaneously sorting their toys by color without being told to do so. Similarly, AI systems using unsupervised learning find patterns and structures in data without explicit labels. Your streaming service uses this approach when it groups similar songs together or suggests new music based on patterns in your listening history that you might not have noticed yourself.

Reinforcement Learning works through trial and error with feedback. Learning to ride a bike involves trial, error, and adjustments—just like AI using reinforcement learning. It makes decisions, receives feedback, and improves over time. This approach has achieved remarkable results, from teaching AI to master complex games like chess and Go to helping smart home devices optimize energy usage based on your habits.

AI can undoubtedly generate art or music that feels creative, but it does so based on patterns without the intuition or emotional spark that drives human creativity.

The implications of these learning methods extend far beyond simple examples. Supervised learning helps AI recognize patterns in medical imagery, assisting doctors in making diagnoses. In finance, unsupervised learning detects fraudulent transactions by identifying unusual patterns. In robotics, reinforcement learning allows machines to learn complex motor skills through repeated attempts. How exciting is that?

Indeed, our journey with AI has evolved from simple commands to sophisticated collaboration. As our understanding has grown from basic interactions to nuanced partnerships, let's explore how AI's brain processes information and transforms raw data into meaningful insights. Now that we understand how we interact with AI, let's explore its inner workings.

Now that you understand how AI works, it's important to engage with it thoughtfully and responsibly. As you start your AI journey, here are some key principles to keep in mind to ensure you interact with AI effectively and ethically.

AI ETIQUETTE ESSENTIALS FOR BEGINNERS

How to Start Your AI Journey Thoughtfully

Understand AI's Capabilities and Limitations

Approach AI with curiosity, but ground your exploration in a solid understanding of its mechanics. Learn how AI works, including its learning models and pattern recognition capabilities. Recognize that AI excels at specific tasks but isn't a general-purpose solution. Use AI for its intended purpose, and don't expect it to perform beyond its training. Always critically review AI-generated outputs, especially in critical fields like medicine or finance, to ensure human oversight.

Engage with AI Responsibly

Cultivate an ethical approach to AI usage. Be mindful of how your use of AI might affect others, especially in professional settings. Respect privacy and autonomy, and never use AI to manipulate or deceive. As AI becomes more integrated into our lives, understanding its learning processes is crucial for responsible engagement. Ask informed questions about the AI systems you encounter, and be aware of your choices about what AI learns and how it acquires knowledge.

Personalize and Optimize Your AI Experience

AI tools can significantly enhance your experience by tailoring content and recommendations to your preferences. You can actively manage this customization by regularly updating your preferences in AI-powered apps and tools. The more feedback you provide, the better the system will align with your needs.

Quick Tip: When using AI in professional settings (such as automated email responses), ensure that your output respects others' privacy and autonomy. Never use AI to manipulate or deceive others.

THE HEARTBEAT OF AI: THE INPUT-PROCESS-OUTPUT CYCLE

At the core of every AI system lies a fundamental process that mirrors our way of interacting with the world. Just as we take in information through our senses, analyze it in our brains, and respond with actions, AI follows a similar cycle: input, processing, and output.

1. Input: The World Through AI's Eyes

An AI system begins with input—the data it receives from the world around it. This data can take myriad forms: images captured by cameras, sounds recorded by microphones, text entered by users, or sensor readings from IoT devices. The AI system's first task is to translate this raw data into a format it can understand and process.

Think of this as your senses gathering information. When you look at a friend's face, your eyes take in visual data. When you listen to music, your ears receive auditory input. When you read a book, your eyes and brain process textual information. AI systems, in their own way, "see," "hear," and "read" the world around them.

2. Processing: Making Sense of the Data

Once the data is in a processable format, the real magic of AI begins. This is where the system's "brain" kicks into gear, applying the patterns and relationships it has learned to make sense of the input.

If the AI has been trained to recognize faces, for instance, it will start to look for the features it has learned to associate with different individuals: the shape of the eyes, the contours of the nose, the curve of the smile. If it's processing natural language, it will break down the input into grammatical structures, analyze the meanings of words, and try to understand the overall context.

This processing stage is where AI's unique capabilities emerge. By leveraging techniques like machine learning, deep learning, and neural networks, AI systems can identify patterns and draw insights that might elude human observers. They can process vast amounts of data in seconds, spotting trends and anomalies that would take us hours or days to discern.

3. Output: AI's Response to the World

The final stage of the AI process cycle is the output or responses that the system generates based on its input processing. This is where AI's learning and analysis are translated into tangible results.

In some cases, the output might be a simple classification or prediction. For example, an AI system analyzing medical images might output a diagnosis, indicating whether a tumor is likely benign or malignant. A system processing financial data might output a fraud alert, flagging a transaction as potentially suspicious.

The output might be a more complex action or recommendation in other cases. For example, an AI-powered virtual assistant might suggest a reply to an email, drawing on its understanding of your communication style and the conversation context. Similarly, an AI system controlling a robot arm might output a series of precise movements, allowing the robot to grasp and manipulate objects with human-like dexterity.

Now that we understand how AI learns, let's examine how it processes and responds to the world around it.

FOUNDATIONS: NEURAL NETWORKS

At the heart of modern AI's learning approaches lies a powerful and elegant system inspired by nature: neural networks. Think of how your brain connects countless dots to recognize a friend's face—AI's neural networks work similarly, spotting patterns in data through repetition and feedback.

AI systems begin with broad input to establish patterns and gradually add finer details with each additional input, building complexity and meaning. This is how AI's neural networks deeply learn. Just as our brains have billions of interconnected neurons working together to process information, AI's neural networks consist of layers of nodes that collaborate to identify patterns and make decisions.

Deep Learning: Building Understanding from the Ground Up

Each layer in a neural network plays a specific role in this intricate process. The input layer receives raw data, like the pixels of an image or the words in a sentence—similar to an artist's first sketch. Hidden layers then process this information, each identifying increasingly complex patterns, much like how an artist refines their work by adding shadows, textures, and subtle details. Finally, the output layer produces the result, whether that's identifying an object in a photo or translating a sentence—the equivalent of the artist's finished art piece.

This layered approach, known as *Deep Learning,* allows AI to tackle increasingly complex tasks. In the early layers, the network may recognize basic shapes, edges, or colors. As information passes through more layers, the network detects increasingly complex patterns, forming connections between features until it can confidently identify what it "sees."

However, it's crucial to understand that while AI's learning process mirrors human learning in some ways, it differs in important aspects. Unlike humans, who can easily transfer knowledge from one domain to another, AI systems are specialized. An AI that masters chess can't automatically apply that learning to driving a car or cooking a meal. Each task requires its own training process, using one or more of these learning approaches.

HOW DEEP LEARNING TRANSFORMS AI

Deep learning is about depth—more layers mean more learning, detail, and refined understanding. Unlike traditional AI, which follows fixed rules, deep learning allows AI to learn through experience, continuously adapting as it processes vast amounts of data. This layered learning approach enables AI to excel at complex tasks, from analyzing medical images with precision to understanding natural language and generating art.

But deep learning doesn't just connect dots—it interprets, refines, and reinterprets patterns until the output reaches near-human recognition levels. It mimics the way humans process information, allowing AI to adapt in ways traditional rule-based systems cannot.

Digging Deeper: How Does Layered Learning Work?

Input Layer: The entry point for data, such as pixels in an image or words in a sentence.

Hidden Layers: Where the real transformation happens—each layer extracts increasingly complex features from the data.

Output Layer: The final step is delivering an answer—whether identifying objects in a photo or translating a sentence.

As data moves through the network, each layer builds upon the patterns recognized by the previous one. Think of it as a game of telephone, but deep learning clarifies and enhances it at every stage instead of distorting the message.

AI has been evolving for decades, with roots in mid-20th-century research and milestones like early neural networks in the 1950s. Machine translation and other AI applications have quietly shaped daily life long before the recent surge in attention. While AI's visibility has grown, its development has been a steady progression rather than an overnight revolution.

THE EVOLUTION OF AI INTERACTION

Our relationship with artificial intelligence mirrors humanity's journey in cross-cultural communication. Just as our ancestors progressed from basic gestures to rich, nuanced dialogue, our interaction with AI is evolving from simple commands to sophisticated collaboration. Understanding this evolution helps us navigate the present and prepare for future developments in human-AI interaction.

The Command Era: Learning a New Language

Think of your early interactions with AI like traveling in a foreign country with only a phrasebook. Each interaction required careful preparation, like a novice language learner practicing pronunciation before speaking. We approached AI with basic commands—"set alarm," "add reminder," etc.—much as a child first learns to make requests with simple phrases like "want juice" before mastering more sophisticated expressions.

This era established its own form of digital etiquette, centered on clear, precise instructions. Like the early days of telephone communication, when operators manually connected calls, these limitations weren't weaknesses but necessary steps in developing a new form of interaction. Each successful exchange built confidence and understanding, creating a foundation for more complex interactions.

The Collaborative Phase: Building Trust and Understanding

Today, we're in a phase of growing sophistication in our AI interactions. Consider how you might let an AI assistant draft routine emails while reserving sensitive communications for personal attention. This mirrors how we delegate tasks to trusted colleagues—with clear boundaries and appropriate oversight. A marketing professional might use AI to generate initial response templates but personally craft messages for delicate situations. Data analysts might employ AI to process information while adding crucial human context to the insights.

The key to this phase is understanding when and how to leverage AI capabilities. We're learning to balance automation with authenticity, much as we balance professional efficiency with a personal touch in human interactions. This phase requires understanding AI's capabilities and limitations, allowing us to make informed decisions about task delegation and oversight.

The Partnership Horizon: Toward Sophisticated Collaboration

The future points toward a more refined partnership with AI, where systems become adept at understanding our working styles and anticipating our needs. This isn't about AI replacing human judgment but rather enhancing it. Medical professionals might use AI to identify patterns in patient data while maintaining the essential human elements of care. Educators might employ AI to personalize learning paths while preserving meaningful student connections.

This evolution demands new frameworks for human-AI interaction—guidelines that help us maintain professional authenticity while maximizing collaborative potential. Success in this era requires understanding AI systems' power and limitations.

UNDERSTANDING THE BOUNDARIES

While AI's capabilities are remarkable, they are bounded by its training and programming. Each AI system is specialized rather than general, mastering specific tasks rather than displaying broad intelligence. For example, an AI might excel at chess but cannot prepare a meal, as each task requires distinct training and optimization.

This understanding helps us set realistic expectations and design effective collaborations. The goal isn't to make AI more humanlike but to leverage its unique strengths while preserving human judgment, creativity, and ethical oversight. As we move forward, success lies in finding the right balance between AI assistance and human guidance, creating partnerships that enhance rather than diminish human capability.

The evolution of our interaction with AI isn't just about technological advancement—it's about developing a new form of digital literacy that will define professional and personal success in the years ahead. By understanding this progression, we can more effectively navigate the present and prepare for future developments in human-AI collaboration.

As I mentioned earlier, we stand at a unique inflection point—the dawn of the age of artificial intelligence. Understanding how AI learns is essential, as we are not passive observers but active participants in shaping this transformative technology. This knowledge equips us to use AI wisely, ethically, and in service of collective human progress. Are you ready to navigate this new frontier with confidence, responsibility, and clear purpose? Let's understand neural networks through our own experience.

THE HUMAN CONNECTION

Our process of learning and growth offers a compelling window into understanding how artificial neural networks function. Just as we build understanding through life experiences, neural networks construct knowledge through successive data processing layers. This parallel reveals profound insights about both human and artificial intelligence.

The Architecture of Learning

Consider how you learned to recognize faces. As an infant, you begin with basic sensory input—shapes, colors, and movements. Over time, you developed increasingly sophisticated ways of processing this information, eventually learning to recognize faces but expressions, emotions, and subtle social cues. Neural networks follow a remarkably similar pattern through their layered architecture.

The Input Gateway

In humans, our senses provide the initial data—sight, sound, touch, taste, and smell. Similarly, a neural network's input layer receives raw data: pixels from an image, sound waves from speech, or text from documents. This is where human and artificial learning begins, with raw information from the world.

The Hidden Depths

Between our sensory input and our ultimate understanding lies a complex web of neural processing. We interpret what we see through filters of experience, cultural context, and emotional memory. Neural networks mirror this through their hidden layers, where each level builds upon the previous one's understanding. Early layers might identify basic patterns, while deeper layers recognize increasingly complex relationships as we progress from recognizing simple shapes to understanding abstract concepts.

The Expression of Understanding

The culmination of this processing manifests in our actions, decisions, and expressions—comparable to a neural network's output layer. Just as our responses reflect the sum of our processed experiences, a neural network's output represents the culmination of its layered analysis. Whether it's recognizing a face in a photograph or translating a sentence, this final step transforms processed information into meaningful action.

The Growth of Understanding

The way neural networks learn reflects our development in surprising ways. Consider how a child builds knowledge:

Early experiences form fundamental understanding patterns, like a neural network's initial training. These basic patterns become the foundation for more complex learning. For example, a child who learns to recognize dogs might start with simple features—four legs, fur, and a tail—before developing a more nuanced understanding that allows them to recognize breeds they've never seen before.

Similarly, neural networks begin with basic pattern recognition before developing more sophisticated capabilities. Each new piece of data adjusts the network's connections, as each new experience shapes our understanding of the world. This process of continuous refinement leads to increasingly nuanced and accurate responses in both human and artificial systems.

From Simple to Complex

Perhaps the most fascinating parallel is how both systems transform simple inputs into complex understanding through interconnection layers. A neural network might take individual pixels and, through its layers, recognize a face, interpret an expression, and identify an emotion. Similarly, we take basic sensory inputs and construct rich, multi-layered understandings of our world.

This layered processing explains how humans and neural networks can handle novel situations. Just as we can understand a sentence we've never heard before by drawing on our layered knowledge of language, grammar, and context, neural networks can make sense of new inputs by applying their layered learning to unfamiliar patterns.

The power of both systems lies not in memorizing specific responses but in developing flexible frameworks for understanding. Each layer adds not just information but new ways of processing and interpreting that information, creating ever more sophisticated capabilities for analysis and response.

Understanding these parallels helps us grasp artificial neural networks' potential and limitations. While they mirror some aspects of human learning with remarkable fidelity, they remain specialized tools rather than general-purpose minds. Their power grows through layered learning, but it stays within the bounds of their specific training and purpose.

This insight leads us to a crucial conclusion: the future of AI lies not in replicating human intelligence entirely but in developing systems that complement and enhance human capabilities through their unique form of layered learning and pattern recognition.

Beyond its practical applications, AI also holds immense potential to profoundly enhance human connection. Imagine a world where language barriers no longer hinder communication, where individuals

with disabilities can interact seamlessly with their surroundings, or where access to education and healthcare is democratized through personalized AI tutors and medical assistants.

AI-powered tools are already making strides in these areas. Real-time translation apps connect people from different cultures, fostering understanding and empathy. AI algorithms analyze social media data to identify individuals at risk of self-harm, enabling timely intervention and support. Personalized learning platforms adapt to each student's unique needs, creating more engaging and effective educational experiences. While concerns about AI's impact on human interaction are valid, it's crucial to recognize its potential to bridge gaps, empower individuals, and foster more substantial, more meaningful connections. The key lies in developing and deploying AI responsibly, prioritizing human well-being and ethical considerations.

THE ART OF FEATURE LEARNING

How AI Delivers Immense Potential

One of deep learning's most powerful aspects is its ability to automatically identify the important features of the data it processes. This is called feature learning.

Let's return to our animal example. The network might first learn to recognize basic shapes like circles and lines to identify a cat. Then, it might learn to identify more complex features like eyes, ears, and tails. Finally, it might learn to combine all these features to recognize a cat.

The beauty of deep learning is that it can do this feature learning automatically without being explicitly programmed. It can find patterns and connections that humans might miss, and it can do so with enormous amounts of data that would take humans a lifetime to process.

The Applications are Endless

There are many impressive AI achievements powered by deep learning. Here are a few:

- Recognizing faces in photos and videos
- Understanding and responding to spoken language
- Translating between languages with near-human accuracy
- Detecting fraudulent transactions in real-time
- Diagnosing diseases from medical images
- Driving autonomous vehicles

As we feed these networks more data and compute power, their capabilities are growing exponentially. They're not just learning to see and hear like humans - in many cases, they surpass the human ability to recognize patterns.

The Future is Deep

As you can see, deep learning is not just another AI term—it's a fundamental shift in how we approach artificial intelligence. Rather than programming computers with specific rules, we teach them to learn and adapt independently, much like the human brain.

This shift opens up countless possibilities, from more personalized technology to groundbreaking scientific discoveries. Imagine more accurate and accessible AI-powered medical diagnoses, customized education tailored to every student's unique learning style, or even new forms of artistic expression generated through human-AI collaboration.

However, this rapid progress also raises important ethical considerations. One key challenge is bias in training data. If an AI system is trained on data that reflects existing societal biases, it may perpetuate or even amplify those biases in its outputs. For example, a facial recognition system trained primarily on images of one demographic group might be less accurate when identifying individuals from other groups. Addressing this requires careful attention to data diversity, transparency in AI algorithms, and ongoing evaluation to ensure fairness and equity.

Another concern is the potential misuse of deep learning, such as developing autonomous weapons or surveillance technologies. As deep learning becomes more powerful, it's crucial to establish clear ethical guidelines and regulations to prevent misuse and ensure that it benefits humanity.

The future of deep learning depends on our ability to address these challenges proactively. By fostering open dialogue, promoting research into AI safety and ethics, and prioritizing human well-being, we can harness deep learning's immense potential while mitigating its risks.

HELLO AI: CAN YOU DO THAT?

AI is a potent tool, but it's not a miracle worker. While it excels in specific areas and has transformed countless industries, it's essential to understand its strengths and limitations. Knowing what AI *is* and *isn't* will help you set realistic expectations and use it effectively.

What AI Is:

- A pattern recognition powerhouse
- A tireless data processor
- A specialized problem solver
- A learning system

What AI Isn't:

- A magical solution to everything
- A replacement for human judgment
- An emotional being
- A general-purpose brain

Our remarkable brain lets us sing our favorite song while thinking about what we will cook for dinner. But AI works differently. Instead of being a jack-of-all-trades like the human mind, it's more like having a team of highly specialized experts. Just as you wouldn't use a hammer to paint a wall, each type of AI has a specific purpose. The key to success isn't finding one AI that can do everything—it's knowing which AI tool best suits each task.

FOUNDATIONS: THREE CORE POWERS

Having explored the foundational concepts of AI - from its historical development to how it works - it's time to shift our focus to the practical capabilities that make AI such a powerful tool in our daily lives. Understanding the three core powers of AI will help bridge the gap between AI theory and real-world applications. Let's review AI's *Three Core Powers*:

1. **Recognizes Patterns**: Like a master detective, AI discovers hidden trends and connections in vast amounts of data, enabling everything from weather forecasting to market analysis.
2. **Automates Tasks:** AI is a tireless worker, handling repetitive tasks with consistency and precision. It frees us so we can focus on more creative and strategic work.
3. **Personalizes Experiences**: Like an attentive assistant, AI learns from interactions to provide increasingly tailored experiences, from content recommendations to scheduling preferences.

Here are some examples:

Digital Assistants (Siri, Alexa, Google Assistant) handle daily tasks and queries.

Content Platforms (Netflix, Spotify, YouTube) curate personalized entertainment.

Analysis Tools assist in fields from medicine and financial markets to meteorology.

Productivity Tools enhance our work through smart features such as Gmail, which completes your sentences or optimizes your route on maps.

I encourage you to take a moment to identify three tasks you perform regularly that drain your time or energy. These could be ideal candidates for AI assistance. Hold on to this list; you'll discover ideas for solutions throughout the book.

THE BOUNDARIES OF AI UNDERSTANDING

AI's pattern recognition differs fundamentally from human understanding. When AI translates between languages, it does not truly comprehend the meaning of words as humans do. Instead, it identifies patterns in how words and phrases typically correspond between languages. This distinction becomes crucial when we consider AI's limitations.

Consider how a child who learns about dogs can quickly transfer that knowledge to understand what makes something "dog-like" or even apply similar principles to understand other animals. AI systems, in contrast, remain confined to their specific training domains. An AI that masters chess cannot automatically apply that expertise to other strategy games, let alone to completely different tasks like cooking or driving.

Today's AI demonstrates remarkable capabilities within specialized domains. It can:

- Generate human-like text based on prompts.
- Create stunning artwork from descriptions.
- Optimize complex logistics operations.
- Enhance photos with remarkable detail.

- Predict maintenance needs in machinery.
- Personalize learning experiences for students.

Each AI system excels at its specific task but lacks the general adaptability humans take for granted. An AI that creates beautiful digital art cannot understand the emotional impact of its creations. A system that helps diagnose diseases cannot comfort patients or consider their circumstances as a human doctor would.

While AI excels in specialized roles, humanity's remarkable adaptability, creativity, and emotional intelligence make us irreplaceable.

BEYOND SPECIALIZED INTELLIGENCE

Your Role in AI's Evolution

As we explore the expanding role of AI, one fundamental truth emerges: Today's AI excels at specific tasks while lacking the general adaptability of human intelligence. While it can generate human-like text, create stunning art, or optimize complex logistics, it operates within predefined boundaries. An AI that translates languages with near-human accuracy cannot grasp their cultural significance, just as a system that detects financial fraud cannot empathize with its victims.

Yet this specialized excellence represents not a limitation but an unprecedented opportunity. AI can create a powerful symbiosis between human creativity and machine capability. We're not just witnessing this transformation—we're actively shaping it. Just as past technological revolutions defined new literacies, understanding and working with AI is essential for thriving in our evolving world.

Our journey through neural networks, learning processes, and AI's core powers has revealed a technology that's both remarkably sophisticated and surprisingly accessible. AI is no longer a futuristic dream—it's a practical tool whose power depends on how we wield it. With this foundational knowledge of how AI learns, processes information, and complements human intelligence, you can move from a passive user to an active participant in the AI revolution.

Remember, every technological revolution has its pioneers—those who step forward to shape how new tools will serve humanity. In the age of AI, that pioneer can be you. The next chapter will transform this understanding into action, exploring practical ways to communicate effectively with and harness AI tools. Effective communication is essential for enhancing human abilities in the new AI-driven world.

As we shape this new tool, we must consider how we guide it—ensuring it serves humanity responsibly and transparently. It's not just about creating better technology; it's about creating a future that reflects our shared values.

THREE
SPEAKING WITH THE FUTURE
THE ART OF AI COMMUNICATION

"The single biggest problem in communication is the illusion that it has taken place."
— George Bernard Shaw

Throughout history, humans have pushed the boundaries of communication—from the first written words to telegrams that crossed oceans, from radio waves that filled the air to video calls that connected continents. Now, we're crossing another extraordinary threshold. For the first time, we're learning to converse with artificial minds that can understand our goals, assist our creative processes, and help us solve complex problems in new ways.

For the average person, this isn't just about learning commands or mastering prompts. It's about developing a new kind of relationship, one that bridges the gap between human creativity and computational power. Every time you interact with AI, you're participating in a dialogue that would have seemed impossible just a few years ago. You're speaking with systems that can understand dozens of languages, process more information than any human could read in a lifetime, and help transform your thoughts into reality.

But the fascinating part is that we're just learning how to have these conversations. My entire approach to AI became more expansive and enriching when I first recognized this. Like early humans discovering the nuances of spoken language, we're at the beginning of understanding how to communicate effectively with artificial intelligence. Those who master this art now will not only be more efficient but also pioneers who help shape how humanity interacts with AI for generations to come.

> Mastering communication with AI systems is among the most crucial skills in modern societies. The quality of your inputs into AI determines the quality of your outputs; thoughtful inputs produce meaningful outcomes.

THE ART OF COMMUNICATION

When you speak to AI, you're not just giving commands to a machine. You're collaborating with a system that can analyze, create, and problem-solve in ways that complement and enhance your abilities. Learning to communicate effectively with AI is like gaining access to a new kind of superpower - one that amplifies your natural abilities and opens doors to possibilities you might never have imagined.

Understanding how to communicate with AI isn't just a technical skill - it's an art form that can transform how you work, create, and solve problems. Just as learning any new language opens up new ways of thinking, mastering AI communication opens up new realms of possibility.

This is paramount during these pivotal times! Think of how often you've had a great idea but struggled to bring it to life, or faced a complex problem but didn't know where to start. AI can be your thinking partner, creative collaborator, and research assistant—but only if you know how to express your needs.

What is the difference between basic and advanced AI usage? I want to take a moment to illustrate this:

Simple vs. Strategic Approaches

Tale of Two Cooks

Think of two people using the same high-end kitchen assistant AI. Tommy types "Give me a dinner recipe" and gets a standard pasta dish. Meanwhile, Mike tells the AI about his family's favorite dishes, available ingredients, and their spice preferences. He asks it to help reimagine those cherished flavors into a quick weeknight meal. While Tommy ends up with a generic dinner, Mike creates a unique fusion dish that becomes his family's new favorite. Same AI, dramatically different outcomes—all because of how they approached the conversation.

Mastering AI with Accuracy

Imagine asking someone for directions. You could say, "How do I get there?" and receive basic turn-by-turn instructions. Or you could mention you're biking, prefer scenic routes, and want to avoid steep hills. It's the same question, but one approach gets you a forgettable commute while the other leads to a memorable journey. That's the difference between basic and masterful AI use.

THE GOLDEN RULES OF AI DIALOGUE

Imagine having a brilliant but highly literal assistant - one with access to vast knowledge but who interprets your requests precisely as stated, without making assumptions about what you might have meant. This assistant won't remember your preferences from yesterday or guess what you're thinking. Instead, it awaits your precise instructions, ready to apply its capabilities exactly as directed.

Communicating effectively with AI continues to evolve as technology advances. Each interaction teaches something new about the power of precise communication and the importance of thoughtful instruction. You'll discover how small adjustments in how you frame requests can lead to dramatically improved results.

Learning AI's language isn't just about mastering a new tool—it's about developing a deeper understanding of communication itself. This can help us express our needs and ideas more precisely and thoughtfully.

The Power of Precision

Clarity isn't just helpful when communicating with AI; it's essential. The more specific and detailed your request, the better the AI can understand and fulfill your needs. Think of it as creating a detailed map for someone to follow rather than pointing vaguely at a destination.

Rule 1: Clarity Is Your Superpower

Basic approach: "Make my recipe better."

This is similar to telling someone, "Just make it tastier," without explaining what you want. Alternatively, consider this more detailed prompt that offers a superior perspective:

"Improve this chocolate cake recipe by making it more moist, reducing the sweetness, and bringing out a richer chocolate flavor." or,

"I'd love this dish with more garlic, a bit less salt, and cooked until the vegetables are still slightly crisp."

The more precise you are, the closer you will come to your desired outcome.

The Power of Thoughtful AI Communication

Consider how tone influences every aspect of human conversation—the distinction between requesting a favor from a friend versus a stranger or explaining something to a child versus an expert. AI communication operates in much the same way. Let's master these nuances.

Rule 2: Context is Your Compass

Basic Approach: "What should I learn next?"

This is like walking into a library and asking, "Where are the good books?" Consider using this effective method instead:

"I'm a beginner photographer mainly interested in wildlife shots. I've mastered basic camera settings. What technical skill should I focus on next to improve my nature photography?"

THE ART OF AI PARTNERSHIPS

When working with any AI, view it as a collaborative session rather than just a simple question-and-answer exchange. The most powerful results often emerge from a dialogue where each response builds on the previous one. This shift from commanding to conversing can completely transform your AI experience.

Rule 3: Think in Conversations, Not Commands

Approach AI like a partner in dialogue—guide it gradually, as you would in a thoughtful conversation, to unlock refined results.

Basic Approach: "Write me a short story."

This is like meeting a creative writing partner and immediately demanding a story without sharing preferences or inspiration. Instead, try this:

"Let's create a short story together. I'm thinking of a mystery set in a small coastal town. The main character is a local baker who discovers unusual messages in fortune cookies. Could you help develop this idea, emphasizing small-town atmosphere and subtle suspense?"

This mirrors the difference between ordering someone to "just tell me a story" and engaging in a creative brainstorming session where ideas can flow and evolve naturally. The more you treat AI as a collaborative partner, the richer and more nuanced your results will be.

FROM RULES TO REFINED DIALOGUE

Now that we understand the fundamental rules of AI communication let's explore what I find most fascinating—the real magic that happens when we learn to build our requests layer by layer. Just as a skilled interviewer knows how to guide a conversation toward deeper insights, we can structure our AI interactions to become progressively more focused and productive. Let's see this artful refinement in action.

Refining Your System: The Art of Ongoing Optimization

Just as a well-designed home requires regular maintenance and occasional updates, your AI-enhanced life benefits from consistent attention and refinement. This isn't about achieving a flawless system but ensuring your technological ecosystem continues serving your evolving needs.

Establish regular check-in points where you deliberately assess your AI integration.

Consider questions like:

- How has this enhancement affected my daily experience?
- Am I spending more time on activities that truly matter to me?
- Have any new friction points or challenges emerged?

- Are there areas where I might benefit from increasing or decreasing AI involvement?

This optimization phase isn't just about adjusting settings or trying new features. It's about deepening your understanding of how technology can best support your personal and professional growth. As you become more comfortable with AI assistance, you might discover new possibilities for enhancement and realize that some early automation choices need refinement or that you do not need any for what you initially thought you did.

The true measure of success isn't how many tasks you've automated or how efficiently your system runs. Instead, it's about whether your technological enhancements are helping create a life that feels more meaningful, balanced, and aligned with your values. Are you finding more time for deep work, creative expression, and genuine human connection? Can you better focus on activities that bring you joy and fulfillment?

As you continue this journey, maintain a spirit of curiosity and flexibility. The landscape of AI capabilities will continue to evolve, offering new opportunities for enhancement. By approaching these changes with a clear sense of your priorities and boundaries, you can make choices that serve your vision of a rich, fulfilling life.

Remember, the goal isn't to create a perfectly optimized existence but to thoughtfully harness technology to enhance your human experience. When done well, AI enhancement should feel like a natural extension of your capabilities, supporting rather than supplanting the qualities that make you uniquely you.

Throughout this book, certain ideas and principles are repeated in different contexts. This is intentional. Mastery comes through reinforcement, and by seeing these concepts applied across various scenarios, you may find unexpected parallels that inspire you. Even if an example doesn't directly relate to your life or work, consider how the underlying approach could be adapted to your own needs. The goal is not just to inform but to spark ideas and new ways of thinking about how you can harness AI as a powerful ally.

THE ART OF REFINEMENT

In the world of AI, refinement is where true mastery begins. It's about moving from simple requests to deep, intentional conversations that yield tailored, meaningful outcomes. It's not just about asking for help but crafting your inquiry in a way that guides AI to deliver precisely what you need. This journey of refinement, much like honing a craft, allows you to unlock AI's full potential and create solutions that feel yours.

Refining your communication with AI transforms ordinary interactions into a dynamic collaboration. The more you refine your prompts and exchanges, the more aligned the results become with your goals, leading to a more fulfilling and efficient use of AI. Here's how you can evolve a simple conversation into a detailed, purposeful exchange:

Step 1:

"Help me plan a garden."

This is a basic, general request to get started.

Step 2:

"Given my small urban balcony and 6 hours of daily sunlight, what plants would thrive?"

By adding specific context—like your space and the sunlight available —you begin to narrow down the AI's response to something more personalized.

Step 3:

"From these options, which are best for growing vegetables year-round?"

Now that the AI knows what plants thrive in your conditions, you refine the question by focusing on your goal of year-round vegetable gardening.

Step 4:

"Now help me design a layout that maximizes my limited space."

Once you've chosen the plants, the next refinement step is to get help optimizing your garden's layout to maximize your space. However, you achieve AI communication mastery by wrapping all the steps into one cohesive prompt.

"I have a small urban balcony with 6 hours of daily sunlight, and I'd like to grow vegetables year-round. Can you help me choose the best plants for these conditions and then design a layout that maximizes my space for optimal growth?"

In this refined prompt, you're giving the AI everything it needs to move seamlessly through the entire planning process. You've developed a much more sophisticated exchange, from selecting plants to designing your garden layout.

This example combines the key details from each of the previous steps—your space, sunlight, the goal of year-round growth, and the need for a functional layout. It's direct and specific, providing the AI with all the context necessary to guide you through the process.

The art of refining your communication with AI is key to unlocking its full potential—allowing you to receive responses that are not just relevant but also deeply aligned with your needs. By using refined prompts, you set yourself up for a genuinely dynamic collaboration with the AI, ensuring that the guidance you receive will be tailored and practical.

DIGITAL ETIQUETTE: CULTIVATING A THOUGHTFUL AI PARTNERSHIP

In AI communication, feedback is pivotal in shaping your interaction and ensuring that the results align with your expectations. Just as in human conversations, where feedback is essential for clarifying misun-

derstandings and improving the dialogue, ,active listening with AI is crucial for refining outcomes. While AI offers vast information and capabilities, it thrives on feedback—something that's often overlooked in the rush to receive quick answers.

Active listening with AI is about more than just receiving an initial response and moving on. It involves the art of iterative refinement, where you continuously assess the output, learn from it, and adapt your request based on what the AI provides. This is an essential practice for mastering AI communication. Just as a skilled communicator adjusts their approach based on the feedback they receive in conversation, engaging with AI requires the same level of attentiveness and flexibility.

The Etiquette of Active Listening

After receiving the first output from the AI, take a moment to assess whether it fully aligns with your needs. Are there elements you could reframe or clarify to refine the AI's response further? Rather than immediately accepting or dismissing the result, consider how you can adjust your request to provide more context or specific direction.

Illustration of Engaged Listening and Iteration

Step 1: *Initial Request*: *"Help me brainstorm ideas for a new product launch in the fashion industry."*

Step 2: *AI Response*: A list of generic product ideas, such as "Eco-friendly clothing" or "Minimalist fashion line."

Step 3: *Reframed Request*: *"Let's focus on a product launch for eco-conscious fashion targeted at millennials in urban areas. Please explore how technology, such as wearable devices or smart fabrics, can play a role in this collection."*

Step 4: *AI Response*: The refined output now provides more tailored ideas, like "Wearable fashion tech integrating health-monitoring devices" or "Smart fabrics with temperature regulation for outdoor activities."

Revisiting your requests based on the AI's output improves your results and encourages a deeper level of engagement and collaboration. It transforms your interaction from a transactional one to a dynamic partnership in which you and the AI adjust and refine your approaches together.

In AI communication, feedback isn't just a tool—it's a core part of digital etiquette. It shows respect for the AI's role as a collaborator. It also ensures that you're not merely using it as a search engine or automated task manager but as a thinking partner capable of elevating your ideas. Adopting this feedback loop will foster a more thoughtful, productive relationship with AI to help you reach higher levels of creativity, insight, and efficiency.

BALANCING AI INTEGRATION AND HUMAN TOUCH

While refining communication with AI allows you to tap into its immense potential, the true power of AI comes when it's harmoniously integrated into your workflow. A refined prompt, like the one we just explored, provides the AI with all the context needed to guide you seamlessly through your desired process. But as you work with AI more extensively, finding a balance that leverages its capabilities while preserving your personal touch is essential.

Mastering AI communication is just one part of a much larger puzzle. As AI becomes increasingly embedded in our lives, maintaining the right balance between its capabilities and human creativity is critical. This section explores how to create a harmonious partnership with AI and one that enhances what makes us uniquely human.

Understanding the principles of AI-human collaboration is essential for successful integration. These core principles serve as guideposts, helping professionals navigate the delicate balance between technological capability and human wisdom.

AI COMMUNICATION & COLLABORATION PRINCIPLES

The way we interact with AI determines its effectiveness. Its outputs are only as valuable as the inputs we provide. Mastering AI communication means learning to guide AI with clarity, intentionality, and ethical responsibility—ensuring that it is a strategic asset rather than an unchecked influence.

Communicating with AI Effectively

AI doesn't read minds; it interprets instructions. The clearer and more precise your prompts, the more useful AI's responses will be. Thoughtful AI communication involves:

- Provide detailed context: AI performs best when given clear parameters, background information, and objectives.
- Refine responses iteratively: Instead of accepting the first AI-generated output, professionals should refine results-based prompts, guiding AI toward more valuable insights.
- Distinguish between automation and other forms of enhancement.: Using AI to support decision-making so that human expertise remains at the forefront.

For example:

A financial analyst using AI for market forecasting might specify, *"Analyze tech industry trends over the past five years, prioritizing sustainability-focused investments."*

A teacher leveraging AI for lesson planning could refine their request from *"Generate a history lesson plan"* to *"Create a student-centered lesson plan on the Renaissance that includes discussion prompts, interactive activities, and assessment criteria."*

By communicating precisely, professionals ensure that AI is an enabler of their expertise rather than a generic automation tool.

Setting Intentional Boundaries in AI Communication

Technology should support professional goals. Strategic interaction requires clear guidelines to maintain control over outputs. Here is what I mean:

- Use AI to draft emails or reports, but ensure tone, personalization, and accuracy with final edits.
- In client interactions, AI-generated insights should be reviewed for context before being shared as professional recommendations.
- Utilize AI for meeting or presentation preparation, not delegation. While using AI for initial research helps streamline work, final decision-making must remain human-driven.

Establish AI interaction boundaries to ensure that AI communication aligns with strategic, ethical, and professional priorities.

Exercising Critical Thinking

AI-generated Content

AI can't fact-check itself—it relies on human judgment to assess its accuracy and relevance.

This is what effective AI communication requires on your behalf:

- Question assumptions: Is the AI-generated insight valid, relevant, and unbiased?
- Verify facts: Cross-check AI responses against credible sources before making data-driven decisions.
- Consider context and perspective: AI might summarize industry trends, but only human expertise can evaluate their impact on a specific business or market.

Here are two examples:

- A legal professional using AI for contract analysis must verify AI-generated risk assessments to ensure legal accuracy.
- A marketing strategist who asks AI for consumer trend predictions should use human insight to filter out superficial or misleading patterns.

Critical thinking remains the cornerstone of AI interaction, ensuring that AI supports well-informed, ethical, and contextually sound decision-making.

CONSIDERATIONS IN AI COMMUNICATION

Responsible AI engagement demands transparency, fairness, and accountability in professionals' use of artificial intelligence insights.

1. Ensure transparency in AI usage by disclosing its role when presenting AI-generated content instead of passing it off as purely human work.
2. Actively identify and correct biases reflected in AI models stemming from existing training data biases.
3. Maintain human oversight in high-stakes decisions, such as medical diagnoses, legal analysis, or financial projections, ensuring that final judgments remain human-driven.

For instance:

AI may flag potential early disease markers in healthcare, but doctors interpret findings and decide on patient treatment plans. Or, in journalism, AI-generated summaries must be verified and provided with context before publication.

Maintaining these best practices in AI communication ensures that AI remains a trusted tool rather than an opaque or unchecked influence.

PRESERVING HUMAN CONNECTION IN AN AI-DRIVEN WORLD

While AI can handle time-consuming administrative tasks like scheduling or coordinating meetings, we must use this technology to free up time for more meaningful face-to-face interactions and relationship-building.

For example, a manager might use AI in sales to forecast market trends or analyze customer data. However, the human touch provided by regular personal check-ins cultivates trust, nurtures client relationships, and drives long-term loyalty. Ultimately, AI should complement our emotional intelligence and creativity.

The key to unlocking AI's true potential lies in thoughtfully balancing its capabilities with the uniquely human qualities that make our connections meaningful. This can improve our personal and professional lives and ensure that technology enhances rather than undermines our humanity and societal needs.

DANCING WITH DIFFERENT AI PARTNERS

Different AI tools require different communication styles. In other words, you wouldn't speak to your professor like you chat with your smart home device. Successful integration of artificial intelligence requires the mastery of this principle.

Virtual Assistants: The Quick-Step Partners

Virtual assistants like Siri, Alexa, and Google Assistant are your efficient, quick-footed partners in the dance of daily routines. These tools excel at managing routine tasks quickly and precisely, making them indispensable for handling everything from reminders to smart home controls.

When you approach virtual assistants, remember that clarity and simplicity are key. The more straightforward and concise your commands, the better the assistant will understand and execute them.

Virtual assistants thrive in the following scenarios:

- **Clear Commands:** Keep it simple and direct, such as saying, "*Set timer for 20 minutes,*" or "*Turn off the lights.*" These commands ensure the assistant knows exactly what to do quickly and without confusion.
- **Specific Questions:** When you need quick answers, virtual assistants are ready. A question like "*What's tomorrow's weather in Chicago?*" gives them a clear direction to provide a direct, helpful response.
- **Smart Home Controls:** Virtual assistants are great at managing your connected devices. For example, a command like "Turn on kitchen lights to 50% brightness" seamlessly adjusts your home environment according to your preferences.
- **Daily Routines:** If you have a regular morning or evening routine, virtual assistants can help you streamline these tasks. For example, you could say, "*Start my morning routine,*" and the assistant would manage the order of your preset actions, like turning on the coffee maker or reading you the news.

Efficiency with Flowing Commands

For more advanced assistants, such as those capable of understanding multi-step tasks, you can create a natural flow of commands that integrate multiple activities simultaneously. This saves time and helps you set the tone for your interactions, making them feel more like a collaborative exchange than a series of isolated commands. For example:

"Hey, I'm starting dinner prep. Turn on the kitchen lights, set a timer for 30 minutes, play my cooking playlist, and remind me to check the oven in 15 minutes."

By stringing multiple requests together, you maximize your assistant's capabilities—managing multiple tasks efficiently without repeating yourself.

LANGUAGE MODELS: THE DEEP CONVERSATION PARTNERS

When you're ready for a deeper conversation, advanced AI models become your sophisticated collaborators. Unlike the quick and efficient virtual assistants, these models excel in handling complex tasks that require deeper analysis, creative brainstorming, technical guidance, or nuanced understanding. These partners are perfect for addressing requests that exceed fundamental interactions and require customized and perceptive responses.

Here's how you can make the most of their abilities:

Deep Analysis: *"Help me understand the key themes in this research paper and their real-world implications."*

Creative Collaboration: *"Let's brainstorm innovative solutions for reducing plastic waste in small businesses."*

Writing Assistance: *"Help me make this technical report more accessible to a general audience while maintaining its key insights."*

Learning Support: *"Explain quantum computing concepts as if you're teaching a high school student, using everyday analogies."*

Project Planning: *"Help me break down this website redesign into manageable phases with clear milestones."*

Code Understanding: *"Walk me through how this function works and suggest improvements."*

Data Interpretation: *"Help me identify patterns in this customer feedback."*

Content Adaptation: *"Help me adapt this blog post for different social media platforms."*

Critical Thinking: *"Let's examine this argument from multiple perspectives."*

Research Organization: *"Help me structure my literature review findings into coherent themes."*

FROM BASIC TO BRILLIANT

Understanding the capabilities of AI language models is one thing; effectively leveraging them is another. The actual value of these models lies in how you communicate with them. While basic prompts might yield generic responses, a refined, detailed request allows you to guide the AI to produce more accurate, insightful, and contextually relevant content.

Let's explore how the difference between a basic and a sophisticated prompt can dramatically improve your results:

Basic User: "Write a business proposal."

This is like asking someone to cook a meal without sharing your dietary preferences or specific ingredients. With limited context, the AI will generate a generic business proposal that might not address your unique needs, market, or goals. Try something different.

"Help me create a business proposal for a sustainable fashion startup. Please focus on our innovative recycling process, a target market of environmentally conscious millennials, and our need for $500K in seed funding. Highlight the success of our pilot program, which resulted in a 25% reduction in fabric waste, and emphasize the social and environmental impact of our approach."

This refined request is much more specific, offering key context and details that direct the AI's focus. It clarifies the target audience, the business's mission, and the desired outcomes, allowing the AI to generate a relevant, engaging, and compelling proposal. This is the difference between receiving a generic, one-size-fits-all document and a customized, strategic pitch that resonates with stakeholders.

By offering more detailed context, you're not just instructing AI to perform a task—you're turning it into a dynamic collaboration that produces more valuable results. The more context you provide, the more effectively AI can respond to your needs, transforming it into a powerful tool for problem-solving, creativity, and analysis.

THE ART OF AI MASTERY: BEYOND BASIC COMMANDS

Imagine conversing with Leonardo da Vinci about your creative project or discussing your business strategy with a team of world-class experts. That's the level of interaction possible when you master AI communication. It's not about issuing commands; it's about fostering a collaborative dialogue. Let's unlock that potential.

The STAR Method: Structuring Your AI Conversations

Think of the STAR Method* as your guide to respectful and effective AI communication. It transforms requests into mini-narratives, providing crucial context for optimal results. This isn't just about getting what you want; it's about engaging with AI in a way that maximizes its capabilities and respects its operational logic. The STAR Method will become second nature with practice, enhancing your AI interactions significantly. Here's how to structure your requests:

S—Situation: "*I'm writing a novel set in ancient Rome, focusing on the social dynamics of different classes.*" (Adds depth)

T—Task: "*I need to describe authentic daily life details, particularly how class distinctions manifested in everyday interactions.*" (More specific)

A—Approach: "*Focus on marketplace scenes and family dinners, highlighting differences in clothing, food, language, and customs based on social standing.*" (More targeted)

* Adapted from the traditional STAR interviewing framework (Situation, Task, Action, Result), reimagined specifically for effective human-AI communication.

R—Result: "*Help me create vivid, historically accurate descriptions that engage all five senses and subtly convey the nuances of class in ancient Rome. Provide citations or sources where possible.*" (Adds academic rigor and emphasis.)

Compare this to a basic request like "Tell me about ancient Rome." Considering the AI's processing needs, the STAR Method transforms a vague request into a focused pathway. The difference in results will be dramatic, and you'll engage with the AI as a true collaborator.

THE POWER OF CONTEXTUAL COLLABORATION

The more context you provide about your goals, constraints, and especially your preferences, the more tailored and valuable your AI interactions become. It's like the difference between getting generic advice and personalized coaching. Think of it as onboarding a new team member – the more information you provide upfront, the more effectively they can contribute. This improves the AI's output and reinforces the interaction's collaborative nature, a key principle of good AI etiquette. By being transparent and specific, you respect the AI's role in the partnership.

To refine the AI's focus further, consider adding examples of what you don't want. For instance, "*Avoid descriptions that rely on common stereotypes about ancient Rome.*"

THE STAR METHOD IN PRACTICE

The STAR Method isn't just a theoretical framework; it's a practical tool for achieving real-world results. Let me share the story of someone I helped that demonstrates its transformative power. The client's details have been changed to protect privacy.

Real Case Study 1: A Restaurant Owner's AI Journey

S—Situation: Eddie, a restaurant owner in a charming Maryland town, saw a surge in catering requests after a website upgrade. While this influx was positive, it threatened to overwhelm his small business. Before implementing the AI solution, Edward tried forwarding catering inquiries to a generic email address, which led to slow responses, missed details, and frustrated customers.

T—Task: Eddie needed to efficiently manage the increased catering inquiries without sacrificing the personalized service his customers valued. He drowned in emails, which affected his menu planning, staff management, and work-life balance.

A—Approach: We implemented a three-phase AI solution:

1. **Foundation:** Analyzed past email patterns, identified common questions, and created AI response templates that captured Edward's voice and brand values.
2. **Implementation:** Deployed an AI email assistant trained in the restaurant's specific language and catering processes. Developed customization protocols for various request types.
3. **Refinement:** Integrated seasonal menu variations, pricing updates, and fine-tuned personalization elements based on customer feedback.

R—Results: The impact was significant:

Quantitative: Response times decreased by half, saving Eddie 4+ hours per week. Catering booking effectiveness increased by 28% and counting.

Qualitative: More consistent brand voice, improved work-life balance for Eddie, increased customer and staff satisfaction, and enhanced capacity for *meaningful* customer interactions.

As you can see, AI freed up time for genuine engagement. Building on this success, Eddie is exploring AI applications for inventory management, staff scheduling, and menu optimization.

Implementation Tips

- Start with your most common email types.
- Maintain human oversight for final approvals (especially initially).
- Keep your AI system updated with menu and pricing changes.
- Actively monitor customer feedback. This demonstrates respect for your AI partner and ensures its continued effectiveness.

The following case studies are illustrative and not based on specific individuals or organizations. While fictional, they're designed to represent common scenarios you may encounter. I hope you can identify similarities to your needs and find them helpful in your journey.

Case Study 2: A Freelancer's Journey

S—Situation:

Maya is a freelance graphic designer who has been receiving more clients through word-of-mouth referrals. However, she struggles to deliver highly personalized designs while managing multiple projects simultaneously. She needs to streamline her process while keeping the work creative and unique.

T—Task:

Maya needs to create a more efficient workflow for design projects without sacrificing the personalization and creativity her clients expect. She wants to use AI to support the brainstorming phase, improve the efficiency of revisions, and maintain a cohesive visual identity for each client.

A—Approach:

Maya integrates an AI design assistant that helps her generate initial mood boards, review and suggest color palettes, and provide typographic options. The AI is trained on her portfolio to understand her style and the preferences of her client base.

1. **Foundation:** Analyzed previous designs to identify common themes, styles, and color palettes. The AI assistant learns her preferences and consistently updates client feedback.
2. **Implementation:** Deployed the AI tool to generate initial design suggestions for new projects based on the brief provided by the client.
3. **Refinement:** Maya regularly provides feedback to the AI, suggesting tweaks, such as adjusting font weight or color saturation. She also keeps the AI updated with her new work and client preferences.

R—Results:

Quantitative: The time spent on brainstorming new concepts decreased by almost half, allowing Maya to dedicate more time to refining the final product. Additionally, the client satisfaction rate increased due to more frequent feedback loops and faster iterations.

Qualitative: The AI helped her maintain consistency across projects and provided many creative options that sparked new ideas. It also helped her manage a higher volume of work without compromising her creative vision. The integration allowed her to focus more on the artistry behind the design.

Implementation Tips:

- Personalize the AI to match your style and ensure it understands your creative preferences.
- Regularly update the AI with new projects and client feedback to maintain the relevancy of suggestions.
- Use AI as a brainstorming partner, not a creative thought replacement. Maintain control of final decisions.

Case Study 3: An HR Manager's AI Journey

S—Situation: Maria is an HR manager at a medium-sized tech company. She oversees recruitment, employee development, and retention. The company is expanding rapidly, and Maria is facing an increasing workload, particularly in hiring. She needs to streamline recruitment while ensuring the best candidate experience and cultural fit for the company.

T—Task: Maria needs to efficiently manage and scale the recruitment process without sacrificing the personalized touch that aligns candidates with the company culture. She wants to ensure a more efficient candidate screening process while still engaging deeply with candidates to assess their fit for the company.

A—Approach: Maria integrates an AI-powered applicant tracking system (ATS) that filters resumes and shortlists candidates based on predefined skills and experiences.

The system is customized to reflect the company's values and cultural needs. She also sets up AI-driven chatbots for initial candidate engagement, allowing candidates to ask questions and schedule interviews at their convenience.

1. **Foundation:** Analyzed past hiring data to identify successful employees' key traits and adjust the system for a more tailored candidate experience.
2. **Implementation:** Deployed the AI system to automatically screen resumes and use data from past hires to rank candidates based on skill and cultural fit.
3. **Refinement:** Regularly provided feedback to the AI tool based on candidate outcomes and employee retention data to refine the system's screening logic. Adjusted the interview questions used by the AI chatbot to match evolving company needs.

R—Results:

Quantitative: Reduced time-to-hire by half, enabling the HR team to process more applications while increasing the quality of hired candidates.

Qualitative: Candidates reported a smoother and more engaging recruitment process, and hiring managers noted higher satisfaction with candidates' cultural fit. Employee turnover in the first six months post-hire decreased by 10%.

Implementation Tips:

- Ensure the AI tool is constantly updated with feedback on its success in matching candidates to the company culture.
- Use AI for initial screenings and scheduling but maintain human oversight for final hiring decisions.
- Regularly refine the criteria used by the AI to adapt to evolving company needs and values.

Case Study 4: A Marketing Manager's AI Journey

S—Situation: Tom is a marketing manager at a consumer goods company. His team handles content creation, social media management, and digital marketing campaigns. The company has been receiving customer feedback but struggles to process and interpret large volumes of comments and suggestions across social media channels, slowing down its ability to respond to customer needs.

T—Task: Tom needs to improve his team's ability to analyze customer feedback quickly, derive actionable insights, and adjust real-time marketing strategies to respond to customer sentiment.

A—Approach: Tom decides to deploy an AI-driven sentiment analysis tool that scans social media posts, reviews, and comments for insights on brand perception. The AI tool is set to identify key themes in customer feedback (positive, negative, or neutral) and automatically categorize them based on specific products or services. Tom also sets up automated reports for weekly team meetings.

1. **Foundation:** Configured the AI tool to track brand mentions and product-specific feedback across multiple channels.
2. **Implementation:** The AI tool was integrated with social media platforms and CRM systems, enabling real-time feedback analysis and the identification of emerging trends.

3. **Refinement:** After noticing that the AI provided more generalized insights, Tom fine-tuned the system by adding specific product lines and customer satisfaction metrics to improve its contextual understanding.

R—Results:

Quantitative: Reduced manual analysis time by 60%, allowing the marketing team to focus on strategy instead of data collection.

Qualitative: Real-time insights led to faster campaign adjustments, with customer satisfaction improving by 15% over three months, as evidenced by customer feedback and product reviews. The AI tool also identified a previously overlooked market segment, which led to a new targeted marketing campaign.

Implementation Tips:

- Regularly update the system to track emerging keywords and themes as customer preferences evolve.
- Use AI for trend spotting and customer sentiment analysis, but ensure that human insight is used to create tailored responses or content.
- Track the long-term effectiveness of marketing adjustments based on AI insights and continue fine-tuning the tool accordingly.

Case Study 5: A High School Teacher's AI Journey

S—Situation: Jane is a high school teacher in a public school who teaches English literature to 11th-grade students. Her class is diverse, with students with varying learning styles, levels of engagement, and individual academic needs. Jane is finding it increasingly difficult to provide personalized attention to each student while managing grading, lesson planning, and administrative tasks.

T—Task: Jane needs to find a way to provide more tailored instruction to her students without overwhelming herself. She wants to use AI to help differentiate instruction for her students, especially to support those who are struggling. She also wants to improve her workflow in grading and lesson planning.

A—Approach: Jane decides to integrate an AI-based learning platform into her classroom. This platform can provide personalized reading comprehension quizzes, track student progress, and offer real-time feedback on assignments. She also begins using an AI grading assistant to help grade essays more efficiently, allowing her to focus on providing targeted support where it's most needed.

1. **Foundation:** Jane identifies areas where AI could support her teaching, such as personalizing quizzes, grading essays, and offering individualized student progress feedback.
2. **Implementation:** She integrates the AI system into her classroom, setting it up to automatically generate quizzes based on the reading material and assess student essays for structure, grammar, and content understanding. Students are encouraged to use the AI feedback to improve their work.
3. **Refinement:** As she reviews the AI's feedback on essays, Jane notices that some feedback on creative writing assignments feels too formulaic. She adjusts the AI settings to address creative expression and narrative voice better, ensuring the feedback aligns with her teaching objectives.

R—Results:

Quantitative: Essay grading time was reduced by 50%, allowing Jane to focus more on providing personal support and facilitating class discussions. The personalized quizzes helped students improve their comprehension scores by an average of 20% over a semester.

Qualitative: Students who struggled with reading comprehension benefitted from targeted quizzes that helped them grasp key concepts. Those with advanced writing skills appreciated the nuanced feedback provided by the AI tool, which encouraged deeper creative exploration. Jane reported feeling less stressed about grading, which allowed her to focus more on fostering a positive classroom environment and engagement.

Implementation Tips:

- Start small by using AI tools for specific tasks (like grading or quiz creation) before gradually incorporating more complex features.
- Review and adjust the AI's feedback regularly to ensure it aligns with your teaching style and your students' needs.
- Ensure students understand the AI's role in their learning and encourage them to use it to supplement teacher guidance.

THE ART OF CONVERSATIONAL AI: MAGIC IN ACTION

This is where the true potential of partnering with AI comes to life. It's not just about *what* you ask but *how* you ask. Think of it as mastering the art of conversation, not just issuing commands. The subject matter is limitless, but the approach transforms a basic inquiry into a master-level dialogue. Let's explore how.

A Designer's Journey: From Basic Request to Master-Level Dialogue

Let's illustrate the power of structured communication with a design example:

Basic Request: "Give me logo ideas for a coffee shop." (Generic and unhelpful)

Power User Dialogue (using a conversational approach):

"I'm designing a logo for an artisanal coffee shop that roasts its own beans. They have a strong commitment to…

Community Connection: They envision their space as a hub for local artists and gatherings.

Sustainable Sourcing: They prioritize ethically sourced beans and eco-friendly practices.

Artisanal Craftsmanship: They take pride in their meticulous roasting process and the quality of their coffee.

Their target audience is urban professionals who appreciate craft and quality. The physical space has an industrial-modern aesthetic with warm wood accents.

Given these details, I'd like to explore logo concepts that:

Reflect on their artisanal roasting process (perhaps incorporating imagery of coffee beans or roasting equipment).

Feel sophisticated yet welcoming, appealing to their target audience.

Work effectively in both large (signage) and small (social media icon) formats.

Could you generate some initial ideas, perhaps focusing on different visual metaphors for "community" and "craft"? I'm particularly interested in how typography might contribute."

Notice how this "dialogue" gives the AI a rich understanding of the project's nuances. It's not just about a logo; it's about capturing the essence of the coffee shop's brand and values.

Etiquette Tip: Cultivate a respectful partnership with AI by communicating clearly and providing ongoing feedback. This collaborative approach unlocks its potential while upholding the principles of digital decorum in the age of intelligent machines.

THE DANCE OF BALANCE: MASTERING AI WITHOUT LOSING YOURSELF

Just as a skilled conductor leads an orchestra without overshadowing the music, your relationship with AI should enhance, not override, your unique human judgment or uniqueness. It's a delicate dance – leveraging AI's power while preserving your own. Let's examine how to maintain this crucial balance by discussing a few common pitfalls.

Common Pitfalls

As you embrace AI, you must be aware of its potential downsides. AI is a powerful tool, but like any tool, it has its limitations and potential for misuse. Being mindful of these common issues will help you use AI responsibly and effectively, ensuring it serves you, not the other way around. Think of these as the "siren songs" of AI – tempting but potentially dangerous if you're not careful. Here are some warning signs to watch for, along with tips to stay on course:

Over-Reliance: The Erosion of Self-Trust

Warning Signs

1. Constantly checking with AI before making even simple decisions.
2. Losing confidence in your own judgment and intuition.

Etiquette Tip: AI should nurture your thinking. Use AI as a sounding board, not a crutch. Remember, your unique human perspective is invaluable.

Privacy Drift: The Slippery Slope of Sharing

Warning Signs

1. Sharing increasingly sensitive information with AI systems without considering the implications.
2. Becoming complacent about your digital footprint and the potential for data misuse.

Etiquette Tip: Treat AI interactions as if you were in a public conversation. Be mindful of what you share, and understand that once shared, data can be challenging to retract. Prioritize your privacy.

Quality Control: Trust, But Verify (Always)

Warning Signs

1. Accepting AI-generated outputs without critical review.
2. Forgetting to fact-check important information, even when provided by AI.

Guidance: Trust AI's capabilities, but *always* verify its outputs. AI is a tool, not an oracle. Your critical thinking and human oversight are essential.

Think of AI like a powerful telescope—it can help you see further and clearer, but you still have to choose where to look and what to focus on. Your judgment, values, and unique human perspective guide the telescope. Don't let technology dictate your choices; let your own wisdom be your compass.

CRAFTING YOUR AI COMMUNICATION STYLE

A Toolkit for Digital Decorum

Now that you know the potential pitfalls, let's empower you with the tools and techniques to master the art of AI communication. Think of this as developing your own "AI fluency," a skill that becomes increasingly valuable as AI technology advances. Just as you've cultivated your communication style across the spectrum of people you encounter, you can refine your approach to interacting with AI, ensuring clarity, efficiency, and mutual respect.

Shaping the Future of Human-AI Collaboration

By practicing the principles of clear communication, providing context, and actively refining your approach, you're not just improving your AI interactions—you're helping to shape a future where human ingenuity and AI capabilities work together to achieve extraordinary things. This collaboration goes beyond simply learning today's tools. It's about actively designing a future where AI serves humanity's highest potential, and you are a co-architect in its evolution.

As we continue to engage with AI, we have a unique opportunity to influence the development of robust AI systems aligned with our ethical values and human-centered goals. Our engagement with AI today contributes to our success and the broader landscape of AI's role in society. This is the transformative potential of mastering AI communication—your thoughtful choices today shape the AI of tomorrow.

We are entering a world where complex ideas flow seamlessly between human minds and artificial intelligence. Creative visions come to life through fluid dialogue, and challenges that once seemed insurmountable become opportunities for innovation and discovery. In this world, AI is integral in solving global challenges, creating opportunities, and enriching human experience.

To shape this future, we must use AI to improve our current efforts while ensuring its systems align with our highest ethical and societal objectives. We must design AI systems that are human-centered, transparent, and aware of their profound impact on society. Our communication with AI today will lay the foundation for the ethical standards, technological frameworks, and societal roles these systems will play in the future.

Here's how this vision could take shape across several key areas:

In scientific research, AI can accelerate the pace of discovery by analyzing massive datasets, identifying patterns, and generating hypotheses. Through this collaboration, AI could help lead breakthroughs in fields like medicine, materials science, and environmental sustainability. Imagine AI supporting researchers in developing new vaccines, designing sustainable materials, or predicting and mitigating the effects of climate change. By shaping how we communicate with AI in these fields, we improve our research practices and ensure these technologies serve the greater good.

In artistic expression, AI can unlock new forms of creativity by collaborating with artists, musicians, and writers to craft novel musical compositions, stunning visual art, or compelling narratives. Picture an AI that works alongside musicians to compose symphonies that evoke complex emotions, visual artists to create breathtaking landscapes that blur the lines between reality and imagination, or writers to build worlds that transport readers beyond their wildest dreams. This is the future where AI is a creatively active partner, helping humans realize artistic visions while remaining aligned with the values of authenticity and human expression.

In problem-solving, AI can offer innovative solutions to global challenges by analyzing complex systems, identifying root causes, and simulating potential outcomes. From alleviating poverty to promoting sustainable development, AI could be crucial in helping policymakers design effective strategies. The future of problem-solving, powered by AI, will be shaped by thoughtful human-AI collaboration—one where creativity, empathy, and human judgment guide the solutions we seek.

But the bigger picture goes even further. Shaping the future of human-AI collaboration isn't just about using AI to enhance our current endeavors—it's about helping shape the systems themselves. As AI technology grows more sophisticated, the designers, thinkers, and communicators who engage with it today will set ethical standards, influence how AI is built, and guide its societal role. Your contributions today will shape the evolution of the AI systems that will define the future.

You are not just a user of AI—you are a co-architect in its evolution. Whenever you thoughtfully engage with AI, provide feedback, and help it evolve, you contribute to a future where AI supports human creativity, fosters social good, and aligns with our collective ethical standards. In this way, AI becomes a collaborative partner rather than just technology, helping us reach greater heights as we co-create.

BRIDGING HUMAN INSIGHT AND COMPUTATIONAL POWER

Mastering AI communication isn't just about learning commands; it's about developing an essential skill set for the future of human achievement—the ability to bridge human insight and computational power. As AI capabilities grow, your communication skills become even more valuable, allowing you to:

- Shape better outcomes by guiding AI with your unique perspectives and values.
- Unlock new possibilities through creative collaboration and problem-solving.
- Guide others in navigating the evolving landscape of human-AI interaction.

Every great leap in human progress has been preceded by advances in communication—from spoken language to written words, from printing presses to digital networks. As we learn to engage meaningfully with artificial intelligence, we are not just witnessing the next significant communication advancement—we are actively creating it. How we speak to AI today, refine our dialogue, and develop ethical frameworks will directly shape tomorrow's systems.

Indeed, your role in this process is more significant than ever. Mastering AI communication today is key to helping design a future where human ingenuity and AI capabilities combine to solve challenges, create opportunities, and realize possibilities we're only beginning to imagine. This is your chance to be a pioneer, shaping a historical transformation in human capability and AI's role in society that will resonate for future generations.

AI COMMUNICATION IN EVERYDAY LIFE

The true power of mastering AI communication isn't just understanding the technology but transforming ordinary moments into extraordinary opportunities. Let's examine how this functions in illustrative scenarios. Below are a few examples of how thoughtful AI interaction can make a difference.

Scenario 1: The Creative Breakthrough

Meet Maya, a novelist struggling with writer's block.

Basic Approach: "Give me ideas for my story."

Master Approach: *"I'm writing a mystery novel where the detective is a botanist. I want to weave plant science into the plot twists. Let's explore:*

How rare plants could be used as clues, ways botanical knowledge could be central to solving the mystery and scientific details that create authenticity and intrigue."

Instead of generic plot suggestions, Maya received tailored insights that blended creativity with scientific accuracy, opening up new story possibilities she hadn't imagined.

Scenario 2: The Learning Revolution

Jeff wanted to learn data analysis for his career. This is an example of proper professional growth in action.

Novice Approach: "Teach me data analysis."

Expert Dialogue: *"I'm in marketing and want to understand customer behavior data. I know basic Excel but want to:*

Learn Python for data analysis, focus on retail customer patterns, and create meaningful visualizations to present insights.

Please guide me through a 3-month learning plan that fits around my full-time job."

Scenario 3: The Home Project Transformer

Meet Wanda, who turned an overwhelming home organization project into a manageable success:

Beginner Approach: "Help me organize my house."

Master Approach: *"I'm tackling a house that's gathered 10 years of memories. I need a system that:*

- *Works for a busy family of four.*
- *Handles both digital and physical items.*
- *Creates lasting organizational habits, not just a one-time fix.*
- *Considers our limited storage space.*
- *Let's start with a step-by-step plan for the kitchen, focusing on daily workflow and family accessibility."*

Result: Instead of generic organizing tips, Wanda received a customized system that transformed her space and her family's daily routines.

The Potential

The most valuable AI interactions explore possibilities you might not have considered. This collaborative approach, where you provide context, refine your prompts, and engage in a genuine dialogue, is the essence of AI etiquette and the key to unlocking its transformative potential.

SPEAKING WITH THE FUTURE, SHAPING PROFESSIONAL SUCCESS

Mastering the art of communicating with AI isn't just about personal efficiency or individual gain; it's about unlocking a new realm of possibilities for transforming professional work and shaping the future of human endeavor. Here are but a few ideas:

- Complex research tasks are completed in a fraction of the time, freeing professionals to focus on strategic decision-making and innovation.
- Creative projects are co-created with AI partners, leading to design, marketing, and product development breakthroughs.
- Routine tasks are automated seamlessly, allowing professionals to dedicate their energy to building relationships and fostering deeper connections with clients and colleagues.

This is the transformative power of speaking with the future—leveraging AI's capabilities to amplify our productivity, enhance our creativity, and redefine the boundaries of professional achievement.

But this transformation isn't just about technology; it's about how we interact with it. By embracing the principles of AI etiquette (clear communication, contextual awareness, and collaborative dialogue), we ensure that AI remains a tool that empowers us rather than a force that diminishes our human touch.

As we step into this new era of professional work, remember that your ability to communicate effectively with AI is not just an advantage; it's an essential skill that will shape your success and contribution to the world. The future of work is not just AI-powered; it's AI-collaborative. Your mastery of this new language of collaboration will determine your ability to thrive in this exciting landscape.

In the next chapter, we'll explore how AI revolutionizes various industries and how you can harness its potential to enhance your career and make a lasting impact. Get ready to discover how the skills you've honed in this chapter can be applied to achieve extraordinary results in the professional world.

THE SEVEN-DAY AI COMMUNICATION CHALLENGE

An Optional Exploration

Consider this your invitation to embark on a journey of personal growth within AI interaction. This seven-day challenge is optional—a flexible toolkit you can adapt to your pace, interests, and goals. Think of it as a "choose your own adventure" guide. There's no need to adhere to a strict timeline; immerse yourself completely, explore the exercises that ignite your curiosity, or take your time over weeks or months, whichever works best for you.

Some might dive in fully, completing each day's challenge with intention. Others might cherry-pick exercises based on what resonates. The beauty of this challenge lies in its adaptability. It invites you to explore various aspects of AI communication and adapt them to your journey.

Most importantly, engage with the challenge naturally and in a way that benefits you. This journey is about crafting your unique communication style that reflects your needs and preferences while embracing the principles of clear, thoughtful communication and digital decorum. By participating, you'll also nurture skills that enhance your personal and professional life, empowering you to work more collaboratively with AI as it becomes an increasingly valuable partner.

The Challenge: Day by Day

Each day's challenge will help you strengthen your intuitive AI communication skills while fostering a collaborative partnership that goes beyond simply issuing commands. These exercises invite you to think strategically, refine your requests, and engage in meaningful conversations with AI.

Day 1: The Clear Request

Challenge: Identify a regularly performed task and rewrite it as an explicit, concise AI request.

Example: Instead of "Help me with emails," try "*Draft a professional email to my colleague confirming our meeting on Friday at 3 p.m.*"

Day 2: The Context Builder

Challenge: To guide the AI's response, add context to yesterday's request by sharing your goals, preferences, and constraints.

Example: "*Draft an email confirming Friday's meeting. Mention it will be virtual and suggest using Zoom unless they prefer another platform. Keep the tone friendly and informal.*"

Day 3: The Refinement Dance

Challenge: Practice using follow-up prompts to refine AI responses. Start with a broad request, then narrow it down based on the AI's initial output.

Example: Begin with "*Summarize this article,*" followed by "*Focus on the section about environmental impact,*" and then perhaps "*Give me three bullet points highlighting the key findings.*"

Day 4: The Creative Collaborator

Challenge: Engage in a creative project with AI as your partner. Describe your vision in detail, explain any constraints, and be open to the AI's suggestions. Embrace the collaborative process.

Example: *"I'm designing a logo for a sustainable clothing brand. I want it to feel modern and minimalist, with earthy tones and a focus on natural imagery. I'm open to suggestions for fonts and visual elements. Can you generate some initial ideas?"*

Day 5: The Problem Solver

Challenge: Present the AI with a real-world challenge. Break it down step-by-step, providing context and desired outcomes.

Example: *"I'm struggling to maintain a healthy work-life balance. I often work late and find it hard to switch off. Can you suggest some strategies for setting boundaries and prioritizing my well-being? I'm interested in time management techniques, mindfulness practices, and tips for creating a relaxing evening routine."*

Day 6: The Strategic Thinker

Challenge: Have a long-form conversation with the AI about a complex goal. Build on its responses, refine your approach, and explore different strategies together.

Example: *"I want to start a small online business selling handmade jewelry. Help me create a 3-month plan to launch this business. Start with market research, then move to marketing and branding, and end with launch logistics and customer service considerations."*

Day 7: The Master Communicator

Challenge: Combine everything you've learned throughout the challenge. Make clear requests, provide rich context, refine your prompts, and critically evaluate the AI's responses.

Example: *"I want to plan a surprise birthday party for my best friend, who loves outdoor activities. I will consider their interests, suggest a location and theme, propose a menu with both vegetarian and non-vegetarian options, and create a playlist that fits the mood. I have a budget of $500 and would like to keep the guest list to around 20 people."*

These exercises will help you build a more intuitive and thoughtful communication style, enhancing your collaboration with AI and guiding you toward a deeper understanding of how to craft requests that truly reflect your needs. Through feedback and reflection, you will develop a more meaningful AI partnership that leads to enhanced creativity, problem-solving, and productivity.

FOUR
ENHANCING DAILY LIVING
AI & HUMAN CONNECTION

… ✦ …

"What is now proved was once only imagined."
— William Blake

EVOLVING WITH AI

Evolving with AI is like a master dancer learning to move with a new partner. Just as a dancer must understand leading and following, we are learning to move harmoniously with AI in our creative expression and daily lives. Sometimes, we lead, articulating our vision with precise prompts and careful guidance; other times, we follow, recognizing when AI offers unexpected insights that merit exploration.

Imagine yourself as a conductor standing before an orchestra where musicians with AI-powered instruments await your direction. The music that emerges isn't purely human or machine but a symphony of possibilities that neither could achieve alone.

Similarly, a potter at her wheel understands that while the clay responds to her touch, it also has a unique nature that must be respected. As we develop our relationship with AI, we must learn its strengths and tendencies and how to work with its distinctive characteristics rather than against them. The art lies not in controlling AI but in harmonizing our intentions with its capabilities.

Thoughtfully integrate AI into your daily routine to create more time for what truly matters.

SMART HOME TRANSFORMATION

For many, AI integration begins with minor changes: a thermostat that adapts to your ideal temperature, a lighting system that adjusts to your routines, or a voice assistant that tracks your schedule.

Integration is often subtle, yet its impact is profound. What begins as small conveniences swiftly transforms into an ecosystem that adapts to our needs, freeing us from mundane tasks and enhancing our comfort. As these tools become part of daily life, they create an ecosystem of seamless support.

Imagine waking up to soft lighting mimicking the sunrise, coffee brewing automatically, and your morning playlist easing you into the day. Later, as you walk through the door after work, the temperature adjusts to your comfort level, and a playlist based on your mood welcomes you home. AI can even help with dinner, analyzing available ingredients and suggesting creative meals, making cooking feel less like a chore and more like an intuitive experience.

These are the quiet, everyday ways AI enhances life. It does so by anticipating needs, easing tensions, and helping create a home that works for you.

Getting Started with AI at Home

This isn't something you need to master overnight. For many, the best way to integrate it is to start with simple, everyday tools that feel natural to their routines. Instead of focusing on which device to buy, consider what aspect of life you'd like to improve first. Do you want more efficiency? Better organization? More seamless transitions between work and home? Let AI serve your needs rather than the other way around.

Some people start by automating their environment—adjusting temperature, lighting, or scheduling. Others begin with AI-powered recommendations for meals, workouts, or wellness. The key is to adopt AI on your own terms in ways that feel comfortable and useful to you.

Just as AI can optimize home routines, it can also support well-being. From personalized fitness tracking to sleep improvement, AI has the potential to enhance efficiency and overall quality of life. How? It can play a transformative role in personal health and wellness.

AI BEYOND WORK

While AI is often associated with professional productivity, its benefits extend far beyond the workplace. It can simplify daily tasks, improve decision-making, and create more time for meaningful human connections.

I hesitated when I first considered AI's role in my personal life. Would it make my home feel overly automated and un-private? Would I lose touch with the simple pleasures of daily routines? These were real concerns; if you share them, you're not alone. However, I discovered a profound truth: the presence of AI in my daily routine simplifies life and allows me to create memorable experiences far more often.

The key to successful AI integration isn't about how much technology you adopt but how thoughtfully you apply it. AI, when used with intention, allows us to reclaim time and energy while preserving the authenticity of our experiences.

Let's explore how AI can serve as a personal assistant, coach, and companion in our pursuit of a fulfilling, balanced, and joyful life.

THE UNEXPECTED JOYS OF AI

When people think about AI, they often focus on efficiency, automation, and problem-solving. However, they usually overlook the small, unexpected joys that AI can bring to daily life. These moments may seem trivial initially, but they contribute to a sense of wonder, connection, and nostalgia.

For example, it helps rediscover forgotten memories through AI-generated photo albums, where old pictures are resurfaced and arranged into beautifully curated timelines. A simple notification might remind you of a trip you took years ago, sparking joy and rekindling stories long tucked away in your phone's storage.

Consider how AI can serve as a serendipitous curator, introducing you to music, books, or films you may never have found. Perhaps it recommends a song that resonates perfectly with your mood or suggests a book that becomes a life-changing read; these little moments of synchronicity add richness to our everyday experiences. They may seem trivial, but they contribute unexpected joys.

Then, there's the delight of AI-assisted creativity. Whether generating whimsical poetry, sketching out imaginative art, or composing personalized bedtime stories for children, AI can surprise us with unexpected bursts of inspiration, reminding us that creativity isn't just about output but the joy of discovery.

Even in the realm of human connection, AI plays an unanticipated role. It might remind us to reach out to an old friend, help us craft thoughtful messages, or facilitate meaningful conversations by surfacing shared memories. When used correctly, it can strengthen human relationships, allowing us to be more present and intentional with the people we care about.

These moments don't make headlines but subtly enhance our lives in ways many take for granted. The unexpected joys of AI remind us that technology, when approached with curiosity and openness, can be a source of delight, connection, and personal enrichment.

AI FOR HEALTH & WELLNESS: YOUR 24/7 HEALTH COACH

Whether it's improving fitness, nutrition, or sleep, AI-powered tools act as an always-available health coach, offering personalized insights that help us lead healthier, more balanced lives.

Imagine waking up to an AI-generated morning wellness plan: a light workout suggestion based on your activity levels, a breakfast recommendation tailored to your nutritional goals, and a meditation session to start the day with focus. Later, AI tracks your hydration levels, reminds you to move after long work sessions, and even helps you wind down at night with a customized sleep routine.

AI transforms your data into meaningful action. Here's how it helps people take control of their health:

- Fitness Tracking: Workout plans adapt based on progress, energy levels, and real-time feedback.
- Nutrition Management: Smart meal planning, ingredient tracking, and recipe suggestions make eating well effortless.
- Predictive Health Analytics: AI can analyze patterns to anticipate potential health concerns before symptoms appear.
- Sleep Optimization: Personalized sleep recommendations, tracking, and bedtime routines to improve rest.

Inspiring Wellness Transformation: From Struggling to Thriving

Sometimes, the most profound changes come not from grand gestures but from having the proper guidance at the right time. A close friend of mine struggled with maintaining a balanced lifestyle. She knew better exercise, good sleep, and healthier nutrition were part of the solution. Nonetheless, practicing them seemed unattainable. She would start workout routines but never stay consistent. She tried meal plans but found them overwhelming. She wanted to sleep earlier but felt exhausted at the wrong times.

Then, she decided to let AI be her accountability partner. First, she used an AI-powered fitness app that adapted to her energy levels and movement history, keeping workouts engaging without being too intense. Then, an AI meal planner simplified grocery shopping, suggesting easy, healthy meals tailored to her goals. AI sleep tracking analyzed her rest patterns at night and provided minor adjustments that gradually helped her feel refreshed.

Six months later, her transformation was undeniable. She had lost weight, regained energy, and built sustainable habits that no longer felt like a burden. AI didn't change her—it helped her change herself. She felt guided.

EMPOWERING PROACTIVE HEALTH WITH AI

A more powerful aspect of AI isn't just tracking health but preventing issues before they arise. Instead of reacting to symptoms, AI helps identify early warning signs, offering proactive recommendations tailored to your personal health data.

Here's where AI is making a difference:

- Predictive Analytics: AI detects subtle patterns in data to identify health risks early.
- Medication Management: Automated reminders, side effect tracking, and medication interaction alerts.
- Telemedicine Integration: AI-powered symptom analysis, virtual consultations, and remote monitoring for personalized health insights.

Imagine a future where AI can alert you to potential deficiencies, suggest lifestyle adjustments before stress takes its toll, and even predict certain health conditions before they manifest symptoms. AI in health isn't just about fitness—it's about creating a longer, healthier, and more proactive life.

AI FOR MINDFULNESS & SPIRITUAL GROWTH

Amid the rapid advancement of AI in productivity, entertainment, and home management, one of its most profound applications is often overlooked: its ability to support mindfulness, self-reflection, and even spiritual exploration. In truth, AI can be a valuable conduit for deepening our connection to ourselves, our values, and the world around us.

Think of it as a quiet guide that gently offers insight, structure, and new perspectives to enrich our inner lives. The same algorithms that tailor recommendations for work or leisure can also be harnessed to cultivate presence, peace, and wisdom.

Enhancing Mindfulness and Reflection

Daily reflection has long been a cornerstone of personal growth, yet many struggle to maintain the habit. AI-powered tools can provide guided prompts based on individual goals, recent experiences, or emotional states inferred from previous entries. These prompts can nudge us toward gratitude, self-awareness, or problem-solving in ways that feel organic rather than mechanical.

Imagine sitting down to write, and instead of facing a blank page, your AI journaling assistant suggests a reflection like: *"What was the most meaningful moment of your day, and why?"* or *"What is something you're holding onto that you might benefit from releasing?"* Over time, these gentle nudges create a personalized archive of growth and insight, helping you recognize patterns in your emotions, aspirations, and values.

AI can also aid in structured mindfulness practices. Applications powered by AI can tailor meditation routines based on stress levels, sleep patterns, or previous sessions. For instance, an AI-driven meditation assistant might suggest a five-minute breathing exercise after detecting elevated stress signals in your voice. It could also adjust your practice based on the time of day, ensuring your morning meditation is energized while your evening routine promotes restfulness.

Deepening Spiritual Exploration

AI can also be an invaluable resource for spiritual seekers, whether religious or philosophical. It can aggregate wisdom from sacred texts, historical commentaries, and contemporary perspectives, offering insights tailored to specific inquiries.

Imagine you are reflecting on a personal struggle and wish to find wisdom from ancient teachings. An AI tool could help surface relevant passages from texts like the Bible, the Bhagavad Gita, the Tao Te Ching, or Stoic philosophy, presenting perspectives that align with your current challenges. In this case, AI acts as a bridge, allowing more profound engagement with spiritual material that might require months or even years of searching.

Similarly, AI-powered discussion tools can facilitate community dialogue by connecting individuals with shared beliefs or questions. Whether through intelligent discussion prompts in spiritual forums or AI-generated summaries of theological debates, technology can make ancient wisdom more accessible to modern seekers.

CURATING CONTENT FOR BALANCE

AI can play a critical role in curating mindful content rather than endless information streams. Instead of bombarding us with news and entertainment, AI can surface articles, podcasts, or videos designed to inspire contemplation, encourage balance, or offer moments of stillness.

Imagine an AI assistant that notices you've been consuming a lot of high-intensity media—perhaps news or work-related content—and suggests balancing it with something more centering: a calming nature video, a poetry reading, or a slow instrumental piece that helps reset your focus. This simple shift can transform how we engage with digital spaces, making them a tool for well-being rather than a distraction.

Ultimately, AI is what we make of it. When used with mindfulness, it becomes a companion in our journey toward greater self-awareness, wisdom, and peace. The key is approaching it as an aid for introspection, as a lantern that helps illuminate the path we already walk.

AI FOR PERSONAL FINANCE: YOUR INTELLIGENT MONEY MANAGER

Just as AI can optimize home routines and enhance well-being, it can also transform how we manage money. Finances can be a significant source of stress, but this technology has the potential to bring clarity, automation, and proactive insights into our financial lives. Whether it's tracking expenses, optimizing savings, or making smarter investment decisions, AI can function as an ever-present financial advisor, guiding you toward stability and growth.

Imagine logging into your financial dashboard and seeing a real-time analysis of your spending patterns, personalized savings recommendations, and investment opportunities tailored to your risk level. AI can provide actionable strategies to help you make informed financial decisions.

Here's how AI is helping individuals take control of their finances:

- Expense Tracking: It categorizes spending, highlights patterns, and alerts you to unusual transactions.
- Savings Optimization: Smart algorithms set goals, suggest automatic transfers and help maximize interest.
- Investment Guidance: AI-driven financial assistants provide portfolio recommendations, real-time market insights, and automated rebalancing for long-term stability.

Achieving financial wellness isn't about earning more; it's about effectively managing what you have. The path to financial freedom sometimes begins with a shift in our approach to money.

Across all aspects of life, home, health, and finances, AI can be a tool that enhances what we already do, allowing us to focus on what matters most while making more thoughtful, more informed decisions.

YOUR AI TRAVEL AGENT: TRANSFORMING THE WAY WE EXPLORE

Another excellent tool AI offers is revolutionizing how we plan and experience travel. Organizing the perfect trip can often feel overwhelming. For example, coordinating flights, hotels, activities, and dining options requires time and research. However, the process becomes effortless and personalized with AI as your travel assistant.

From discovering hidden gems to optimizing your itinerary, AI can curate travel experiences tailored specifically to you. Whether planning a once-in-a-lifetime vacation or a spontaneous weekend getaway, AI tools help remove the guesswork, ensuring smooth logistics, great deals, and unforgettable experiences.

How AI Enhances Travel Planning

AI assists travelers in multiple ways, from planning to real-time support:

- Personalized Trip Planning: It suggests destinations, optimizes itineraries, and curates activities based on your preferences and past travel history.
- Smart Booking Assistance: AI tracks flight deals, recommends hotels, and compares price trends to help you book at the right time.
- On-the-Go Support: It provides real-time itinerary updates, local recommendations, and instant language translation, making travel seamless.

A Dream Vacation: AI Creates the Perfect Getaway

Travel planning can be stressful, but AI transforms it into an intuitive, hassle-free experience. When a couple set out to celebrate their 10th wedding anniversary, they wanted a trip combining relaxation, adventure, and cultural immersion, but they had no idea where to start.

After answering a few questions about their travel style, AI analyzed their past trips, preferences, and budget to suggest Costa Rica, which provided a perfect blend of beaches, rainforest hikes, and rich local culture.

Their AI assistant found the best flight and hotel deals in this case, automatically tracking price drops. It also designed a personalized itinerary, balancing relaxation with adventure while providing real-time dining, local events, and sightseeing recommendations.

When they arrived at their destination, AI continued to enhance their experience by offering insider tips on local attractions, translating menus, and even suggesting spontaneous detours that led to some of their favorite memories. What once felt overwhelming became effortless and exciting, letting them focus on the experience rather than logistics.

THE PRESENT FUTURE: A DAY IN THE LIFE...

Integrating AI into our daily lives represents a technological shift and a fundamental evolution in how we experience and interact with our world. This section reviews how AI can help with our daily routines while preserving and amplifying our essential humanity.

Morning Rhythm: The Art of Beginning (6:00 a.m. - 9:00 a.m.)

Your day begins with a gentle awakening at 6:45 a.m. when AI works harmoniously with your natural rhythms. By analyzing your sleep cycles, the system determines your optimal wake time and coordinates with your calendar to ensure you're well-rested for important events. The experience is multi-sensory: room lighting gradually shifts to match the natural sunrise, while personalized wake-up sounds are chosen based on your sleep quality, creating a peaceful transition to wakefulness.

Your morning wellness routine begins at 7:15 a.m. AI draws from data about your previous day's stress levels to suggest a customized meditation session. Your physical well-being is addressed through a personalized stretch routine that targets specific areas of muscle tension, while mood-aware music selections enhance your morning energy. Weather conditions are factored into workout recommendations, ensuring your exercise routine is effective and practical.

Your day starts with an informed start at 8:00 a.m., with a thoughtfully curated selection of news and updates filtered for relevance and potential impact on your life and work. Your schedule receives a priority-based overview with suggested adjustments for optimal flow. Even nutrition becomes more intentional, with breakfast recommendations tailored to support your day's activities. Your commute is optimized based on real-time traffic conditions.

Professional Focus: Enhancing Human Capability (9:00 a.m. - 5:00 p.m.)

As you transition into your professional day at 9:30 a.m., AI becomes a thoughtful partner in productivity. Your tasks are prioritized in harmony with your natural energy levels, ensuring you tackle challenging work when you're at your peak. Contextual briefings that provide the necessary information make meeting preparations more insightful. While AI handles routine tasks in the background, it proactively gathers resources for upcoming projects, allowing you to focus on work that requires human creativity and judgment.

The midday break at 12:30 p.m. transforms into a mindful pause in your day. Rather than just a simple lunch hour, it becomes a carefully considered wellness opportunity. AI suggests meal options that balance nutritional needs with personal preferences while identifying natural breaks in your schedule for quick wellness activities. Perhaps most importantly, it recognizes opportunities for meaningful social connections.

By 3:00 p.m., when many traditionally experience an energy dip, your work enters a creative collaboration phase. AI enhances brainstorming sessions by providing real-time research support and identifying patterns that might spark innovation. The system's ability to recognize subtle shifts in team energy and mood allows for intelligent workflow adjustments, ensuring that collaborative time remains productive and engaging.

Personal Time: Nurturing Life Beyond Work (5:00 p.m. - 10:00 p.m.)

As the workday transitions to personal time at 5:30 p.m., AI helps manage life's practical aspects with subtle sophistication. Shopping lists evolve based on your meal preferences and patterns while your home environment adjusts for optimal energy efficiency. Family schedules are coordinated with care, suggesting activities that align with everyone's interests and energy levels. Maintenance reminders arrive proactively, helping you stay ahead of household needs without feeling overwhelmed.

The evening hours around 7:00 p.m. become an opportunity for enrichment and connection. Based on your interests and energy levels, AI suggests personalized learning opportunities and creative hobbies that might appeal to you. Cultural experiences are recommended thoughtfully, while social connection opportunities are identified in ways that feel natural and unforced. This time becomes a canvas for personal growth and meaningful interaction, supported but not directed by technology.

As bedtime approaches, your environment gradually transitions to support restful sleep. The AI system helps create optimal sleeping conditions while suggesting relaxation routines that suit your preferences. Assistance with next-day preparation comes gently, ensuring you can rest easy, knowing tomorrow is thoughtfully planned. This winding-down period exemplifies how AI can enhance our natural rhythms rather than disrupt them.

This vision of daily life demonstrates how technology can support our human experience without dominating it. Each interaction is designed to let us enjoy our natural capabilities and preserve the spontaneity and personal connection that make life meaningful. The key lies in thoughtfully integrating AI support in ways that promote our essential human experiences.

Integrating AI into our routines makes it easy to focus on its tangible benefits—efficiency, organization, and convenience. But beyond the practical applications, there's a more profound question: How do we ensure that it benefits the most human aspects of our lives? Our relationship with AI is not just about what it does for us but also about how it shapes our choices, creativity, and connections. This is where the proper balance between technology and human agency is found.

THE HUMAN ELEMENT IN AN AI-ENHANCED LIFE

Technology is often discussed in terms of efficiency, productivity, and optimization, but beneath these practical benefits lies something far more profound: the way AI can support and help to foster the deeply human aspects of life: our choices, connections, creativity, and well-being. The real question is not whether AI can assist us but how we remain intentional in shaping that partnership to enrich our humanity.

Understanding Personal Agency in the Age of AI

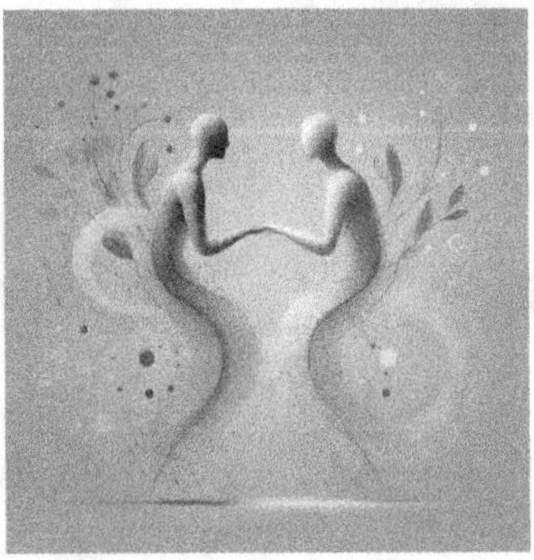

Personal agency is at the heart of a healthy relationship with AI. It is the ability to make deliberate, intentional choices about how technology integrates into our lives. AI is not meant to dictate our actions but to adapt to our values and preferences, serving as a flexible tool rather than an authority.

Consider this: AI might suggest a faster, more efficient route to work, but you may choose the scenic path instead, valuing the peace of a morning drive over pure optimization. During a family dinner, an AI calendar assistant might remind you of an upcoming meeting, but you silence notifications, choosing presence over productivity. These seemingly small decisions reflect a larger truth: technology should better human experience, not silently rule our routines.

Personal agency is also about balance. Some days, AI assistance might be indispensable, streamlining schedules, filtering information, managing logistics, and freeing up mental space for more meaningful pursuits. Other times, we do things manually, not because AI can't help but because the joy of hands-on effort, problem-solving, or creating from scratch is intrinsically valuable. True empowerment comes from knowing when to lean on AI and when to rely on ourselves.

Nurturing Authentic Social Connections

If misused, technology can feel like a wedge between us, replacing direct interaction with filtered, digital exchanges. But when used thoughtfully, it can remove tension from relationships by allowing us to be more present, engaged, and intentional in the connections that matter.

Imagine an AI that helps coordinate family schedules so that dinner together is no longer an afterthought. Or an assistant that reminds you of a friend's milestone, not with a generic notification, but with context: "It's been six months since you last spoke. Why not send a thoughtful message?" As you can see, these tools facilitate our connections.

However, not all moments benefit from digital mediation. Some experiences demand pure, uninterrupted presence—the warmth of a shared silence, the unspoken understanding of a hug, the emotional weight of a difficult conversation. AI may be helpful in our relationships, but human intention gives them depth. Knowing when to engage and when to unplug ensures that technology serves as a bridge, not a barrier.

Preserving Creative Expression in a Digital Age

Creativity isn't limited to artists or musicians; it's woven into everyday life. Our daily choices require imagination, from crafting a heartfelt message to planning a unique event. AI can serve as a creative partner, offering fresh perspectives and breaking creative blocks, whether helping draft a letter, generating dinner ideas, or inspiring a home project. It can enhance the moments when inspiration feels elusive, helping us bring more thoughtfulness and joy to our daily creations. All this while you keep your originality. It helps by sparking new ideas when inspiration runs dry.

Consider a person struggling to write a meaningful speech for a loved one's milestone. AI can suggest structure, themes, and even sentimental phrasing, helping shape their raw emotions into something impactful. A home cook looking to experiment might turn to AI for inventive ingredient pairings, finding culinary inspiration in unexpected places. Even in personal projects like decorating a space, brainstorming gift ideas, or crafting a unique playlist, AI can act as your creative extension, offering new perspectives without overriding your vision.

The key is maintaining the integrity of our voice, vision, and emotional depth. AI should never dictate creativity; instead, it should serve as a springboard for our expression, enhancing the process while leaving the final choices to us. By treating AI as an idea generator rather than a decision-maker, we ensure that technology supports the human essence of creativity instead of overshadowing it.

PRIORITIZING HOLISTIC WELL-BEING

In the race for efficiency, it's easy to overlook the simple yet essential rhythms of human well-being. Physical health, mental clarity, and emotional resilience form the foundation of a fulfilled life, and technology should only help to promote habits that sustain them.

Well-being in an AI-enhanced world means knowing when to engage and when to unplug. It means setting boundaries—choosing quiet

moments over noise, movement over stagnation, and introspection over instant answers. AI can suggest a meditation break, but the depth of that stillness comes from your decision to be present.

Rather than being led by technology's pace, we must be conscious architects of how it fits into our well-being. We must ensure that efficiency never comes at the cost of presence and that automation never erodes the value of personal effort.

Finding Harmony with AI in Personal Life

Just as we have social norms for human interaction, developing a code of etiquette for AI is crucial for maintaining our authenticity, safeguarding our well-being, and using these powerful tools responsibly. It's not just about what these tools can do but how we interact with them.

AI etiquette is essential for several reasons. First, it aids in establishing healthy boundaries, preventing undue overreliance on technology. Second, it ensures that we utilize AI to prioritize interpersonal relationships. Third, privacy is another critical aspect, as adequate etiquette safeguards our privacy and that of those around us. Adhering to AI etiquette allows us to enjoy AI's benefits while remaining aligned with our core values. Ultimately, it enables the development of a technological partner that effectively meets our needs.

AI FOSTERING HUMAN CONNECTION

As AI integrates more deeply into our lives, one truth remains evident: Technology works best when it strengthens human bonds instead of promoting isolation. AI is not meant to distance us from one another. Instead, it must help smooth our interactions, making it easier to connect in meaningful ways.

Think of AI as a social facilitator that supports relationships by helping us be more present, intentional, and engaged with the people who matter most. Whether organizing schedules, remembering special moments, or even offering insights to enhance conversations, AI can enrich our human connections in ways we may not have imagined.

How Does AI Strengthen Social Bonds?

Intelligent Scheduling & Communication: It helps coordinate family time, social events, and important milestones, ensuring no birthday, anniversary, or gathering is overlooked.

Shared Experiences & Group Engagement: AI suggests activities, organizes events, and even curates shared digital memories to bring families and friends closer together.

Relationship Support & Emotional Insights: These tools remind users to make thoughtful gestures, suggest personalized gifts, and offer insights into conflict resolution and relationship health.

Technology Meets Tradition: A Modern Family's Story

Despite their best efforts, a once close-knit family drifted apart as the demands of modern life took over. The parents juggled work and household responsibilities. Irregular shifts made family dinners rare, and the children were consumed by school and extracurriculars. The warm, unplanned moments that once defined their home became fewer and further between.

They attempted to bridge the gap through group chats and video calls, but conversations felt rushed and disconnected. Milestones were acknowledged with quick messages rather than heartfelt celebrations, and their cherished traditions faded into memory. They weren't growing apart intentionally; they were struggling to stay connected.

Then, they decided to embrace AI-powered family management tools.

Their smart home assistant became an invisible yet impactful presence, syncing schedules and highlighting windows of opportunity for family meals and quality time. The shared digital calendar shifted from a source of stress to a tool for togetherness, revealing moments where they could reconnect.

AI's subtle nudges encouraged small but significant changes. Movie nights returned with personalized recommendations that spanned generations, sparking long conversations. The daughter's dance recitals were no longer missed because AI adjusted everyone's commitments weeks in advance. The family found themselves not only spending more time together but also genuinely engaging with one another.

Six months in, their home felt different, not more automated, but more alive. The presence of AI had done something unexpected: it had encouraged them to be more present. They learned when to embrace technology and when to set their devices aside, cherishing moments of laughter, shared meals, and late-night conversations.

This family's story is about technology helping them rediscover their uniqueness. Their home again became a place of warmth, not just through automation but also through the simple joy of being together.

A THOUGHTFUL APPROACH TO AI IN RELATIONSHIPS

As you can see, AI has the potential to bring people closer if used intentionally. It facilitates meaningful connections through coordinated gatherings, memory-sharing, or smoothing life's logistics. It can serve as a quiet assistant, creating space for what truly matters: being present with the people we love.

Let's explore some more principles of AI etiquette, from setting appropriate boundaries to navigating social situations. I'll provide practical guidelines for mindful integration to create a balanced, authentic life in the age of artificial intelligence. I am confident that you will find this information helpful and meaningful.

UNDERSTANDING APPROPRIATE BOUNDARIES

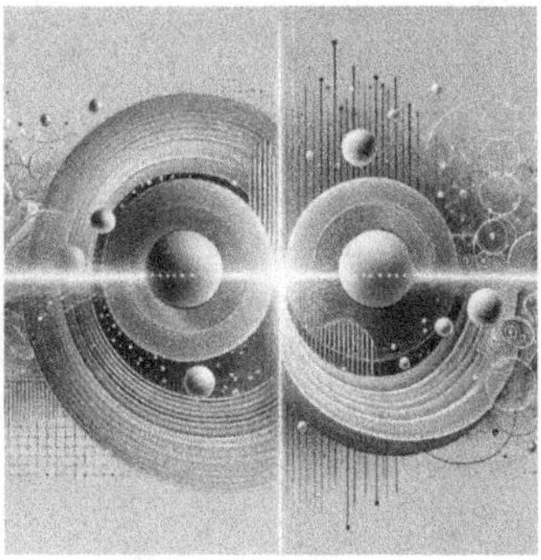

Thoughtful use is key to ensuring that AI complements instead of complicates your life. Just because AI can assist with something doesn't mean it should. It's essential to approach AI interactions with mindfulness, balancing convenience with judgment.

Let's explore the boundaries of appropriate AI use, starting with tasks where it excels.

Personal Organization

1. Schedule management: "AI, help me plan my week."

2. Task reminders: "Remind me to call Mom at 6 p.m."

3. Essential planning support: "What's the best route to the office?"

Information Assistance

1. Research help: "Find information on healthy meal planning."

2. Learning support: "Explain quantum computing concepts."

3. Fact-checking: "Verify the source of this news article."

Language Development

1. Pronunciation practice: "How do I say this word correctly?"

2. Conversation scenarios: "Let's practice business English dialogue."

3. Writing improvement: "Help me make this email more professional."

Creative Support

1. Brainstorming ideas: "Suggest topics for my next blog post."

2. Format suggestions: "Help me outline my presentation."

3. Process guidance: "What are the steps for planting a garden?"

Professional Growth

1. Skill assessment: "What skills should I develop for my field?"

2. Interview preparation: "Practice common interview questions."

3. Industry insights: "What are emerging trends in my industry?"

AREAS TO AVOID

Artificial intelligence is competent but isn't intended to take precedence over human intuition, emotional support, or professional judgment. While the examples below may not match your experiences, they remind you to stay mindful. If a situation feels similar, it's worth evaluating whether relying on AI is the best choice.

Emotional Dependency

1. Using AI as a therapist: "I'm feeling sad; make me feel better."
2. Relying on AI for emotional support: "You're my only true friend."
3. Replacing human connections: "I don't need real friends; I have you."

Personal Decisions

1. Life-changing choices: "Should I quit my job and move to Bali?"
2. Relationship advice: "Should I break up with my partner?"
3. Medical decisions: "What medication should I take for this?"

Private Information

1. Sensitive personal details: "Here's my social security number."
2. Family members' information: "Let me tell you about my sister's problems."
3. Financial data: "My credit card number is..."

COMMUNICATION GUIDELINES

How we communicate with AI sets the tone for a healthy relationship with technology. Here's how to interact with grace and purpose:

Effective Communication Principles

1. Clear Boundaries

Appropriate: *"I'd like help organizing my schedule for the week."*

Inappropriate: "Tell me what to do with my life."

2. Specific Requests

Practical: *"Help me plan my tasks for tomorrow."*

Impractical: "Fix everything that's wrong in my life."

3. Maintaining Agency

Empowering: *"Suggest some healthy dinner options."*

Disempowering: "Tell me exactly what I should eat."

Remember, you're in charge. AI is a tool to support you, not control you. You can establish a balanced, beneficial relationship with AI by communicating clearly and purposefully.

DAILY LIFE INTEGRATION: MINDFUL AI USAGE

Before relying on AI, take a moment to reflect. Thoughtful AI usage starts with asking the right questions to ensure it aligns with your values, enhances your autonomy, and respects the boundaries of human connection and privacy. Here are some guiding considerations to help you navigate when and how to use AI effectively.

Before Using AI, Ask:

1. Is this task appropriate for AI?

Does it involve personal decisions or sensitive information? Is it something I should be doing myself? Would AI assistance enhance or diminish this experience?

2. Would human interaction be better in this situation?

Is this a matter that requires human empathy and understanding? Would I benefit more from connecting with a real person? Is AI the most authentic choice here?

3. Am I maintaining my privacy and the privacy of others?

Does this involve sharing sensitive personal details? Could this impact the privacy of my family or friends? Have I set appropriate boundaries around what I share?

4. Does this support my autonomy and agency?

Am I relying on AI to make decisions for me? Is this empowering me or creating dependency? Will using AI here enhance or diminish my capacity?

Example Scenarios

Good Practice:

"AI, help me create a cleaning schedule that fits my weekly energy levels."

Why it works: You're using AI as a supportive tool while maintaining control over your routines.

Avoid:

"AI, tell me how to live my life."

Why it doesn't work: This shifts responsibility entirely to AI, undermining your autonomy.

Better Choice:

"AI, suggest healthy recipes based on my dietary preferences and goals."

Why it works: AI provides tailored suggestions, empowering you to make informed decisions.

Avoid:

"AI, decide all my meals for me from now on."

Why it doesn't work: Over-reliance on AI here diminishes personal agency and involvement.

By pausing to reflect before engaging AI, you ensure these tools support your well-being and align with your values, fostering a balanced relationship with technology.

FAMILY AND SHARED SPACE ETIQUETTE

When used thoughtfully, technology can bring us closer to friends and family. However, if we're not mindful, it can just as easily create tension or disconnect in shared spaces. This is especially true of AI, which often interacts directly with our voices and preferences.

Using technology thoughtfully in shared spaces means respecting those around us. Loud notifications, invasive voice commands, or unshared decisions can make others feel overlooked or excluded and be disruptive. By establishing clear guidelines, we ensure that technology serves as a tool for connection and productivity rather than a source of disruption or conflict.

Respectful Usage Guidelines

In Common Areas

1. Use AI at appropriate volumes that don't disrupt others.
2. Honor quiet hours and focused work times.
3. Get an agreement from others before using shared devices.
4. Be mindful of others' privacy when they're present.

During Family Time

1. Prioritize human interaction over AI engagement.
2. Keep AI assistance brief and purposeful.
3. Include others in AI-assisted activities when appropriate.
4. Set boundaries for AI usage during meals and gatherings.

Privacy and Consideration: Important Boundaries

1. Keep personal AI conversations private.
2. Avoid sharing family information without consent.
3. Consult others before making AI-assisted household decisions.
4. Respect individual preferences for AI interaction.

Mindfulness about technology fosters respect, collaboration, and harmony within a household. When considering how our tech usage affects others, we strengthen relationships and create an environment where everyone's needs and boundaries are acknowledged. This applies to AI and all devices and systems that affect our daily lives.

Etiquette Tip: Technology should not interrupt family life. These guidelines help balance technological convenience and meaningful human connection in your home.

TEACHING CHILDREN AI ETIQUETTE

Learning appropriate interaction with AI is a crucial life skill for children growing up in an AI-enabled world. Just as we teach internet safety and social media literacy, guiding children in AI etiquette empowers them to become responsible digital citizens who can harness these tools while maintaining healthy boundaries.

Age-Appropriate Guidelines

Young Children (Under 12)

For younger children, simplicity and supervision are key:

1. Always supervise AI use with clear parental controls and time limits.
2. Use real-world analogies for rules (e.g., "Just like we don't share our address with strangers, we don't share personal information with AI.").
3. Highlight AI's limitations by explaining that it can make mistakes like people.
4. Teach polite interaction while emphasizing that AI is not a friend or emotional support.
5. Encourage creativity and make sure AI complements original thinking.

Tweens (11-13)

As children grow, focus on building independence and critical thinking:

1. Guide them in exploring AI tools for homework and creative projects.
2. Teach fact-checking and verifying AI-generated information.
3. Discuss AI bias and the importance of diverse information sources.
4. Help them recognize appropriate versus inappropriate uses of AI.
5. Foster awareness of digital footprints and long-term privacy implications.

Teens (14+)

For teens, the emphasis shifts to deeper engagement and ethical considerations:

1. Encourage the purposeful use of AI in academic, creative, and personal pursuits.
2. Develop their critical thinking skills to evaluate AI outputs and recommendations.
3. Discuss AI ethics and responsible innovation.

4. Highlight the importance of balancing AI use with real-world relationships and personal growth.
5. Prepare them for AI's role in future careers and teach them to recognize misinformation and AI bias.

TEACHING STRATEGIES

1. Use real-world scenarios or examples to illustrate key points.
2. Create family projects that integrate responsible AI use.
3. Keep communication open—encourage questions and discussions about AI experiences.
4. Model responsible behavior in your AI interactions.
5. Review and adapt guidelines as technology evolves and your children grow.

Teaching AI etiquette is about helping children build confidence and independence in navigating technology. By encouraging them to trust their instincts, set boundaries, and know when to seek human advice, you're equipping them to handle challenges responsibly.

This isn't a one-time lesson; it's an ongoing dialogue that evolves as your child grows and technology advances. Lead by example and foster a healthy, balanced relationship with AI in your household.

PRIVACY IN SHARED ENVIRONMENTS: HEALTHY HABITS

Integrating AI assistants and smart devices can enhance convenience in shared living environments, but it also introduces unique privacy challenges. Whether in a family home, a shared apartment, or a dorm, being mindful of how and where you use AI is essential to maintaining trust, respecting personal boundaries, and fostering a harmonious living space.

The Importance of Mindful AI Use

Shared spaces are built on mutual respect and responsibility. Misusing AI, such as oversharing personal information, inadvertently involving others in your interactions, or compromising device security, can create discomfort or strain relationships. Thoughtful AI etiquette ensures that technology doesn't become a source of tension. Here are some simple suggestions to help you practice good etiquette.

Essential Privacy Guidelines

1. Consider Your Surroundings

Who else is present? Be mindful of who might overhear sensitive or private information. For example, asking an AI assistant about personal matters or finances in a shared space might make others uncomfortable.

What's visible? Ensure that screens or devices don't unintentionally display private information to those nearby.

Is this the right place? Consider whether the living room or kitchen is appropriate for your AI interaction or if moving to a private room would be more respectful.

2. Reflect on the Information You're Sharing

Is it sensitive? Consider whether your interaction involves personal or confidential details like health, finances, or work-related topics.

Does it involve others? Avoid sharing details about housemates, friends, or family members without their consent—directly or indirectly.

Can it wait? If the AI interaction isn't urgent, consider waiting until you're in a more private space to ensure everyone's comfort.

3. Secure Device Access

What device are you using? If it's a shared device, be cautious about storing personal preferences or search history.

Are settings optimized? Regularly check privacy settings to ensure your interactions remain secure and aren't accessible to others.

Should you clear the history? After using shared devices, consider clearing interaction logs to prevent accidental disclosure of sensitive information.

SOCIAL SITUATIONS AND AI

As AI assistants become more prevalent, guidelines on appropriate use in social contexts become more critical. A few simple principles can help ensure that AI doesn't detract from human connection, whether in a professional meeting or dinner with friends.

Proper Etiquette for Different Settings

In Social Gatherings

Constantly checking your phone, having loud cellphone conversations in public, or playing music without headphones in public is rude. Thus, AI interactions during social events need careful consideration to prevent disrupting meaningful human connections. Follow these guidelines to maintain social harmony:

1. Keep AI interactions brief and purposeful.
2. Involve others and avoid private side conversations with AI.
3. Explain your AI use if it's unusual for the setting.
4. Be ready to put AI away when it's time to engage fully.

In Professional Situations

The workplace also demands a balanced approach to AI that enhances productivity while maintaining professionalism and respecting workplace dynamics. Consider these essential practices:

1. Use AI for appropriate task assistance, not personal matters.
2. Be transparent about when you're using AI tools.
3. Respect colleagues' preferences around AI use.
4. Ensure AI interactions maintain your professional image.

Ultimately, the key is to be mindful of your environment, prioritize the people you're with, and ensure that AI remains a tool that enhances rather than detracts from real-world interactions.

PROMOTING RESPECTFUL TECHNOLOGY USE

1. Communicate Expectations

Set clear household guidelines for AI use in shared spaces. Discuss topics like: When is it appropriate to use AI assistants (e.g., during quiet hours)? Which devices are personal versus shared, and how should they be used? What types of information are off-limits for shared spaces?

2. Lead by Example

Demonstrate thoughtful AI etiquette in your interactions. For instance, lower the volume when using voice assistants, move to a private area for personal queries, and avoid disrupting shared activities with unnecessary interactions.

3. Balance Technology and Human Connection

While AI can streamline tasks, it should take a step back during meaningful interactions with housemates or family members. Prioritize face-to-face communication and shared experiences over convenience.

When AI is used respectfully, it enhances shared living without infringing on personal boundaries. Taking a moment to assess your surroundings, reflect on what you're sharing, and secure your devices ensures privacy for yourself and others. This builds trust and sets the tone for a harmonious living environment where technology supports, rather than disrupts, everyday life.

AI Etiquette: Technology should facilitate ease and efficiency in shared spaces, not cause discomfort. By practicing mindful AI use, you can create a living space where everyone feels respected and valued.

SHARING AI ETIQUETTE WITH OTHERS

When introducing AI guidelines to others, take a gradual approach that builds understanding through relatable examples and clear principles. Just as we learned to navigate social media and smartphone etiquette together, we can help each other develop better, healthy AI habits that respect the technology's potential and essential human boundaries.

1. Start with the Fundamentals

- Frame etiquette around simple, relatable principles.
- Emphasize the "why" behind privacy protection and boundaries.
- Give concrete examples of appropriate vs. inappropriate uses.
- Highlight common pitfalls to watch out for.

2. Lead by Example

- Model the behavior and habits you're trying to teach.
- Narrate your decision-making around AI interactions.
- Be open about your learning process and challenges.
- Invite reflection and discussion on developing shared norms.

Remember that adopting new etiquette takes time and practice. Be patient with yourself and others, celebrate successes, and keep the focus on progress over perfection. But do your part.

BUILDING COMMUNITY IMPACT: COLLABORATIVE AI LEARNING

The journey of integrating AI into our lives becomes richer and more meaningful when shared with others. While personal growth with AI is valuable, creating a positive community impact amplifies these benefits across networks of people, fostering environments where everyone can learn, grow, and adapt together. This guide explores how you can transform your AI journey into a force for community empowerment.

The Power of Knowledge Sharing

Knowledge sharing in the context of AI adoption isn't about positioning yourself as an expert—it's about being a thoughtful guide who helps others navigate their journeys. Think of yourself as someone who has explored specific paths and can now help others avoid common pitfalls while discovering their growth opportunities.

Consider the small business owner who discovered how AI could streamline inventory management. By sharing their experience—including the initial struggles, the learning process, and the eventual benefits—they provide a realistic roadmap for others in similar situations. This kind of authentic sharing helps demystify AI technology and makes it more accessible to everyone.

The art of effective knowledge sharing involves meeting people where they are. For instance, when helping a senior neighbor learn to use AI assistants for daily tasks, you might start with simple applications like setting reminders or making lists. As they grow more comfortable, you can introduce more advanced features based on their interests and needs. This gradual approach builds confidence and ensures sustainable adoption.

Create an ongoing dialogue about AI in your professional and social circles. Why? First, it normalizes discussions about technology integration, reducing anxiety and resistance. Second, it creates opportunities for mutual learning—often, someone's question will spark insights that benefit the entire group. Finally, it helps identify common challenges and collaborative solutions.

Fostering Collaborative Growth

Learning about AI is most effective in a community. Whether formal or informal, learning circles provide structure for continuous development and foster supportive relationships among participants.

Consider starting with something as simple as a monthly coffee meetup where people share their experiences with AI tools. These gatherings might begin with essential tips and tricks but often evolve into deeper discussions about how technology influences various aspects of work and life. The key is creating an environment where people feel comfortable asking questions, sharing successes, and addressing challenges.

Professional learning circles offer even greater value by enabling the focused exploration of AI applications in specific fields. For example, healthcare professionals might meet regularly to discuss how AI can enhance patient care while maintaining the human touch essential to their work. These discussions often lead to innovative solutions that benefit entire professional communities.

A shared resource library naturally emerges from collaborative learning. What begins as a simple collection of helpful articles and tutorials can evolve into a comprehensive knowledge base that reflects the community's collective experience. This ensures that these resources remain accessible and relevant, allowing individuals at different stages of their AI journey to benefit.

Diversity in collaborative learning isn't just about inclusion—it enriches everyone's experience. When individuals from various age groups, professional backgrounds, and levels of technical expertise come together, they bring unique perspectives that challenge assumptions and spark creative solutions.

Making Broader Societal Contributions

What begins as individual or small-group learning can extend to a broader societal impact. As your understanding of AI grows, so does your ability to contribute meaningfully to discussions about technology's role in community life.

When AI implementation is discussed in your workplace or community organizations, your practical experience becomes valuable input. You can help bridge the gap between technical possibilities and human needs, ensuring AI adoption decisions consider real-world impacts on different community members.

Supporting responsible AI practices requires both personal choices and community advocacy. Choosing and recommending tools that prioritize privacy and ethical behavior helps establish responsible standards. This might involve researching privacy policies, supporting AI solutions with transparency, or advocating for ethical guidelines in organizations.

Addressing the digital divide becomes a natural extension of community involvement. Your experience helping individuals learn about AI can scale into broader initiatives, such as volunteering at local libraries or community centers. These efforts might start small—perhaps with a workshop on using AI for job searches or educational support—but can grow into comprehensive programs serving diverse community needs.

Clear, honest discussions about AI are essential for community impact. Helping people understand AI's potential and limitations—without hype or unnecessary fear—ensures realistic expectations and practical approaches to adoption. Your real-world insights provide valuable context, enabling others to develop informed perspectives and responsible strategies.

Starting Your Community Impact Journey

Making a difference doesn't require deep technical expertise or grand initiatives. Start with what you know and the people around you. Perhaps begin by helping a colleague understand how AI can simplify their workflow or by organizing a small discussion group in your neighborhood. These initial steps often lead to expanding circles of impact as others feel empowered to share their learning journeys.

The key to sustainable community impact is approaching it as a collaborative learning experience rather than a one-way knowledge transfer. Each interaction is an opportunity for mutual growth and understanding. As you share what you've learned, remain open to new perspectives and insights from others. This reciprocal approach fosters resilient learning communities that can adapt and grow as AI technology evolves.

Building Lasting Impact

As your community impact expands, consider how to make your efforts sustainable and scalable. Documenting successful approaches, developing reusable resources, or mentoring others can help build knowledge-sharing networks. The goal is to create ripple effects of learning and empowerment that extend beyond your direct involvement.

Every person you help understand and effectively use AI contributes to a more informed and capable community. These individual interactions, multiplied across networks, create a future where AI adds to empowerment rather than division or uncertainty.

CREATING YOUR AI-ENHANCED FUTURE

Imagine starting a home renovation project. You wouldn't start by tearing down walls or installing new fixtures at random. Instead, you'd carefully consider what you need, how each change you make would affect your daily life, which spaces need the most attention, and how to preserve the cherished aspects of your home while enhancing its functionality. Crafting your future embraces a similar philosophy. It involves thoughtfully designing a life where technology feeds your capabilities while preserving what makes you unique.

Begin by examining your daily routines. Where do you encounter repetitive tasks that drain time and energy? Where do you crave more efficiency without sacrificing personal engagement? AI thrives when applied to high-friction, low-satisfaction tasks like scheduling, organization, and data retrieval, freeing you to focus on more profound, rewarding activities.

At the same time, it's essential to define boundaries. Just as you designate certain rooms as quiet spaces, establish areas where AI should and shouldn't be used in your life. Family meals, personal reflection, and creative endeavors might be places where human engagement remains irreplaceable.

A CALL TO EXPERIMENTATION

The best way to understand AI's role in your life is not through theory but through experience. Consider this an invitation, an experiment of sorts, to see what happens when you let AI take on a small role in your day-to-day routine. Let it be a companion on your journey, illuminating the way for human efforts and thoughtful experiences.

Start with something simple. Perhaps you can ask an AI assistant to summarize your emails in the morning to see how much time it saves. Or maybe you let it generate a meal plan for the week, offering inspiration where routine might have dulled your creativity. Observe whether the changes are liberating you or creating unforeseen challenges. What surprises you most?

Next, take AI somewhere personal. Let it suggest a journaling prompt at the end of the day and see where your reflection takes you. Try an AI-powered creative tool to write a poem, compose music, or generate artwork with it, just for the fun of seeing what emerges. Engage with AI not as an all-knowing authority but as a sparring partner for your imagination. Have fun, and let your creativity run.

As you go through this experiment, ask yourself: Where and how does AI enhance my life? Where does it feel unnatural? What aspects of my routine benefit most from its support, and where do I prefer to remain fully human-driven? You may find that AI effortlessly takes over tasks you once dreaded or provides insights you hadn't considered. You may also discover areas where its presence feels intrusive, where the joy of a process lies in doing it yourself, which is good.

By the end of this journey, you'll have a clearer sense of what AI means for you, not based on abstract discussions but on lived experience. You'll know which aspects of AI are worth embracing, which should be approached with caution, and how to make it work for your life on your terms. Ultimately, AI is about enriching life in ways both big and small.

BUILDING MINDFULLY: GRADUAL INTEGRATION

Using home renovation as a metaphor, consider AI adoption as building an addition to your home. It should be methodical and intentional, ensuring each new element connects seamlessly with existing structures. Start with small wins. Perhaps that means using AI for meeting summaries, grocery planning, or fitness tracking. The key is gradual, meaningful integration.

As you explore AI's role, reflect regularly on its impact. If you like, keep a simple mental journal noting changes in productivity, stress levels, and emotional well-being. This repetitive approach ensures that AI enhances your life without diminishing your autonomy or sense of self.

Action Steps: Integrating AI into Your Life

1. Start Small

- Choose one area of your life to enhance with AI.
- Experiment with different tools and find what works for you.
- Gradually expand to other areas as you get comfortable.

2. Set Boundaries

- Decide what information you're comfortable sharing with AI.
- Establish clear limits on AI access and control.
- Create tech-free zones and times for human connection.

3. Personalize

- Take the time to customize AI to your unique needs and preferences.
- Regularly review and adjust AI settings as your needs change.
- Remember, AI is a tool—you're the one in charge.

4. Focus on Enhancements

- Use AI to streamline tasks and create space for what matters.
- Look for ways AI can facilitate human interaction.
- Prioritize authentic experiences and genuine connections.

5. Reflect and Adjust

- Regularly assess how AI is impacting your life.
- Make adjustments to ensure AI is serving you, not vice versa.
- Remember, the goal is a life well-lived—with or without AI.

How could you use AI today to free up more time for what truly matters?

LIVING BETTER WITH AI

The main point I want to convey is that the journey to a life with AI is about creating space for what truly matters. From smart homes to health coaching, financial planning, and travel adventures, AI can be your partner in crafting a more fulfilling life.

As we've seen, AI has the power to transform our personal lives in countless ways. From creating a smart home that anticipates our needs

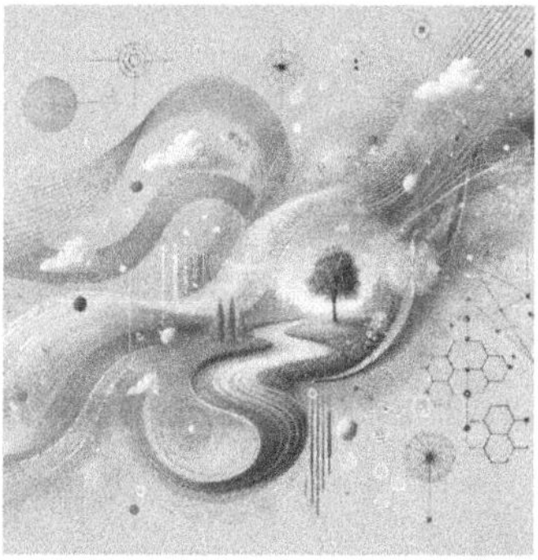

to offering personalized health and financial guidance, from making travel a breeze to enhancing our leisure time, AI can be a powerful tool for living life on our terms.

However, the key is to use AI wisely as a facilitator of human connection. By striking the right balance and staying true to our values, we can harness its capabilities to create more space and time for what truly matters: authentic experiences, meaningful relationships, and a life well-lived.

Make AI your personal assistant, coach, and intelligent companion. But always remember that you're the one in charge. With AI by your side and human connection at your core, there's no limit to the life you can create. Here's to living better with AI and some actionable advice.

KEY TAKEAWAYS

Privacy & Boundaries

Think of AI privacy like any significant relationship—be intentional about what you share, protect those close to you, and establish clear boundaries that feel right for your life. As with any other digital tool, consider how your AI use affects shared spaces and relationships.

Balance & Authenticity

Let AI enhance what matters most. Keep human connections at the center of your life while thoughtfully using AI to support your goals. Stay true to your values and judgment—AI should complement your authentic self, not override it.

Mindful Integration

Context matters in AI interaction, just as it does in human communication. Pay attention to when and how you use AI, developing habits that fit naturally into your daily life without disrupting the people and spaces around you.

Growth & Communication

Share your AI journey with others, learning and adapting together. Have open conversations about what works and what doesn't, and help each other develop healthy practices that serve everyone's needs.

YOUR PERSONAL AI ETIQUETTE GUIDE

By embracing these principles, you shape how AI is a meaningful tool in your life while honoring the people and spaces around you. This isn't just about developing good habits—it's about expressing your values in an evolving digital world.

Remember, AI etiquette isn't meant to restrict your use of these powerful tools. Instead, it ensures that AI truly enhances your life authentically and meaningfully. When you're intentional about AI integration, establish healthy boundaries, and keep human connection at the center, you can harness the benefits of this transformative technology while staying true to yourself.

Here is your comprehensive guide to improving your life with AI. Remember the human touch as you integrate these powerful tools into your life. With AI as your assistant and authenticity as your compass, you're well on your way to a more fulfilling, balanced, and joyful life. With the right mindset, the experience can be truly extraordinary. Let's examine this further in the next chapter.

FIVE
THE NEW ECONOMY OF POSSIBILITIES
A VISION FOR THE FUTURE

"The future belongs to those who blend human wisdom with artificial intelligence. It's not about replacement, but renaissance."
— Dr. Sarah Chen, AI Research Director at Stanford

What benefits can you expect from incorporating AI in a professional setting? Beyond excelling in your field, AI opens doors for exploring passions and interests that inspire you. This new economy values versatility, where professionals can learn faster, adapt more fluidly, and apply their skills across multiple domains. AI enables us to become both specialists and explorers, fostering innovation and personal growth in ways that were once challenging to achieve.

Consider this: What if your professional capabilities expanded overnight? You can have an assistant who organizes your day, highlights key insights, and drafts reports, all before you've had your first cup of coffee. AI makes things more efficient and unlocks new strategic thinking, creativity, and impact dimensions. In this chapter, I will show you how AI can take your work to levels you might never have thought possible.

The rapid pace of change today poses a continual challenge to keep up, adapt, and grow. But it's also an opportunity for those who are ready to evolve. Think of it as a professional AI revolution, a rocket booster for your career! Artificial intelligence transforms how we work and solve problems, changing everything from routine tasks to complex decision-making processes.

We'll explore illustrative examples from industries like strategic advisory, creative fields, and healthcare to show how the technology is being thoughtfully integrated. I'll also share practical frameworks for implementing AI, ensuring quality, and tackling industry-specific challenges. Whether you're just dipping your toes into AI or looking to deepen your current integration, this chapter offers the insights and guidance you need to evolve your practice for the AI era.

Despite the rapid technological revolution, you don't have to be a victim of this change. You can be the master of your destiny and the architect of your future-proof career. Now is the time to prepare for continuous learning, strategic thinking, and proactive growth.

THE THREE PILLARS OF PROGRESS

Your advancement in AI mastery rests on three fundamental pillars: clear goals, regular assessment, and continuous learning.

First and foremost, **clear goals** serve as your north star. Rather than vague aspirations, successful practitioners set specific, measurable objectives that align with their professional vision. These goals should include what you want to achieve and when you expect it. Establishing concrete progress indicators creates a framework that transforms abstract ambitions into actionable steps.

The second pillar, **regular assessment**, ensures you stay on course. Think of it as your professional GPS; it regularly checks your position against your intended destination. This isn't about harsh self-judgment but about maintaining awareness of your growth. As you track your advancement against milestones, you'll naturally discover key learnings that inform your journey. Sometimes, these insights will lead you to adjust your strategies, and that's not just okay—it's essential for optimal growth.

Continuous learning, the third pillar, keeps you relevant and growing in this rapidly evolving field. The AI landscape shifts constantly, with new developments emerging by the hour. Successful professionals don't just keep up; they actively build upon their foundation of knowledge, continually connecting new insights with previous experiences. Each success becomes a stepping stone to greater understanding and capability.

THE NEW PROFESSIONAL PARADIGM

Professional excellence is no longer defined solely by technical proficiency or the speed at which tasks are completed. Instead, it's about the capacity to harness technology as a powerful tool to enhance your unique skill set. AI is here to celebrate human brilliance and to enable you to focus on what truly matters: unlocking creativity, honing strategic insight, and building more profound and meaningful human connections.

Excelling in this new landscape is about developing the adaptability, resilience, and growth-oriented mindset necessary to integrate these tools into your daily work. Professional excellence also includes continuously learning, thinking critically, and leveraging AI to bring out the best in your work while continuing to evolve in your field.

This is where an evolution-ready mindset comes into play. In a world of constant change, this mindset views new technologies as catalysts for growth, not challenges. By cultivating an evolution-ready mindset, you transform change into an opportunity to thrive. You're adapting to new tools and proactively reimagining your professional path by maximizing AI use.

THE EVOLUTION-READY MINDSET

Adaptability and Strategic Integration

Change is not a threat; it is an opportunity. Every new AI tool can be a catalyst for your growth. That's the power of an evolution-ready mindset. It is a perspective that turns disruption into momentum.

The most accomplished professionals of the future won't be those who react to change; they'll be the ones who anticipate it, embrace it, and strategically position themselves as leaders. This means developing technical proficiency, adaptability, foresight, and a commitment to lifelong learning.

How Transformation Growth Happens

The path to long-term career success in the AI era follows a cycle of learning, adapting, and leading. By focusing on these key adaptability skills, professionals can stay relevant and actively shape the future.

Technology evolves rapidly, but your ability to learn faster than the speed of change keeps you future-proof. Growth begins with a deep understanding of where you stand today and where you need to go. Know your strengths and gaps. Identify the skills AI can enhance and the ones that require human expertise.

1. Laser-focus your growth: Prioritize learning AI tools that align with your career goals rather than getting distracted by every new development.
2. Uncover your blind spots: Stay curious and open to feedback; sometimes, the most valuable insights come from what you don't yet know.
3. Chart your course to mastery: Develop a structured learning

roadmap that helps you integrate AI seamlessly into your profession.

As AI transforms industries, the real advantage isn't knowing every tool; it's developing the mindset to evolve with the changes. Adaptability isn't just about keeping up; it's about staying ahead with confidence.

AI is transforming industries at an unprecedented pace, and the professionals who thrive are the ones who stay flexible, spot trends early, and pivot with confidence. The days of rigid career paths are over—adaptability is the new stability. Instead of fearing change, ask: How can AI improve this process? The most successful professionals don't wait for disruption; they anticipate it, experiment with it, and use it to their advantage.

STRATEGIC TOOL SELECTION: USING AI WITH PURPOSE

Success in the AI era is about using the right tools with intention and not about adopting every available one. Professionals who get the most out of AI don't chase trends; they strategically integrate technology where it adds real value. AI should be an extension of your expertise, not a disconnected tool that disrupts your workflow.

Knowing when AI enhances your impact and when human expertise must take the lead is key. Not every process benefits from automation, and not every tool will serve your goals. Thoughtful selection and seamless integration allow AI to complement your skills rather than overshadow them. In a world flooded with AI options, discernment is your greatest asset.

FROM MASTERY TO LEADERSHIP

Adapting to AI is just the beginning—true future-proofing happens when you move beyond using AI to leading its implementation. At first, this means mastering AI-assisted workflows and using automation to optimize tasks without losing critical thinking. Over time, you become a strategic implementer, identifying new AI opportunities, combining AI insights with human expertise, and advocating for ethical AI practices.

The fundamental shift happens when professionals evolve into AI leaders. The ones who shape the future aren't just using AI; they integrate it into business models, mentor others, and ensure its responsible adoption. They understand not just where AI is today but where it's going.

The professionals who stay ahead aren't competing with machines; they're refining the skills AI can't replicate: strategic thinking, creativity, leadership, and ethical judgment. The future belongs to those who think flexibly, act intentionally, and use AI efficiently and wisely.

Moving Beyond Basic Interaction

The evolution from basic AI usage to true professional partnership represents a fundamental shift in our work with artificial intelligence. As professional relationships develop from initial encounters to trusted collaborations, your relationship with AI can mature into a sophisticated alliance that enhances your expertise.

CREATING AI PARTNERSHIPS: UNDERSTANDING THE DYNAMICS

A successful professional partnership with AI begins with recognizing complementary strengths. While humans excel at understanding context, making nuanced judgments, and solving problems creatively, AI brings rapid analysis, pattern recognition, and consistent processing of large datasets. This combination of capabilities creates powerful collaboration opportunities that exceed what humans or AI could achieve alone.

AI is like a powerful instrument in your professional orchestra. As the conductor, you determine when to leverage its computational power and when to rely on human judgment. The key lies in thoughtfully blending these capabilities by creating harmonious workflows that maximize human insight and AI efficiency.

Practical Partnership Principles

A clear definition of a chosen role forms the foundation of an effective AI partnership. Understanding which tasks benefit most from AI assistance and which should remain exclusively human-driven helps create productive workflows. For hybrid situations, establish clear protocols that outline how human judgment and AI analysis work together.

Quality assurance is essential throughout the partnership. Develop verification processes for AI outputs while upholding professional standards through careful human oversight. Create feedback loops that facilitate continuous improvement, allowing human and AI contributions to evolve and strengthen over time.

Professional partnerships must remain adaptive as AI capabilities evolve. Stay flexible in allocating tasks and regularly reassess your partnership's effectiveness. This dynamic approach ensures that your collaboration remains productive as technology advances and professional demands change.

Consider how this partnership manifests in different professional contexts. An investment advisor might use AI to analyze market trends but apply human judgment to understand how these trends affect individual client situations. In creative fields, a graphic designer might collaborate with AI for initial concept generation but rely on human creativity and client understanding to refine and personalize final designs.

These partnerships demonstrate how AI can cement professional expertise. By thoughtfully combining human wisdom with AI capabilities, professionals can achieve new levels of excellence while maintaining the essential human elements that define their practice.

CAREER EVOLUTION PLANNING: A THREE-HORIZON FRAMEWORK

As a creative entrepreneur, I have always embraced curiosity, which consists of constantly seeking, learning, and acting with an open and flexible mindset. This approach has been vital in navigating the ever-evolving landscape of innovation. I encourage you to adopt the same mindset as you plan your career evolution in the AI era.

The future won't wait for you to react to change. To thrive, you need a proactive, strategic approach. By staying curious and adaptable, you can align your goals with emerging opportunities and develop the skills to set you apart.

Let's explore the Three-Horizon Planning Framework, which offers a clear roadmap for helping you balance today's immediate demands with the long-term aspirations that will define your professional journey.

Horizon 1: Mastering the Present

Before you can innovate, you need a solid foundation. This phase is about gaining fluency in AI and integrating it seamlessly into your daily work. Develop proficiency in the tools that enhance your workflow, automate routine tasks, and boost efficiency. Define clear metrics to track your progress and ensure AI adds measurable value to your work.

AI Etiquette: Start small. AI should complement your expertise. Be transparent about how you use AI to ensure trust and clarity in your contributions.

Horizon 2: Building Tomorrow's Capabilities

Once AI becomes a natural part of your workflow, it's time to expand your reach. Staying ahead of emerging AI advancements allows you to refine processes, apply AI across different areas, and lead initiatives that showcase innovation. The goal here isn't just to use AI efficiently—it's to create smarter, more versatile workflows that demonstrate your adaptability.

AI Etiquette: Collaboration is key. Foster a culture where AI-driven solutions are shared across teams, ensuring innovation remains human-centric and accessible.

Horizon 3: Shaping the Future

Beyond personal mastery lies leadership. The professionals who shape the future aren't just using AI; they're defining its role in their industries. This phase is about positioning yourself as an AI thought leader who designs solutions that add real value, mentors others, and ensures responsible AI adoption on a broader scale.

AI Etiquette: Lead with empathy and mindfulness. AI should serve progress, not just efficiency. Thoughtful integration ensures that innovation aligns with human values, fostering trust and long-term success.

Turning Plans Into Action

Having a vision is only part of the journey. To translate this framework into meaningful progress:

Align strategically: Ensure your goals support organizational priorities while reflecting your growth aspirations.

Track your success: Regularly assess milestones, measure your impact, and refine your approach.

Adapt to change: Remain flexible, updating your plans as AI evolves and new opportunities arise.

With a structured approach, you'll remain relevant and set the standard for thoughtful and ethical AI integration. This framework isn't just about advancing your career—it's about shaping a future where technology and humanity work together to create lasting impact.

DEVELOPING YOUR AI INTERACTION SKILLS

The evolution of AI fundamentally changes how we work, communicate, and solve problems. As these systems continue to evolve, developing strong AI interaction skills becomes crucial for professional success.

AI enhances human insight, creativity, and strategic thinking. Professionals who thrive in new technological environments don't rely solely on automation; they leverage it as a collaborative tool that frees them to focus on complex decision-making, innovation, and problem-solving.

Mastering the New Social Language

Just as human etiquette has evolved from formal Victorian manners to today's more fluid social codes, our interaction with AI continues to develop and refine. The key to mastering this new social language is not memorizing rigid rules but understanding fundamental principles that remain constant even as technology evolves.

Effective AI interaction begins with clarity of expression. While early AI required exact commands, modern systems understand more natural language. However, the underlying principle remains unchanged: the more precise your communication, the better your results.

Consider these different ways of expressing the same intent:

- Basic: "Set timer for 10 minutes."
- Natural: "I need a timer for the design team meeting."
- Contextual: "Help me stay on schedule during the client presentation."

Each approach has its place, and mastering when to use each style marks the difference between basic competence and true fluency.

Building Sophisticated Dialogue

As AI systems become more capable, our interaction patterns naturally become more nuanced. However, this evolution doesn't eliminate the need for clear communication—it simply adds layers of sophistication. Think of it as similar to developing fluency in a language, where you progress from basic phrases to complex ideas while still relying on fundamental grammar rules.

THE ART OF PRECISION

The way you frame AI interactions directly impacts their effectiveness. Thoughtful, well-structured prompts lead to more relevant, actionable insights, while vague requests often yield generic results. Consider these examples of refined AI interaction:

Financial Analysis: Instead of "Analyze these market trends," try: "Analyze market trends in the Asia-Pacific region, focusing on emerging technologies and their impact on sustainability-driven investments over the past two quarters."

Strategic Planning: Instead of "Help me prepare for my client meeting," try: "I'm meeting with a healthcare client exploring AI integration. Identify the main discussion points regarding AI's role in clinical settings, balancing opportunities with patient care considerations."

By clarifying intent and adding context, you transform AI from a generic assistant into a precision-driven tool that aligns with your strategic needs.

A Fashion Industry Illustrative Case Study

AI improves ideation and problem-solving most effectively when requests are framed with precision and context. Refining AI prompts in creative industries, where innovation and market trends intersect, can mean the difference between generic suggestions and groundbreaking insights.

The following illustrative case study demonstrates how strategic refinement transforms AI from an essential brainstorming tool into a powerful innovation partner that delivers targeted, actionable results aligned with real-world business needs.

Initial Engagement: A product development manager begins with a broad request: *"Help me brainstorm ideas for a new product launch in the fashion industry."*

First Response: The AI provides general suggestions like "eco-friendly clothing" and "minimalist fashion line." While these ideas aren't wrong, they lack the specificity for meaningful action.

Strategic Refinement: Understanding the need for more context, the manager reframes the request: *"Let's focus on a product launch for eco-conscious fashion targeted at millennials in urban areas. Please explore how technology, such as wearable devices or smart fabrics, can play a role in this collection."*

Improved Outcome: This refined approach yields more actionable insights, including specific concepts like "wearable fashion tech integrating health-monitoring devices" and "smart fabrics with temperature regulation for outdoor activities."

Let's highlight the progression from general to specific questioning, the integration of market context—such as millennial urban consumers—and the ability to combine multiple relevant factors like eco-consciousness, technology, and fashion. The refined prompt emphasizes how ideas evolve from basic concepts into innovative solutions.

This example demonstrates how professional AI etiquette is about structuring our interactions to achieve better outcomes. Each refinement adds layers of context that help AI understand what we're asking for and the broader professional context in which the request is made.

BALANCING AI INTEGRATION AND HUMAN TOUCH

Learning the art of balancing AI capabilities with human essence is paramount. This section explores how to create harmonious partnerships with AI while preserving and enhancing what makes us uniquely human.

Embrace artificial intelligence as a highly skilled apprentice. Someone eager to learn, capable of remarkable tasks, yet needing thoughtful guidance and human wisdom to unlock its full potential. This apprentice fuels the master craftsperson's abilities by managing complex preparatory tasks, enabling the master to concentrate on the craft's most subtle and creative elements. The relationship is dynamic: sometimes the apprentice leads with computational precision, other times stepping back to allow human intuition to guide the process.

The most sophisticated aspect of modern AI is its ability to support emotional and social well-being. This goes beyond simple scheduling and task management to encompass a holistic understanding of human needs and relationships. By monitoring patterns in your work intensity, communication styles, and physical activity, the system develops an awareness of your emotional state and energy levels.

For example, after a series of demanding meetings, the system might gently suggest a short walk, understanding the importance of physical movement for mental clarity. It helps maintain work-life balance during hectic periods by ensuring professional demands do not overshadow personal commitments. It might remind you about an important family member's event or suggest blocking time for exercise, understanding that these elements are crucial for long-term well-being and productivity.

PERSONALIZATION AS CONTINUOUS LEARNING

AI is like a profoundly perceptive assistant. It remembers your preferences and anticipates how they evolve in different contexts. This is the essence of AI personalization: a dynamic learning process that adapts

to your work habits, communication style, and decision-making needs over time.

Consider how this unfolds in daily work: AI doesn't just sort emails by sender or subject—it learns which messages truly matter, elevating the ones that require your attention while managing routine correspondence. During your morning commute, it provides detailed industry briefings, yet later in the day, when your schedule is packed, it shifts to concise, high-priority updates—all without explicit instruction.

This kind of adaptive intelligence is present in the tools we use:

- A smart calendar that reshapes your schedule based on past patterns and real-time priorities.
- A smartwatch that detects activity levels and suggests timely movement breaks.
- An email assistant that streamlines your inbox, ensuring urgent matters are addressed first.
- A virtual assistant that curates insights, adjusting its delivery based on your focus mode—whether in meetings, commuting, or deep work.

AI's contextual awareness extends even further. While working from a café, it might analyze ambient noise and suggest an optimal spot for a video call. During research-heavy projects, it automatically bookmarks sources, connects related insights, and organizes findings to mirror your thought process.

Through continuous interaction and adaptation, AI shifts from a passive tool to an intuitive enabler, enhancing efficiency, focus, and decision-making without disrupting your natural workflow.

CREATING A HUMAN-CENTERED AI PRACTICE

Success with AI integration demands a structured approach that thoughtfully balances automation with human connection. At the daily level, create an intentional framework that harmonizes AI assistance with meaningful human interaction. Your morning planning should start with a review of your AI-suggested schedule, taking time to identify which moments require your direct human presence. Consider these high-touch points carefully and set clear intentions for human connection throughout your day.

As you move from planning to execution, focus on thoughtful task assessment. Evaluate each activity through the lens of appropriate AI integration, looking for opportunities to maximize human value. This balanced approach ensures that you leverage technology while preserving essential personal elements. With this foundation in place, turn your attention to cultivating meaningful connection points throughout your day. Schedule deliberate person-to-person interactions, using AI to create space for these essential moments while maintaining an authentic presence in key relationships.

INDUSTRY TRANSFORMATIONS

The AI revolution is adding new tools and reimagining how we work. Let's examine how AI is transforming key industries.

Strategic Advisory & Finance

For years, strategic advisors and financial professionals relied on time-intensive manual processes to analyze market trends, assess risks, and develop recommendations. Decision-making often lagged behind real-world shifts, and the insights were outdated when they reached clients. Also, identifying emerging patterns required weeks of research, leaving firms reactive rather than proactive. The limitations of this traditional approach meant businesses were often caught off guard by economic shifts, competitive pressures, and sudden disruptions.

Personalization was also a challenge. Without real-time insights, advisors had to rely on broad, one-size-fits-all strategies that lacked the nuance required to serve clients with distinct needs. Crafting tailored recommendations took extensive effort, making it challenging to scale high-touch advisory services. Meanwhile, administrative burdens—from financial modeling to trend analysis—left professionals with less time to focus on strategic thinking and client engagement.

AI has reshaped financial decision-making. Instead of static reports, advisors now get instant insights into market shifts, industry trends, and competitor strategies. AI models don't just analyze past performance; they forecast future risks and opportunities, allowing firms to anticipate change before it happens.

Proactive decision-making has replaced reactive adjustments. With predictive analytics, professionals can spot trends before they fully emerge, allowing for more strategic foresight. Instead of scrambling to respond to disruptions, firms leverage AI to build strategies that preempt them.

Personalization has reached new heights. AI-powered analytics allow advisors to precisely tailor financial recommendations, risk assessments, and strategic roadmaps. Reports that once took hours to compile are now generated instantly, offering deep, client-specific insights backed by vast datasets.

At an operational level, AI automates repetitive tasks like data collection, report creation, and performance tracking. This efficiency allows professionals to focus on the human side of their work—delivering high-value strategic guidance, strengthening client relationships, and fostering long-term growth.

HEALTHCARE TRANSFORMATION

Few industries are as deeply rooted in human connection as healthcare. At its core, the provider-patient relationship is built on trust, empathy, and personalized care. AI is reshaping this field—not by disregarding human expertise but by enhancing its impact through greater precision, proactive engagement, and real-time insights.

For years, healthcare operated in a reactive model. Patients sought care only when symptoms appeared, diagnostic processes were lengthy, and treatment plans often followed standardized protocols rather than personalized approaches. The constraints of limited face-to-face time, overburdened systems, and episodic care meant that providers struggled to deliver genuinely individualized treatments.

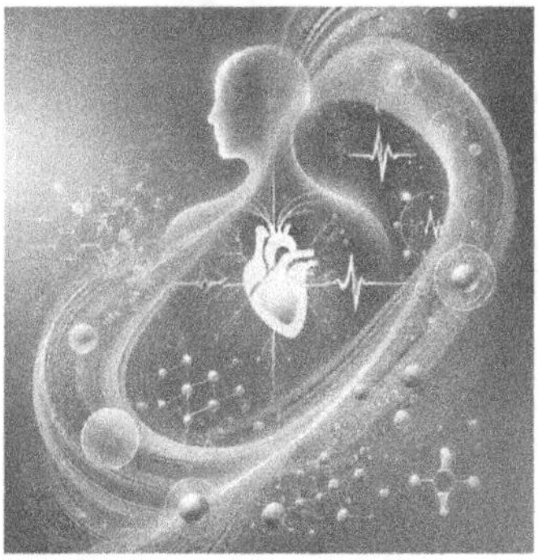

Traditional diagnostics relied heavily on manual evaluation, lab tests, and clinician experience. While effective, these methods were time-consuming and prone to delays. A patient might wait days or weeks for test results when an illness could progress undetected. Early intervention opportunities were often lost, leading to more complex and costly treatments later.

Treatment planning faced similar challenges. Standard medical guidelines, though essential, did not always account for individual differences in family history, lifestyle, or evolving health risks. Personalized medicine was a promising idea, but it wasn't easy to scale. Meanwhile, patient monitoring remained largely episodic—most conditions were only addressed during scheduled appointments, leaving gaps where complications could arise unnoticed. Chronic disease management, in particular, suffered from this lack of continuous oversight, often leading to unnecessary hospitalizations.

AI has moved healthcare from a reactive system to a proactive, data-driven model. Diagnostics that once took days can now be performed in seconds. AI-powered imaging tools detect early signs of disease with greater accuracy, analyzing thousands of cases to recognize subtle patterns that the human eye might miss. Machine learning models flag potential risks in lab results before symptoms appear, allowing for earlier intervention and better patient outcomes.

Patient engagement has also evolved. AI-powered assistants streamline administrative processes, ensuring that providers spend less time on paperwork and more time on direct patient care. Communication tools and digital health assistants use AI to facilitate real-time communication, offering patients guidance between visits and ensuring they remain engaged in their own health management. Medication adherence, once a persistent challenge, is now improved through automated reminders and AI-generated alerts that help prevent lapses in treatment.

Treatment plans are no longer one-size-fits-all. AI integrates family history data, lifestyle factors, and real-time health metrics to create precision medicine strategies tailored to each patient's needs. These personalized approaches result in more effective treatments with fewer side effects, dramatically improving long-term health outcomes.

Continuous patient monitoring has also become a reality. Wearable devices track vital signs and activity levels live, transmitting data to AI systems that detect warning signs before a condition worsens. Instead of waiting for the next appointment, providers can intervene when early symptoms emerge, reducing hospital readmissions and preventing avoidable complications. Chronic disease management has shifted from crisis response to ongoing, proactive care.

By integrating AI as a strategic tool, healthcare professionals can focus on what matters most: compassionate, informed, and effective patient care. Those who embrace AI as a technological advancement and a transformative partner will lead the next era of healthcare excellence.

STRATEGIC AI INTEGRATION: SUSTAINING EXCELLENCE AND TRUST

Integrating AI into professional practice isn't just about efficiency—it's about sustaining relevance and elevating quality. Excellence isn't a fixed benchmark but a continuously evolving pursuit, and professionals who thrive in AI-powered environments understand that AI, when applied with intention, enhances precision, strengthens decision-making, and fosters trust. Without strategic oversight, however, AI can dilute expertise rather than refine it.

Successful professionals use AI and shape its role to match their values and goals. They establish evolving quality benchmarks, ensuring AI is a refinement mechanism rather than a shortcut. Instead of treating AI as an unquestioned authority, they build validation processes that balance efficiency with accuracy. Their success isn't measured by automation rates alone but by AI's tangible impact—how it improves decision-making, elevates service quality, and reinforces professional credibility.

A key part of this process is practicing active judgment. AI-generated insights must be evaluated with discernment, ensuring recommendations align with real-world context and strategic objectives. AI may detect patterns in market trends, but human expertise is essential for interpreting cultural shifts, consumer behavior, and economic nuances. AI can produce vast amounts of data-driven insights, yet only professionals can connect these insights to larger strategic goals. Instead of treating AI outputs as absolute truths, critical thinkers evaluate assumptions, ensuring that AI's recommendations reflect real-world complexities rather than surface-level correlations. AI should function as a trusted advisor, not a final decision-maker.

Trust remains the foundation of professional relationships. Professionals who integrate AI responsibly understand that simply implementing these tools isn't enough—they must demonstrate their value in ways that reassure and inform. Rather than stating that AI speeds up processes, they illustrate how it enhances personalization, decision-making, and service quality. AI-assisted work must meet the same rigorous standards as fully human-driven efforts, reinforcing that technology should never compromise excellence.

Above all, trust requires clear accountability. AI may assist in analysis, automation, and forecasting, but the professional remains the final authority. Thoughtful quality assurance ensures that AI processes align with mindful, fair, and strategic principles. Keeping professional judgment at the core of AI integration safeguards standards and strengthens client relationships, reinforcing confidence in an increasingly AI-powered world.

YOUR FUTURE-READY PROFESSIONAL PRACTICE

The professional world is profoundly transforming, driven by AI's ability to magnify how we think, create, and deliver value. Thriving in this new landscape requires more than adaptation—it calls for strategic innovation and leadership. AI should not dictate your professional trajectory; instead, it should serve as a tool that aligns with your vision and promotes your expertise.

A future-ready professional strategically integrates AI. In other words, they do it with intent. This journey unfolds in three key phases:

Laying the Foundation: Building AI Fluency

The first step in integrating AI is clearly understanding its capabilities, strengths, and limitations. This knowledge allows professionals to make informed decisions about AI's role in their work. Mastery doesn't mean adopting every emerging tool; it's about identifying where AI creates meaningful impact without diluting expertise.

Begin by evaluating how AI can enhance your workflow. Think about the inefficiencies it can address, how it can aid decision-making and the tasks it can streamline or personalize for better efficiency. Many professionals start with AI-assisted research, analytics, or communication tools. However, the real value comes when AI integrates smoothly into strategic thinking—enabling professionals to concentrate on high-impact work that necessitates human insight.

Action Step: Identify one area in your workflow where AI could boost efficiency or insight and investigate a tool that meets that requirement.

Fostering Innovation: Pushing Boundaries

Once the foundation is set, AI integration moves beyond optimization and becomes an innovation catalyst. This phase is about exploration, experimentation, and refinement. Professionals who push boundaries with AI discover new efficiencies, elevate creativity, and gain deeper insights.

Those who experiment with AI-streamlined workflows develop a mindset of continuous learning. For example, a financial analyst might refine market predictions using AI-powered forecasting, while an architect could use generative design tools to develop sustainable structures with greater precision. The key is intentionality—not using AI for novelty but for its potential to elevate quality, depth, and impact.

At this stage, it's crucial to reflect:

- Is AI enhancing your work in ways that align with your professional goals?
- Does it create more profound value for clients, colleagues, and your industry?
- Beyond efficiency, is AI improving decision-making, personalization, or long-term outcomes?

True success isn't measured by the number of tools used but by the meaningful advancements they enable.

Action Step: Test one new process improvement this week, measure its impact, and refine your approach.

LEADING THE TRANSFORMATION: SHAPING AI'S ROLE IN YOUR INDUSTRY

AI integration isn't just about personal success—it's about actively shaping the future of your profession. The most forward-thinking professionals don't passively adopt AI; they set the standards for its responsible and strategic use, ensuring that it elevates—not diminishes—the integrity of their field.

Effective leadership in the AI era isn't just about using the technology but defining how it should be used. It means advocating for thoughtful adoption, where AI enhances expertise rather than diluting it. It involves mentoring peers and sharing real-world insights to help others navigate AI's complexities. It's about influencing best practices and ensuring AI is applied to drive meaningful impact.

Those who take this approach aren't just keeping up with change—they're leading it. Position yourself at the forefront of work by discussing AI governance, refining industry standards, and contributing to responsible innovation.

Action Step: Find one way to share your AI insights. It can be mentoring a colleague, joining an industry discussion, or helping refine best practices in your organization. The future of AI in your profession is being written right now; thus, it should be a part of the conversation.

A Catalyst for Professional Excellence

AI transforms industries by elevating precision, efficiency, and strategic decision-making. From designing sustainable cities to advancing medical research, professionals use AI to push boundaries, refine workflows, and accelerate innovation.

Architects leverage generative design to create sustainable, functional structures. AI optimizes layouts, energy use, and traffic flow, enabling rapid iterations while maintaining environmental responsibility.

Legal professionals streamline research, contract analysis, and case predictions with AI-powered tools, freeing them to focus on advocacy and legal strategy.

Financial advisors use AI for portfolio management and market forecasting, identifying risks and opportunities with real-time data insights.

Scientists and researchers analyze vast datasets and generate hypotheses faster, driving breakthroughs in medicine, engineering, and climate science.

In every profession, use AI with intention; don't just keep up with change—define it.

THE FUTURE OF WORK

AI transforms the fabric of professional practice by redefining how we think, create, and innovate. Success in this new professional world isn't about blindly embracing automation—it's about using these tools with intention. The professionals who thrive in this new paradigm see AI as expanding their skills.

Rather than limiting human capability, AI serves as a catalyst for efficiency, personalization, and strategic excellence. The future of professional work is about refining and amplifying expertise. Those who approach AI with curiosity and strategic foresight will unlock new levels of creativity, insight, and problem-solving.

This shift isn't about technology for technology's sake—it's about freeing professionals to focus on what truly matters: innovation, connection, and delivering lasting value.

EMBRACING THE NEW ECONOMY OF POSSIBILITIES

AI integration isn't a one-time shift—it's an ongoing process. The tools will change, but what truly matters is staying curious, adaptable, and committed to doing great work. Every step forward in AI adoption should be intentional and aligned with your professional vision. The goal isn't technology for technology's sake—it's about expanding your capabilities, refining your insights, and ensuring that AI remains a tool that serves your expertise, not the other way around.

Success comes from balance: knowing when to use AI for efficiency and when to rely on human insight, ethics, and creativity. The most impactful professionals will integrate AI with intent, using it as a catalyst for innovation rather than a crutch.

Mastering AI is not about control—it's about orchestration. Successful professionals learn to seamlessly integrate AI into their workflows, leveraging its strengths while elevating their uniquely human qualities.

The future of work doesn't belong to machines. It belongs to those who know how to use them wisely. Those actively participating in this transformation won't just navigate change—they will define it.

SIX
FUTURE-PROOFING YOUR CAREER
PROFESSIONAL EVOLUTION

"The illiterate of the 21st century will not be those who cannot read and write, but those who cannot learn, unlearn, and relearn."
— Alvin Toffler, Futurist and Author

HARNESSING AI'S POTENTIAL

Just as a telescope sharpens our vision without replacing our eyes, AI can enhance our analytical and creative strengths while relying on human judgment, intuition, and ethical reasoning.

The most effective use of AI comes from understanding its role as a collaborator. As discussed in prior chapters, AI can precisely analyze medical images in healthcare practices. For example, it can flag abnormalities that might otherwise go unnoticed. However, the doctor combines this data with the patient's history, lifestyle factors, and medical expertise to make informed decisions. Similarly, in creative fields, AI can generate initial ideas or variations. Still, the human artist or writer who provides the emotional depth, cultural context, intentionality, and passion transforms a concept into something meaningful.

To harness AI's potential, we must balance automation and human judgment. Yes, AI excels at processing vast amounts of data, optimizing logistical operations, and identifying patterns in ways that far exceed human capacity. From detecting fraud in financial transactions to predicting inventory needs in supply chains, AI enables professionals to work smarter, not harder.

However, AI's strengths lie in logic, pattern recognition, and efficiency—not nuance, ethics, or emotional intelligence. While it might be able to filter through thousands of résumés, it cannot assess a candidate's passion or office cultural fit. While it can assist in generating customer service responses, it lacks true empathy in complex interactions. In creative fields, AI can structure content and suggest improvements but cannot compare to human storytelling's originality, intuition, or emotional depth.

The key to thoughtful AI integration is understanding where automation adds value and when human oversight is essential. For example, AI can summarize reports and fact-check data in journalism, but the journalist ensures the story carries depth, context, and ethical responsibility. AI can automate tasks in business, but strategy, creativity, and innovation still rest in human hands.

Professionals who learn to integrate AI with discernment rather than blindly rely on it will shape the future of work.

But how does this balance play out in real-world applications? The following section explores practical examples of AI integration, demonstrating how professionals can use AI strategically while ensuring that authenticity, responsibility, and the human touch remain at the core of their work.

THE AI MASTERY ETIQUETTE: FROM FOUNDATIONS TO LEADERSHIP

Thriving in an AI-powered world isn't just about keeping up with new tools—it's about growing alongside them, strategically evolving your skills, and embracing a leadership mindset in this technological revolution. AI is not just something to use; it's something to integrate thoughtfully, ensuring that your strategic thinking, decision-making, and creativity remain at the forefront.

Mastering AI is a progressive journey of learning, experimentation, and leadership, not a sprint. Those who stay adaptable, refine their expertise, and align their growth with AI advancements will keep pace with the future of work and help shape it.

FUTURE-PROOFING THREE-TIERED FRAMEWORK

Mastering AI is not an overnight transformation; it is an intentional, evolving journey that unfolds in three phases. This progression isn't just about technical expertise; it's about growing alongside AI, refining your strategic thinking, and ensuring that technology enhances rather than overshadows human ingenuity.

At the heart of this journey are three guiding principles that will help you integrate AI into your professional evolution:

1. **Set Clear Goals**: Identify how AI integrates into your work and align its application with your career aspirations and vision.
2. **Assess Your Growth**: Regularly assess AI's impact, refine your strategies, and adapt to evolving needs.
3. **Commit to Continuous Learning**: Stay adaptable by embracing AI advancements, enhancing your skills, and sharing insights with others.

By following these pillars, you'll master it with purpose and integrity. So, where do you begin? Let's break this down into the mastery levels shaping your journey from AI learner to AI leader.

Level 1: Laying the Foundation

Every AI-driven career begins with a strong foundation. In this stage, you experiment, explore, and build confidence using AI tools. At this point, AI is a supportive assistant, not a decision-maker. Use it to enhance your work and hone your expertise.

The key to success is learning by doing—integrating AI into your workflow, recognizing its strengths and limitations, and refining your approach as you go. You might start by using AI to automate repetitive tasks, assist with research, or streamline communications. However, the real skill lies in analyzing AI-generated insights critically and ensuring that the outputs align with your standards.

How do you know you are at this level?

- You've created simple AI-driven workflows, saving time on repetitive tasks.
- You're documenting efficiency gains and tracking improvements in quality and productivity.
- You feel confident experimenting with AI, refining outputs, and identifying best-use scenarios.

At this stage, AI etiquette is about transparency and discernment. One should always be open about where AI is used and critically consider its suggestions.

Level 2: Expanding Impact Through Strategic Integration

Once AI becomes a natural extension of your workflow, the next step is to use it strategically. AI shifts from a helpful tool to a thought partner at this stage, offering insights for decision-making, strategy, and innovation.

Now, AI isn't just automating simple tasks—it's enhancing creativity, optimizing performance, and helping you make more informed choices. Whether predicting market trends, analyzing consumer behavior, or improving operational efficiency, AI becomes a powerful ally in expanding your professional reach.

Achieving success at this stage appears as follows:

- You are optimizing AI-driven workflows across different areas of your work.
- You train others in AI best practices, sharing insights and expanding AI adoption.
- You actively contribute to strategic discussions about AI implementation, positioning yourself as a valuable resource in your industry.

AI etiquette is about collaboration. It involves using AI to empower teams. Thoughtful integration ensures that automation enhances work without sacrificing creativity or critical thinking.

Level 3: Leading the AI Future

AI is part of your workflow and leadership approach at the highest level. You mentor others, shape AI strategies, and lead innovation efforts. At this stage, AI mastery is about how you guide and influence the responsible use of AI in your field.

You move beyond using AI for efficiency and begin leveraging it for transformation. You solve complex challenges, pioneer new AI applications, and shape industry standards.

In other words,

- You mentor and educate others on responsible AI adoption.
- You actively shape AI policies within your organization or industry.
- You develop new AI-driven solutions, influencing how AI is used broadly.

AI etiquette at this level is about integrity and accountability. It involves advocating for ethical AI use, fostering education, and ensuring that AI aligns with business values, social responsibility, and human creativity.

THE PATH TO MASTERY: USING AI WITH PURPOSE AND LEADERSHIP

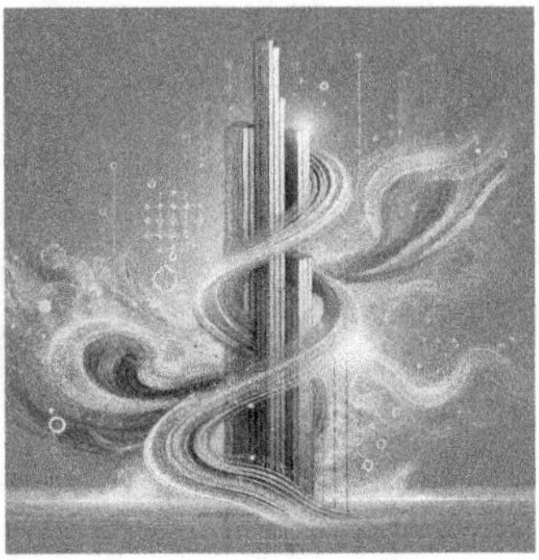

AI mastery is not about how many tools you know but how effectively you use them. The accurate measure of success isn't in automation alone but in the impact this technology has on your ability to think strategically, lead confidently, and shape the future of work.

Throughout this journey, the most future-proof professionals will be those who don't just adapt to AI but actively define its role in their careers.

So, where do you stand on this journey? Are you still laying the foundation, integrating AI into your workflow, or stepping into leadership? The key is to keep evolving wherever you are; stay curious, refine your approach, and make yourself uniquely valuable.

The choice is yours. Will you let AI shape your career, or will you take the lead in defining AI's role in your professional future?

DEVELOPING PROFESSIONAL AI SKILLS

While soft skills remain the backbone of professional success, mastering technical AI skills is just as crucial in today's evolving workplace. AI is a career accelerant, a force that can optimize workflows, enhance decision-making, and free professionals from repetitive tasks. Thus, the key to professional success is learning to interact with AI strategically.

Like most things in life, mastering AI doesn't happen immediately. It's a progressive process, moving from foundational skills to advanced strategies that refine AI's role in your work. Learning how to communicate effectively with AI, personalize its output, and integrate it seamlessly into your workflow will provide both efficiency and a strategic advantage in your career.

Laying the Foundation: Learning to Work with AI

We have discussed that AI can analyze data, generate insights, and automate tasks, but without precise guidance, it is just a tool that produces semi-generic results.

Because clear communication is the secret sauce in using AI, professionals who learn how to structure prompts and refine AI-generated content will always get higher-quality results than those who use AI passively. Developing an intuitive sense of when to trust AI outputs and when to intervene ensures that AI becomes the reliable assistant you need, not an unchecked authority.

To enhance your foundational skills, consistently seek opportunities to automate repetitive tasks, support research efforts, and improve communication efficiency. The goal is to build confidence in using AI while maintaining a critical mindset: verifying information, ensuring accuracy, and making informed, responsible decisions based on AI insights.

A professional who masters this foundational level will find that AI saves time, enhances creativity, expands problem-solving abilities, and improves overall efficiency.

OPTIMIZING AI FOR STRATEGIC INTEGRATION

Once AI is integrated into daily workflows, the next step is fine-tuning its performance and expanding its role beyond simple automation. In the same way, an experienced manager brings out the best in their team, a skilled professional knows how to get the most out of AI by refining its inputs, improving accuracy, and adjusting outputs based on real-world applications.

At this point, AI can effectively assist with decision-making, forecasting trends, and optimizing strategic processes. However, the most successful professionals at this stage don't just use AI passively; they customize it to fit their needs.

Those who expand their AI knowledge explore personalized AI solutions, integrate AI across multiple platforms, create automation that streamlines work, and even fine-tune AI-generated content for a specific audience. At this level, AI moves from being a productivity booster to a strategic tool that enhances critical thinking, creativity, and innovation.

The professionals who excel at this stage are not just using AI to assist them—they are using AI to extend their reach, uncover insights faster, and make more informed decisions.

MASTERING AI FOR TRACKING PROGRESS AND DRIVING INNOVATION

The final stage of AI mastery is about ensuring that AI works meaningfully for you. Those who track their progress, measure AI's impact, and refine their approach stay ahead of the curve rather than getting lost in AI trends that don't deliver real value.

At this stage, professionals adapt to AI advancements and contribute to how AI is used in their industry. AI mastery is about leadership, influence, and ethical responsibility, whether by sharing insights, leading discussions, or helping shape best practices.

Do not accumulate tools to have them; understand how to use them purposefully. The most future-proof professionals adopt AI and know how to blend it with human insight, creativity, and societal responsibility.

THE FUTURE OF WORK IS YOURS TO DEFINE

So, where does AI fit into your career? The most crucial step is the one you take today. Whether you're refining your current role or stepping into new opportunities, understanding how AI applies across different fields will help you confidently navigate this evolving landscape.

The future of your work is about how you choose to engage AI.

CONCRETE IMPLEMENTATION STRATEGY FOR DEVELOPING AI SKILLS

Developing AI interaction skills requires structured learning and adaptability. To engage with AI effectively, professionals should consider a personal competency framework, a guide for enhancing their understanding, communication, and ethical considerations.

This framework consists of the following three essential dimensions:

Technical Literacy

Developing a foundational understanding of AI's capabilities and limitations is essential for working with it confidently. Knowing what it can and cannot do helps prevent over-reliance on automated outputs while ensuring its use remains practical and informed. Likewise, knowing what you can and cannot do effectively will guide you strategically in using AI.

Staying updated on emerging trends is valuable, but filtering information wisely is equally important. Rather than feel pressured to keep up with every new development, focus on advancements that align with personal or professional needs.

Adaptive Communication

Effective AI interaction requires strategic communication. Clear, precise prompts lead to more relevant and accurate outputs, while iterative refinement ensures that AI-generated content meets expectations. However, the most essential skill is recognizing when human intervention is necessary and understanding that AI is a partner in creativity and decision-making rather than an independent source of truth.

Ethical Discernment

As AI becomes integrated into daily workflows, establish personal and professional guidelines for its use to ensure that interactions with technology align with core human values. Regularly assess how AI influences your work—whether in decision-making, creative processes, or professional communication. This helps maintain transparency, accountability, and integrity. Ethical engagement with AI involves adhering to external regulations and ensuring that technology is a tool for enhancement rather than distortion.

By developing technical literacy, adaptive communication, and ethical discernment, professionals can ensure that their engagement with AI is intentional, strategic, and responsible. The technology is most powerful when used with awareness and purpose—not as an unquestioned authority, but as a means to elevate human potential while staying true to professional and personal values.

CORE AI SKILLS EVERY PROFESSIONAL NEEDS

AI is only as effective as the way we engage with it. We have learned that the more intentional and precise we are in our interactions, the better results we'll achieve. Let's explore the fundamental skills that will help you best use AI.

Mastering AI Communication: Prompt Engineering

Think of AI as an intern—it's eager to help but relies on clear and specific instructions to deliver the best results. Crafting precise AI prompts is an art; mastering them will determine whether you get valuable insights or generic responses. It will also assess how future-proof your career is likely to be. Let's add more layers to the skill sets for success that we have already discussed.

- Approach AI with clarity and structure; vague instructions lead to ambiguous results.
- Experiment with different phrasing to fine-tune responses and optimize outputs.
- Develop templates for commonly used prompts to streamline your workflow.
- Understand that iteration is key; refine your approach if the first response isn't proper.

Ensure Accuracy: AI Fact-Checking & Quality Control

While it is an incredible tool, AI isn't infallible. It can misinterpret context, generate hallucinated facts, or reflect biases from training data.

- Always verify AI-generated outputs, especially when working with data-driven insights.
- Verify information with trustworthy sources before using AI-generated content for professional purposes.
- Be aware of AI limitations and trust your judgment if a claim sounds questionable.
- Establish feedback loops to enhance AI output time.

INTEGRATE AI INTO YOUR WORKFLOW: SMART AUTOMATION

AI uncomplicates your workflow. The goal is to reduce repetitive tasks so you can focus on high-value, creative, and strategic work. Therefore,

- Identify which tasks AI can automate and where your input is still required.
- Establish standard procedures for AI-assisted tasks; consistency is key.
- Establish fallback procedures for situations when AI tools fail or malfunction.
- Regularly audit your workflow to ensure AI improves efficiency and does not create more work.

Navigate AI Risks: Be Aware of Bias

With great power comes responsibility. Because AI is a powerful tool, ensure it is used transparently, responsibly, and without unintended bias.

- Acknowledge AI's influence on data privacy and put necessary safeguards in place.
- Remember that built-in biases exist—AI learns from human data, which means it can inherit human prejudices.

- Ensure ethical oversight when utilizing AI for decision-making, particularly in hiring, finance, and legal matters.
- Stay informed about AI regulations and best practices. This field constantly evolves, and staying ahead will help you remain compliant and responsible.

PUTTING AI TO WORK: YOUR AI TOOLBOX

Each case study in this section highlights a unique story of transformation, demonstrating how AI can streamline processes, boost productivity, and enhance decision-making across various professions.

Whether a sales professional strengthens client relationships, a content creator refines their strategy, or an entrepreneur optimizes operations, these case studies showcase the new strategic partner in professional evolution.

As you examine each case study, think about how the Three-Tiered Mastery Framework and the principles of Digital Decorum, such as respect, collaboration, and thoughtful integration, come to life in real-world applications.

Remember that AI's impact goes beyond individual tasks. It shapes entire career trajectories. As seen in the following examples, professionals who strategically integrate AI move through distinct stages:

- Laying the groundwork by utilizing AI as an assistant to boost efficiency.
- Harness AI to improve decision-making and foster creativity through strategic integration.
- Through leadership and transformation, fostering innovation and clarifying AI's role in the industry.

Each illustrative case study shows how AI adoption progresses through these levels, providing a roadmap for how professionals can evolve with AI rather than compete against it.

Case Study 1: Sales Mastery Through AI-Powered Insights

Adaptation: These AI-driven sales strategies can also be utilized in customer service, consulting, real estate, or any profession where building relationships and making data-driven decisions are crucial.

Level 1: Laying the Foundation—AI as an Assistant

Balancing administrative work with client relationships is a constant challenge in sales. A sales professional managing a growing portfolio of leads finds that routine tasks like scheduling follow-ups and logging interactions consume valuable time that could be better spent on meaningful client conversations.

AI-powered CRM automation was introduced to streamline these processes, handling data entry, outreach scheduling, and engagement tracking. AI-assisted sentiment analysis also helped refine messaging by identifying client needs based on past interactions.

Impact: By allowing AI to manage logistical tasks, the professional regained time to cultivate stronger relationships, emphasizing high-value conversations instead of getting bogged down in administrative work details.

AI Etiquette: AI should enhance communication, not be used in place of your authenticity.

Level 2: Strategic Integration—AI as a Thought Partner

Once AI became integral to daily workflows, it evolved into a decision-support tool. By utilizing predictive analytics, AI improved lead prioritization by identifying the best outreach opportunities based on previous interactions and purchase behavior.

AI also provided real-time sales insights, offering data-driven recommendations on when and how to engage with clients. This facilitated a more strategic approach to relationship building, ensuring that each interaction was well-timed and relevant.

Impact: Rather than simply reacting to customer needs, the professional anticipated them, resulting in more effective and timely engagements.

AI Etiquette: Leverage AI insights to enhance intuition. Your judgment should always steer AI-driven recommendations.

Level 3: Leading the AI Future: AI for Sales Leadership

At an advanced level, AI is no longer just assisting; it is a catalyst for coaching and leadership. Professionals use AI-driven performance analytics to mentor their team, share insights on effective strategies, and train others in AI-assisted sales techniques.

AI-powered simulations and conversation analysis also helped refine negotiation tactics, offering real-time feedback on communication effectiveness.

Impact: Sales professionals close deals faster and cultivate more profound, long-term client relationships while establishing new industry standards for AI-powered sales strategies.

AI Etiquette: Leading in AI industries involves promoting transparent, mindful, and responsible AI use.

Case Study 2: AI as a Content Strategy Partner

Adaptation: These AI-powered strategies apply to digital marketing, publishing, journalism, branding, or any profession that relies on audience engagement and storytelling.

Level 1: Laying the Foundation: AI as a Creative Assistant

Content creation requires consistency and creativity, yet professionals often get bogged down by research, ideation, and editing. A content strategist facing high output demands begins using AI to brainstorm ideas, refine drafts, and optimize writing workflows.

AI-assisted writing tools provide structural suggestions, summarize research, and help generate variations of existing content, allowing the strategist to iterate faster while maintaining creative control.

Impact: Rather than spending too much time on technical refinements, the creative professional concentrated on developing engaging narratives and a high-level creativity vision.

AI Etiquette: AI supports originality. Always infuse content with personal expertise and creativity.

Level 2: Strategic Integration: AI for Data-Driven Content Strategy

As AI was integrated into content creation, it also became part of audience analysis and performance monitoring. AI tools now analyze engagement patterns, recommend optimal posting times, and suggest content variations tailored to various audience segments.

Impact: The strategist no longer relied solely on intuition—AI provided clear, actionable insights that informed content decisions, ensuring maximum reach and impact.

AI Etiquette: Communicate the role of AI in crafting content. Trust is built on authenticity. Although AI may be essential for refining the content, the original voice must be yours.

Level 3: Leading the AI Future—AI for Thought Leadership

At the mastery level, AI shapes industry-wide strategies. The content strategist now mentors others in AI-assisted marketing, leads workshops on responsible AI use, and contributes to discussions on AI's evolving role in content ethics.

AI is also used for trend forecasting, helping to identify emerging topics before they gain traction. This allows strategists to establish themselves as early voices in industry conversations.

Impact: AI-driven content strategies increase engagement and position the professional as an industry leader and educator in AI adoption.

AI Etiquette*:* Future-proofing a content career isn't just about AI adoption—it's about responsible integration that keeps human creativity at the center.

Case Study 3: AI for Small Business Owners—Streamlining Operations & Growth

Adaptation: These AI-driven efficiencies apply to e-commerce, hospitality, creative entrepreneurship, and any field where efficiency, customer engagement, and growth strategy are crucial.

Level 1: Laying the Foundation—AI for Automation

A small business owner juggling multiple responsibilities needs a way to reduce workload without sacrificing quality. AI-powered tools are introduced to automate customer interactions, streamline scheduling, and manage basic inquiries through chatbots.

Impact: Routine tasks become effortless, allowing entrepreneurs to focus on business growth and customer relationships.

Level 2: Strategic Integration—AI for Smart Decision-Making

After implementing automation, AI became essential in managing inventory, predicting demand, and optimizing marketing efforts. AI-driven insights helped the business adjust stock levels dynamically while targeted advertising tools analyzed customer preferences to refine marketing efforts.

Impact: AI saves time, improves decision-making, guarantees better inventory control, and optimizes marketing investments.

Level 3: Leading the AI Future—AI for Business Growth & Innovation

At the leadership level, AI is integrated into long-term business strategies. The entrepreneur educates peers on AI adoption, experiments with tailored AI-driven solutions, and actively influences their industry's best practices for AI integration.

Impact: AI supports business growth and helps redefine how small businesses operate in an AI-driven economy.

THE FUTURE OF WORK IS YOURS TO SHAPE

These examples showcase how AI enhances strategy, creativity, and efficiency. Where do you see yourself on this journey? Are you still building your foundation, integrating AI strategically, or leading innovation in your industry? The key to success is evolving with AI on your terms.

Now that we've examined some essential AI skills professionals need, the next question is: How do these skills lead to career growth? Skills alone do not define success; what truly matters is how you apply them in real-world situations.

AI-DRIVEN GROWTH ACROSS PROFESSIONS

So, how does this evolution unfold in different careers? Let's explore how AI shapes professional growth across some industries, mapping the journey from AI adoption to leadership.

Marketing: From Data to Experience Design

A marketing professional just starting to use AI might automate content scheduling, refine ad targeting, and generate campaign insights, freeing time for more creative and strategic work.

As their expertise deepens, AI becomes a true thought partner, providing predictive analytics that shape data-driven strategies. Instead of reacting to trends, AI anticipates them by understanding customer behavior before the market shifts.

At the highest level of experience, AI is a cornerstone of experience design. Marketers in leadership roles use AI to craft hyper-personalized customer journeys, blending human creativity with AI-driven precision to create seamless brand experiences.

Adaptation: This trajectory also pertains to public relations, branding, and digital media.

Data & Analytics: From Insights to Decision-Making

A data analyst beginning their AI journey may use it to automate reports, detect patterns in large datasets, and visualize trends more efficiently.

As they integrate AI more deeply, their role expands to include working with AI-powered forecasting models, which provide decision-makers with strategic insights beyond raw numbers.

Eventually, they move beyond analysis into building AI-driven decision systems that shape entire organizations, influencing everything from financial strategy to operational efficiency.

Adaptation: These AI-driven approaches also benefit fields like finance, business intelligence, and market research.

Creative Fields: Blending Artistry with AI

For a creative professional, AI starts as a supportive tool, assisting with photo editing, video production, copy generation, and ideation. The goal is to improve workflow efficiency, providing more time for artistic endeavors refinement.

As they gain confidence in AI's capabilities, they move into AI-driven storytelling, where AI tools help personalize content, refine audience engagement strategies, and even co-create original works.

At its peak, AI evolves into a medium for creating innovative artistic experiences—from generative design to interactive installations, pushing the limits of what's possible in visual, written, and digital arts.

Adaption: These innovations reshape game design, filmmaking, and UX/UI development industries.

Healthcare: From Assistance to Innovation

A physician new to AI may begin with diagnostic tools that help analyze scans, identify patterns, and suggest treatment options. These tools ensure that final decisions remain in human hands.

Over time, they move beyond individual cases, leveraging AI to optimize hospital workflows, reduce administrative burdens, and enhance patient care efficiency. AI helps flag early disease markers, allowing for preventative interventions before symptoms arise.

At the leadership level, AI becomes a force for medical innovation. It powers personalized treatment plans, predictive medicine, and AI-driven drug discovery, transforming healthcare globally.

Adaptation: These advancements also impact nursing, medical research, and healthcare administration.

Law: AI as a Legal Ally

A legal professional in the early stages of AI adoption might use it to speed up research, analyze case law, and summarize contracts, significantly reducing time spent on repetitive tasks.

With further implementation, AI becomes an asset in litigation strategy and compliance automation, helping firms detect risks, predict case outcomes, and optimize legal workflows.

In leadership, AI is no longer just about efficiency—it's about access to justice. Forward-thinking professionals help design AI-powered legal tools that simplify complex legal processes, making legal services more accessible and equitable.

Adaptation: These innovations extend to corporate law, compliance, and intellectual property rights.

Engineering: AI for Smart Innovation

Engineers early in their AI adoption may use it to optimize designs, run simulations, and improve predictive maintenance, saving time and reducing errors in structural planning.

As AI becomes a core part of their workflow, they integrate intelligent automation and AI-driven quality control, making projects more efficient, cost-effective, and resilient.

With expert leadership, AI can enhance projects and redefine them. AI-driven engineering pioneers develop smart infrastructure, energy-efficient solutions, and intelligent systems that shape the future of cities, transportation, and sustainability.

Adaptation: These concepts apply to mechanical, civil, electrical, and aerospace engineering.

MEASURING PROGRESS AND SUCCESS

Because progress is not a single destination, tracking it ensures that your efforts lead to meaningful outcomes. Growth in this space isn't about accumulating tools or automating every task—it's about continuously refining your expertise, expanding your ability to make strategic decisions, and ensuring that AI assists and supports your professional capabilities.

The objective measure of success isn't just efficiency—it's impact. How has AI changed the way you work? Are you solving problems more effectively? Are you creating new opportunities for yourself and others? These are the benchmarks that define true mastery.

Efficiency is one indicator of progress. If a reporting task that once took four hours now takes thirty minutes with AI, that's a measurable improvement. But what matters most is how you use the time saved to refine your skills, explore creative solutions, or take on leadership opportunities. AI isn't just about working faster; it's about working more innovatively and strategically.

Beyond efficiency, skill development is a key marker of AI fluency. Mastery isn't about knowing every AI tool but about understanding how and when to apply AI effectively. Are you integrating AI seamlessly into your workflow? Are you using it to solve complex challenges? Can you clearly communicate AI-driven insights to colleagues or lead initiatives that inspire confidence in AI adoption? These questions help assess whether AI is genuinely expanding your professional capabilities.

However, progress isn't linear. Some days will bring breakthroughs, while others may feel like stagnation. What matters is maintaining forward momentum, staying adaptable, and recognizing the compounding effect of small improvements. The most successful AI professionals aren't the ones who aim for instant mastery—they're the ones who embrace continuous learning, strategic experimentation, and a willingness to evolve.

Ultimately, success in AI isn't just measured in technical proficiency or automated workflows. It's reflected in how well you lead, innovate, and create a meaningful impact in an AI-powered world.

Celebrating Progress

As you grow professionally, celebrating progress means more than just enjoying a moment; it's an essential practice for sustaining motivation and momentum in the challenging journey of AI mastery. These celebrations are fuel stops on a long expedition, offering the energy and confidence to keep moving forward. But how do we approach this thoughtfully?

Throughout your career, work, or any activities you engage in, start by documenting your wins, no matter how small. That first successful automation, the project that saved your team hours, or the moment you solved a particularly challenging problem are all worthy of recognition. Documenting achievements builds your confidence, provides evidence of your growth, and creates a resource to draw from when tackling future challenges.

Sharing your successes with peers is equally important. This isn't about boasting; it's about contributing to a shared knowledge base where your experiences can inspire and guide others. Your wins might spark ideas for colleagues or provide valuable insights into overcoming similar challenges.

Consider building a portfolio highlighting your growth and impact as your achievements accumulate. This may encompass case studies, metrics showing enhanced efficiency, or testimonials from colleagues who have gained from your efforts. Formal recognition, such as certifications, awards, or speaking engagements, can further solidify your reputation and contributions to the field.

AI Etiquette: *When celebrating success, recognize the contributions of others. A collaborative and supportive environment ensures that progress is shared and valued as a group.*

YOUR JOURNEY AHEAD

Professional growth in AI isn't about reaching a final destination—it's about embracing a continuous journey of learning and improvement. The levels of mastery described earlier are not rigid benchmarks but flexible guideposts, helping you map your progress and identify your next steps.

Each person's journey is unique. Some may advance quickly through certain stages, while others take more time to master key concepts. What matters most is maintaining steady progress and creating a meaningful impact within your sphere of influence.

As you progress, think about the footprints of your journey, tangible markers of how far you've come:

- Quantifiable Milestones: These may include optimizing workflows, automating repetitive tasks, or attaining measurable enhancements in efficiency outcomes.
- Skill Expansion: New capabilities arise through training or necessity, each serving as a building block for future success.
- Project Accomplishments: Completed projects serve as examples of obstacles overcome, solutions developed, and value generated.
- Professional Growth: A more intricate tapestry of relationships, leadership opportunities, and influence that goes beyond mere metrics.

Leadership often emerges organically, not solely through titles, but during instances when others turn to you for guidance or choose to follow your example. These instances shape not only your career but also your character. Recognition follows in various forms: formal awards, peer respect, or the gratitude of those you've mentored and supported.

Finally, consider the influence you've cultivated. This manifests in how your ideas spread, your suggestions are implemented, and your approach becomes integral to your organization's methodology. Influence isn't taken; it's earned through consistent demonstration of judgment, expertise, and thoughtful action.

BUILDING MOMENTUM

Success isn't about perfection but about progress. Small wins build momentum, and each step brings you closer to realizing your potential.

Think about this course and concentrate on both short-term gains and long-term development:

Start Today: Map your existing AI capabilities and areas for development. Outline your learning path and pinpoint key milestones. Seek quick wins where AI can immediately impact your work; set clear metrics to track your progress.

First 30 Days: Concentrate on establishing your foundation through focused learning. Enhance one routine task with AI to achieve noticeable results. Create a support network of mentors and peers, and thoughtfully document your initial successes and insights.

90-Day Horizon: Master role-specific AI applications that align with your goals. Take the initiative to lead an AI integration project. Create opportunities for team AI development and share your journey to inspire others in their pursuit of growth.

Remember, growth is about applying what you've learned and continuously asking, "What's next?" The AI landscape evolves constantly, and your commitment to learning will keep you at the forefront of innovation. Stay curious, stay inspired, and embrace the endless possibilities ahead.

Your journey is unique, and countless resources are available to support you every step of the way. Explore what resonates with your goals, experiment with new ideas, and connect with others who share your passion. The path to AI mastery is ongoing, but with dedication and the right approach, you're well-equipped for the journey ahead.

AI INTEGRATION ACROSS PROFESSIONS

From sales to marketing to small business management, AI's role is clear: it enables greater efficiency, smarter decision-making, and creative expansion. Successful professionals in an AI-powered world embrace these tools strategically, using them to remove barriers and enhance their capabilities.

The future of work isn't just about AI. It's about the choices we make in how we engage with it. Those who see AI as a collaborator—a tool to amplify strengths rather than a competitor to resist—will be the ones who lead in their fields, shaping industries rather than reacting to them.

AI is an invaluable tool across industries, from business to creative work. Instead of resisting or fearing it, choose to engage with it strategically. It is not about removing the human element but about removing tension, stagnation, inefficiency, and barriers to innovation.

As you reflect on the insights from this chapter, consider how AI can become a seamless part of your professional and personal growth. The question is not whether AI will change how we work—it already has. The real question is: How will you choose to engage with it? Will you let it passively shape your career, or will you take control, using it to elevate your expertise, enhance your efficiency, and confidently lead?

AI is changing the work landscape, but ultimately, people define its impact. Our decisions today will determine whether AI becomes a tool for empowerment or just another layer of automation.

We have a choice. How we engage with AI now will shape our careers and the future of work itself.

SEVEN
AI ETIQUETTE ACROSS INDUSTRIES
CREATIVE APPLICATIONS

... ✦ ...

"The journey of a thousand miles begins with a single step."
— Lao Tzu

FUTURE TRENDS AND PREPARATION

To thrive in the AI age, professionals must master two essential elements: adapting to emerging technologies and preserving the irreplaceable human touch. As AI reshapes industries at an unprecedented pace, its role is no longer just about automation; it is about exponentially increasing human expertise and expanding what's possible across creativity, science, sustainability, and business.

AI is no longer a distant concept—it is woven into the fabric of our daily work. It is revolutionizing how we create, design, teach, cook, and solve some of the world's most pressing challenges. The question isn't whether AI will transform industries—it already has. The real challenge is how we, as professionals, entrepreneurs, and creators, will harness its potential while preserving the depth, intuition, and artistry that make us uniquely human.

AI AND THE ARTIST: A NEW KIND OF CREATIVE PARTNER

Nowhere is AI's transformation more profound than in creativity. AI has evolved into a catalyst, pushing the boundaries of artistic expression and redefining collaboration. From generating breathtaking visual art to composing emotionally resonant music, AI challenges us to reconsider what creativity truly means in the digital age.

Artists who once relied solely on traditional tools now collaborate with AI, experimenting with novel techniques that blend human vision with machine precision. This evolution raises important questions: How do we credit AI's role in the creative process? How do we maintain artistic integrity while embracing these powerful tools?

Navigating Visual Creation with AI

The landscape of AI-powered visual creation has expanded dramatically with tools that generate increasingly sophisticated and nuanced artwork. These systems create original visual content, from abstract concepts to photorealistic images, using advanced machine-learning models trained in various artistic styles and techniques.

When incorporating AI into visual creation, consider the origin of the training data and respect the rights of original artists whose work may have influenced the AI's capabilities. Proper attribution is both a legal requirement and an ethical consideration. Develop a thoughtful approach to prompting and iteration, taking time to understand how your inputs shape the output.

Establish clear guidelines about AI usage early in collaborative visual projects. Discuss with all involved how AI tools will be used and ensure everyone is comfortable with and informed about AI's role in the creative process. Document creative decisions and their reasoning, mainly when AI plays a significant role.

When using images or artwork created with the assistance of AI, transparency is key. Proper attribution ensures clarity and acknowledges AI's role in the creative process. Below are simple guidelines and recommendations for appropriate crediting:

Be Transparent: Mention that the artwork was created or enhanced with the help of AI. For example:

"This image was generated using [Tool/Platform Name]."

"Created with the assistance of AI technology from [Tool/Platform Name]."

Provide Context: If applicable, describe your contribution to the process. For example:

"This artwork was generated using [Tool Name], with prompts and adjustments provided by [Your Name]."

"I collaborated with AI to design this piece using [Tool Name]."

Respect Copyrights: Ensure that the AI tool or platform you use allows commercial or public use of its outputs. If required, include any specific attribution guidelines set by the platform, such as:

"Image generated using [Tool Name], as per [Tool's Attribution Policy]."

Optional Detail: For readers curious about the process, you can briefly share how AI contributed:

"This image combines my concept with AI-generated elements, refined using [specific adjustments]."

Acknowledging AI's role encourages ethical use and sets a thoughtful example for others navigating creative work in the AI age.

THE EVOLUTION OF MUSICAL CREATION

AI tools that can understand and generate complex musical structures have transformed the musical landscape, enabling new forms of composition and performance. These systems can create complete compositions while maintaining musical coherence and emotional resonance, understanding intricate elements such as structure, harmony, and genre-specific characteristics.

However, transparency is essential when incorporating AI into musical creation. Acknowledge the tool's role while respecting traditional musicianship. In live performances featuring AI-generated elements, inform your audience appropriately without letting technical details overshadow the artistic experience. In collaborative settings, ensure all participants understand and are comfortable with AI's involvement.

The democratization of music creation through AI tools introduces new etiquette considerations. As these tools make sophisticated musical capabilities more accessible, respecting their strengths and limitations is crucial. When sharing AI-assisted musical compositions, be clear about the collaborative nature of the work while celebrating the unique fusion of human and artificial creativity.

Building Respectful Creative Partnerships

Just as AI transforms visual art, it also redefines collaboration in music and other creative disciplines. The most promising developments arise when human creativity and AI capabilities work in synergy. This partnership works best when guided by clear principles of authenticity, attribution, and respect.

At the heart of creative AI partnerships lies authenticity. While AI can enhance your work, your unique artistic voice should remain central. Documenting your creative journey—including AI and human contributions—ensures transparency with your audience. This documentation also becomes part of your creative story, helping others understand how AI tools can complement human artistry.

Respecting copyright and attribution requirements is equally important. Using AI does not exempt creators from traditional intellectual property considerations. Stay informed about licensing terms and any obligations that AI tools impose on your work. Understanding these requirements builds trust within the creative community and ensures your work remains ethically and legally sound.

Beyond individual practice, fostering open dialogue about AI's role in creative communities is essential. Sharing experiences, insights, and challenges allows artists, musicians, and creators to collectively shape best practices for AI-enhanced creativity. This ongoing conversation ensures that AI is integrated thoughtfully and respectfully into artistic practice, supporting innovation while maintaining the integrity of expression.

The future of AI in creativity is about expanding human artistic possibilities. The key lies in mastering AI tools while ensuring their use respects our artistry and remains mindful of AI's computational capabilities.

As AI-driven creative tools evolve, so will the etiquette surrounding their use. It is crucial to stay informed about developments in your field and adapt your practices accordingly. More than ever, creators belong to a broader community working together to integrate AI mindfully and effectively.

THE FUTURE OF AI-POWERED CREATIVITY

AI revolutionizes creative expression in previously unimaginable ways. These systems can now generate comprehensive virtual worlds with distinct characters and narratives that operate under their own physical laws. More remarkably, AI tools democratize creativity, enabling anyone—regardless of experience—to produce captivating artwork, compose moving musical pieces, or craft elegant designs.

This creative revolution raises important considerations. We must preserve meaningful roles for human artists while harnessing AI's capabilities. Questions surrounding creative attribution and intellectual property become increasingly complex as the lines between human and machine contributions blur. Additionally, it is crucial to ensure this technological shift promotes diversity and equitable access within creative fields.

Addressing these challenges requires ongoing collaboration across various industries. Artists, engineers, policymakers, and the wider public must work together to develop practical frameworks that balance innovation with accountability. What remains clear is AI's unparalleled potential to expand creative boundaries and encourage new forms of artistic collaboration.

Success in the future lies in balancing experimentation with thoughtful consideration. By embracing innovation and responsibility, we can transform AI into a tool that enriches our creative landscape, making it more inclusive, dynamic, and meaningful for all.

AI IN ENTREPRENEURSHIP

Harnessing the Power of AI for Business Innovation and Growth

Just as AI transforms creativity, it also revolutionizes entrepreneurship. Business leaders and startups use AI to launch new ventures, streamline operations, and develop cutting-edge products. AI is no longer just a tool—it is a business partner, enabling entrepreneurs to make data-driven decisions, automate complex processes, and optimize customer engagement.

Across industries, companies leverage AI to automate workflows, analyze vast amounts of data, and personalize customer experiences. Entrepreneurs who understand AI's capabilities can build more innovative business models, predict market trends, and develop creative solutions that set them apart.

AI's most significant business advantage is its ability to analyze and predict consumer behavior. By leveraging machine learning algorithms, companies can create more tailored services, automate marketing efforts, and optimize supply chains, ensuring efficiency, cost savings, and customer satisfaction.

Identifying AI Opportunities: Finding Your Niche

The first step in leveraging AI for entrepreneurship is identifying the right opportunities and the areas where AI can create significant value and differentiation for your business.

Some key factors to consider when identifying AI opportunities include:

- **Industry Dynamics**: What are your industry's major pain points, inefficiencies, or unmet needs that AI could address? Are there areas where traditional approaches are failing to deliver results?
- **Data Availability**: Do you have access to large, high-quality datasets that could be used to train and optimize AI models? Are there opportunities to collect or acquire new data enabling valuable AI applications?
- **Technological Feasibility**: Are the AI technologies needed to address your identified opportunities sufficiently advanced and accessible? What are the technical requirements and limitations of implementing AI in your specific use case?
- **Market Demand**: Like any product, is there a clear and compelling value proposition for an AI-powered solution in your target market? Are customers willing to pay for the benefits that AI can provide?
- **Competitive Landscape**: What are other companies in your industry doing with AI, and how can you differentiate your approach? Are there untapped opportunities or gaps in the market that you could address with AI?

By carefully evaluating these factors, entrepreneurs can identify high-potential areas for AI innovation and develop a clear strategic vision for their ventures.

BUILDING AI-POWERED PRODUCTS

From Vision to Reality

The journey from identifying an AI opportunity to launching a successful product requires a delicate balance of technical expertise, strategic thinking, and human-centered design. This transformative process demands careful consideration of several crucial elements shaping your product's success.

The Foundation: Data Strategy and Infrastructure

A robust data strategy lies at the heart of every successful AI product. This strategy isn't merely about collecting vast amounts of information; it's about curating high-quality, relevant data to train your AI to deliver meaningful results. Your data strategy should address the immediate needs of model training and the long-term requirements for continuous improvement and adaptation.

Success begins with identifying the precise data needed to solve your target problem. This requires a deep understanding of your domain and the nuances of AI capabilities. Consider what data you need today and what you'll need as your product evolves and scales. Establish rigorous data collection, validation, and preparation processes that ensure quality and ethical compliance.

The Engine: Algorithmic Excellence

Selecting the right algorithms and technical approaches forms the engine of your AI product. This choice isn't merely technical; it's strategic. Your chosen algorithms must align with your business goals, data availability, and performance requirements. Whether you're implementing deep learning for complex pattern recognition, traditional machine learning for structured data analysis, or natural language processing for communication interfaces, your choice must be guided by capability and practicality.

The selection process must include thorough experimentation and validation. To test different approaches, create proof-of-concept implementations, always considering the real-world constraints of computing resources, latency requirements, and scalability needs.

Infrastructure: Building for Scale

The foundation of a successful AI product extends beyond algorithms to encompass the entire technical infrastructure. This includes the computing power needed for training and deployment and the sophisticated ecosystem of tools and platforms that support development, monitoring, and maintenance. Modern cloud platforms offer unprecedented access to scalable computing resources, but choosing the proper infrastructure requires careful consideration of costs, performance requirements, and security needs.

Your infrastructure choices should consider future growth and evolution. Consider not just your current needs but your future scale. Build systems that can adapt and grow with your success, incorporating redundancy and failover capabilities. The right infrastructure choices early on can prevent costly redesigns later.

The Interface: Crafting the User Experience

The most sophisticated AI technology is useless without an intuitive, engaging user experience. This is where technical capability meets human needs, where algorithms transform into solutions that users trust and value. Successful AI products make complex technology accessible and valuable through thoughtful interface design.

Design your user experience with transparency and trust in mind. Users should understand what the AI is doing and why, with clear feedback about system confidence and limitations. Build interfaces that guide users naturally through interactions, providing context and explanation where needed. Remember that your users aren't AI experts—they're people looking to solve problems or improve their lives.

Evolution: The Continuous Improvement Cycle

Perhaps the most crucial aspect of AI product development is understanding that the launch is just the beginning. AI products are living systems that must grow and evolve with use. Establish robust processes for monitoring performance, gathering feedback, and implementing improvements. Create systems that learn from data, user interactions, and real-world applications.

Set up clear metrics for success and systems to track them. Monitor not just technical performance but user satisfaction and business outcomes. Use this information to guide the continuous refinement of your models and user experience. Build feedback loops that help your product get better with every interaction.

MARKET STRATEGY: BRINGING YOUR PRODUCT TO LIFE

The final piece of the puzzle is your go-to-market strategy. This encompasses everything from pricing and positioning to distribution and customer acquisition. Your plan should clearly articulate your value proposition and differentiate your offering in an increasingly crowded market.

Consider your pricing strategy carefully: it must reflect the value you deliver and the costs of operating and improving your AI system. Build relationships with early adopters who can provide valuable feedback and testimonials. Create a straightforward narrative about how your AI solution transforms your users' worlds.

Remember, successful AI products aren't just technically sophisticated; they're carefully crafted solutions that solve real problems in ways that users find natural and valuable. By paying attention to these elements and how they work together, you can build products that work well and make a difference in people's lives.

While the opportunities in AI entrepreneurship are transformative, they also present distinct challenges that require careful navigation. Success in this rapidly evolving field demands innovation, strategic foresight, and a commitment to good business practices.

CRITICAL CHALLENGES AND STRATEGIC SOLUTIONS

Ethical and Social Implications

AI can reinforce biases, erode privacy, and create societal disruptions. Entrepreneurs must adopt a proactive approach to responsible AI development. This begins with embedding ethical guidelines directly into the development process, from selecting diverse and representative datasets to implementing systems that prioritize explainability and accountability. Creating technology that benefits society is a foundation for building trust and ensuring sustainable growth.

Navigating the Regulatory and Legal Landscape

AI operates in an evolving legal framework where rules surrounding data privacy, intellectual property, and algorithmic accountability constantly emerge and shift. Success requires staying attuned to local, national, and international regulatory changes. Forward-thinking entrepreneurs develop robust compliance strategies for data handling while engaging legal counsel to navigate complex laws and anticipate future regulatory shifts. Taking these proactive measures early can prevent costly legal challenges and build a strong foundation for growth.

Addressing the Talent and Skills Gap

The shortage of skilled AI professionals poses a considerable challenge for growing ventures. Successful entrepreneurs address this with multifaceted strategies for talent development and acquisition. Partnerships with academic institutions can create valuable talent pipelines, while robust internal training programs help upskill existing team members. The rise of remote work has opened new possibilities for accessing global talent pools. Most importantly, fostering a culture of learning and innovation helps attract and retain top-tier talent despite fierce market competition.

Safeguarding Intellectual Property

Intellectual property often represents the core of AI startups' value proposition and competitive advantage. A comprehensive IP strategy begins by identifying the crucial aspects of AI technology that warrant protection. This might include pursuing patents for unique algorithms or processes, establishing trademarks for brand protection, and implementing strategic non-disclosure agreements to safeguard proprietary knowledge. A well-crafted IP strategy protects innovations, signals professionalism to investors, and creates barriers to imitation.

Securing Funding and Investment

The technical complexity and substantial initial costs of AI ventures make funding particularly challenging. Successful entrepreneurs approach this challenge by developing compelling, data-backed business cases that clearly articulate their value proposition. They typically explore multiple funding avenues, from venture capital and angel investors to government grants and strategic partnerships. Building strong relationships with potential investors and demonstrating early traction through pilot projects or customer feedback can significantly improve funding prospects.

Adapting to Market Evolution

The AI landscape evolves dizzily, with new technologies, competitors, and consumer expectations constantly emerging. Successful entrepreneurs are keenly aware of industry trends and breakthroughs while remaining open to pivoting their strategy based on market feedback. Continuous learning and adaptation aren't just advantages—they're necessities for long-term survival and success in this dynamic field.

A Framework for Success

Navigating the challenges of AI entrepreneurship requires more than technical expertise; it demands a holistic strategy that balances innovation, responsibility, and adaptability. By approaching these challenges with foresight and determination, you can unlock AI's full potential to drive transformative change.

The path to success in AI entrepreneurship isn't just about building cutting-edge technology—it's about creating solutions that resonate with people, solve meaningful problems, and stand the test of time. Successful entrepreneurs understand that each challenge presents an opportunity to strengthen their venture's foundation and contribute to the responsible advancement of AI technology.

Preparing the Workforce of Tomorrow

The need for AI literacy and education grows as AI becomes an integral part of industries. AI transforms how we teach, learn, and upskill individuals to prepare the next generation of professionals.

AI IN EDUCATION

Transforming How We Learn and Grow

AI-powered personalized learning platforms analyze student performance and tailor educational experiences to individual needs. Adaptive learning systems ensure that students receive the right level of challenge, helping them build critical thinking and problem-solving skills more effectively.

Additionally, AI assists educators in grading, generating lesson plans, and tracking student progress, allowing them to focus more on mentorship and engagement rather than administrative tasks. Integrating AI into education enhances learning and bridges gaps in access to quality education.

Personalized Learning: Tailoring Education to Each Student

Personalized learning ranks among the most transformative educational applications of AI. It leverages algorithms and machine learning to craft educational experiences uniquely suited to individual students' needs, capabilities, and passions. This technology brings us closer to realizing an educational paradigm in which learners benefit from adaptive, personalized instruction that responds to their distinct learning styles, pace, and objectives.

AI-powered educational platforms analyze how students learn and adjust their guidance accordingly. They can suggest personalized study materials, adapt language lessons to match skill levels, and provide real-time math support to improve understanding. These tools help students progress at their own pace, making learning more effective for everyone.

Case Study: From Virtual TA to Personalized Learning Partner

Georgia Tech's 2016 *"Jill Watson"* initiative demonstrated AI's transformative role in education. Developed as part of the online Master of Science in Computer Science (OMSCS) program, Jill was an AI-powered teaching assistant designed to respond to student questions in online forums. Initially unaware of Jill's AI nature, students found her responses remarkably effective, highlighting AI's potential to enhance learning.

This experiment was a technological achievement and a glimpse into AI's ability to improve education by handling routine support tasks. The initiative evolved into a broader vision for AI-driven learning systems that personalize assessments, foster critical thinking, and support skill development. AI complements educators, freeing teachers to focus on mentorship and deeper learning, while AI assists with administrative and repetitive tasks.

Intelligent Tutoring Systems: Providing Guidance and Support

Another key application of AI in education is intelligent tutoring systems (ITS). These AI-powered tools provide students with real-time guidance, feedback, and support as they learn. Unlike traditional educational software, which typically follows a fixed, one-size-fits-all approach, ITS can adapt to each student's needs and provide targeted support when needed.

These systems demonstrate their value across various subjects and skills. AI tutors offer step-by-step guidance through complex problems and tailor their explanations according to student responses and prevalent misconceptions in mathematics. For writing development, intelligent systems analyze essays in real-time, providing feedback on everything from grammar and syntax to argument structure and evidence use. In science education, these tutors engage students in natural language conversations, helping them grasp complex concepts through interactive dialogue and personalized explanations.

In essence, intelligent tutoring systems assist students in maintaining engagement and motivation while working independently by offering responsive, personalized support. This immediate feedback loop fosters a more dynamic learning environment where students can advance independently while receiving continuous guidance and encouragement.

Creative Learning Unleashing Student Expression with AI

While AI in education often emphasizes personalized learning paths and assessment, its potential to transform creative expression in the classroom is equally significant. AI tools open up unprecedented opportunities for students to explore, create, and innovate in unimaginable ways.

Reimagining the Creative Classroom

Artificial intelligence can serve as a creative catalyst in learning environments. It can help create a place where students use AI tools to visualize their stories, compose original music, and solve real-world problems in their communities. This empowers students to become confident creators and innovators.

CREATIVE TOOLS IN EDUCATION

Visual Arts and Design

AI-powered design platforms enable students to transform their ideas into visual reality. These tools support everything from generating images prompted by written descriptions to sophisticated graphic design and digital storytelling. Students explore machine learning concepts while developing artistic skills, making the technology both a creative medium and a learning tool.

Music and Sound

AI music creation tools offer students new ways to explore sound and composition. These platforms combine music theory with artificial intelligence, allowing users to experiment with composition, create original soundtracks, and understand music through hands-on creation. Students can compose, arrange, and produce music regardless of their traditional musical training.

Coding and Interactive Creation

Interactive platforms engage students with AI concepts through hands-on applications. Learners create AI-powered applications, explore machine learning principles through coding exercises, and develop computational thinking skills. These tools make complex technology accessible, enabling students to become creators rather than just consumers of AI.

Storytelling and Writing

AI-enhanced writing platforms help students develop their narrative skills. These tools support creative writing through various approaches, from generating illustrations for student stories to offering writing prompts and story development assistance. Students can publish and share their work in multiple digital formats, fostering creativity and digital literacy.

PRACTICAL APPLICATIONS IN THE CLASSROOM

Project-based learning thrives when enhanced by AI capabilities. Students process environmental data to identify patterns and trends, visualize historical events and timelines in new ways, and develop AI-assisted solutions for local community challenges.

Artificial intelligence tools also facilitate cross-disciplinary integration. Students explore mathematical concepts by creating artistic patterns, grasp physics principles through digital music composition, and deepen their understanding of literature via AI-assisted visual interpretation. This interdisciplinary approach helps them recognize connections across traditionally separate subjects.

Furthermore, AI transforms collaborative learning experiences. Groups utilize AI tools to enhance their brainstorming and ideation processes, create digital showcases of their work, and develop rich multimedia stories together. These collaborative projects help students master both subject matter and valuable skills in teamwork and creative problem-solving.

Skills Development Through Creative AI

Students interacting with AI in creative contexts can cultivate essential competencies. Through hands-on experience, they strengthen critical thinking and problem-solving skills while building digital literacy and technical fluency. This approach nurtures creative confidence and artistic expression while fostering a nuanced understanding of AI's capabilities and limitations. As students collaborate on new projects, they refine their communication skills and cultivate an entrepreneurial spirit.

THE POWER OF PRESENT LEARNING

The Essential Experiences That Shape Us

While AI tools offer remarkable capabilities for education, nothing surpasses the fundamental power of direct observation, present-moment engagement, and hands-on connection with the subject matter. The most profound learning happens when students fully immerse themselves in their studies, whether examining a leaf's intricate structure, feeling the texture of clay between their fingers, or experiencing the resonance of a musical instrument.

These immediate, tangible experiences forge neural pathways and emotional connections that technology alone cannot replicate. When students gaze through a microscope for the first time, plant a seed and watch it grow, or successfully solve a complex equation after multiple attempts, they develop not just knowledge but also intuition, persistence, and wonder.

AI should never minimize these essential experiential moments. Thoughtfully combining traditional hands-on learning with technological tools may create an educational environment that honors innovation and the timeless value of direct experience. The goal is to harness AI's capabilities while preserving the irreplaceable magic of discovery through personal engagement.

Best Practices for Implementation

Educators can maximize the impact of creative AI by thoughtfully integrating it into their teaching practices. The most successful approaches begin with simple, accessible tools that complement existing curricula. Teachers should create an environment that welcomes experimentation and views challenges as learning opportunities. By emphasizing the creative process over final products and fostering peer collaboration, educators help students develop both technical skills and creative confidence.

Schools play a crucial role in facilitating the success of this integration. By investing in professional development, they effectively prepare teachers to utilize innovative AI tools. Designated spaces for showcasing AI-enhanced student work celebrate achievements and inspire creativity. Clear guidelines for appropriate AI use help maintain academic integrity while promoting exploration. Strategic partnerships with technology experts and creative professionals offer valuable insights and opportunities for authentic learning experiences.

Balancing AI Implementation with Traditional Learning

AI tools in education should complement traditional learning methods. Through the mindful integration of technology, the goal is to promote critical thinking and deepen understanding. When students combine AI capabilities with foundational learning practices, they develop richer cognitive skills and a more nuanced understanding of concepts.

This balanced approach allows learners to strengthen their foundational abilities while using AI to explore more complex ideas and challenges. For example, students should first grasp basic mathematical concepts through traditional problem-solving before using AI to tackle advanced applications. In writing, they should develop their own voice and critical thinking skills while using AI to refine and explore different perspectives.

Future Possibilities

The future of creative learning with AI holds extraordinary potential. As these tools evolve and become more accessible, they will unlock new forms of expression we have yet to imagine. Success lies in focusing on human creativity while leveraging AI to enhance exploration.

The goal isn't to have AI create for our students but to empower them to build with AI, developing the skills, confidence, and creative mindset they'll need for future success.

ENSURING EQUITABLE IMPLEMENTATION

The effective integration of AI in education necessitates careful implementation at both institutional and systemic levels. Important considerations include:

Access and Infrastructure

Educational institutions must ensure equitable access to AI tools and resources across all student populations. This includes addressing technical infrastructure needs and providing appropriate support systems for underserved communities.

Professional Development

Educators need comprehensive training and ongoing support to integrate AI tools effectively. This includes understanding the technical aspects and pedagogical implications of AI in education.

Guidelines and Ethics

Clear frameworks for ethical AI use in educational settings are essential. These frameworks should address data privacy, appropriate use of guidelines, and student rights while ensuring transparency in AI tool selection and implementation.

Collaborative Implementation

Success requires engagement from multiple stakeholders, including state leadership, which sets the vision and provides resources; district administration, which handles local implementation and adaptation; teachers, who manage classroom integration and feedback; families, who provide support and engagement; technology partners, who offer tools and technical expertise; and higher education, which contributes to research and teacher preparation.

Educational transformation through AI isn't just about technology; it's about reimagining learning for the future. Institutions are critical in ensuring this transformation is equitable, effective, and sustainable. A systematic approach while remaining flexible to local needs can create education systems that serve all students.

How to Measure Success

To ensure effective implementation, institutions should track the following:

- Student engagement and achievement.
- Teacher satisfaction and effectiveness.
- Technology access and utilization.
- Cost-effectiveness and sustainability.

- Equity in implementation and outcomes.
- Long-term student success indicators.

The future of education is not just about adopting new technologies; it's about creating systems that empower every student to thrive in a rapidly changing world. Through thoughtful leadership and collaborative implementation, we can build education systems that are more personalized, engaging, and effective for all learners.

AI changes not only how we learn but also how we eat, cook, and experience hospitality. The restaurant industry is experiencing a technological revolution, from AI-driven kitchen automation to personalized dining experiences.

AI IN THE RESTAURANT AND FOOD INDUSTRY

Transforming the Dining Experience

AI-powered systems manage inventory, automate food preparation, and ensure quality control in commercial kitchens, reducing waste and improving efficiency. AI also transforms the customer experience, offering personalized menu recommendations and even automated service interactions.

Sustainability is another key advantage: AI helps track food waste, optimize energy use, and improve supply chain management, making restaurant operations more eco-friendly and cost-effective.

Revolutionizing Kitchen Operations

The modern restaurant kitchen is becoming an AI-powered command center. Intelligent kitchen management systems are revolutionizing how restaurants handle food preparation, inventory, and quality control. These systems use computer vision and sensor technologies to monitor real-time cooking processes, ensuring food preparation consistency and reducing waste.

Advanced AI systems can accurately predict cooking times, adjusting for variables like ingredient freshness, kitchen temperature, and order volume. This precision improves food quality and optimizes kitchen workflow. Intelligent systems can now coordinate multiple dishes within a single order, ensuring everything arrives at the perfect temperature and at the right time.

Inventory and Supply Chain Intelligence

One of the most significant challenges in restaurant management is inventory control and supply chain optimization. AI systems are transforming this aspect by providing predictive analytics that can forecast ingredient needs based on historical data, seasonal trends, and even weather patterns. How?

Intelligent inventory systems continuously monitor stock levels, automatically generating orders when supplies run low. They can adjust order quantities based on predicted demand, accounting for upcoming events, weather forecasts, and local trends. This intelligence extends to supply chain management, where AI helps restaurants build more resilient and efficient supplier networks.

ENHANCING CUSTOMER EXPERIENCE

AI-powered innovations transform the front-of-house experience by creating more personalized and efficient service models. Digital menus can now adapt based on inventory levels, time of day, and customer preferences. These systems can also make intelligent recommendations based on dietary restrictions, past orders, and weather conditions.

Voice AI and natural language processing enable more sophisticated interactions between customers and ordering systems, whether in person or through digital channels. These systems can handle complex modifications to orders, answer ingredient questions, and provide detailed recommendations while maintaining a natural, conversational flow.

Food Safety and Quality Assurance

AI revolutionizes food safety protocols through advanced monitoring and detection systems. Computer vision systems can identify potential contamination risks, monitor food storage conditions, and ensure proper handling procedures are followed. These systems provide continuous monitoring far exceeding what human inspection alone can achieve.

Temperature monitoring systems use IoT sensors and AI analysis to maintain optimal storage conditions and alert staff to potential issues before they become problems. Machine learning algorithms can predict equipment maintenance needs, preventing breakdowns that could compromise food safety or disrupt service.

Sustainability and Waste Reduction

Environmental awareness is becoming increasingly important in the restaurant industry, and AI offers powerful tools for sustainability. Intelligent waste management systems use computer vision to track what's being discarded, helping restaurants identify patterns and adjust ordering and preparation accordingly. These systems can reduce food waste by:

Machine learning algorithms analyze patterns in food waste data to suggest menu modifications, portion adjustments, and preparation techniques that minimize waste while maintaining quality. This technology also helps restaurants track their environmental impact and make data-driven decisions about sustainability initiatives.

Labor Optimization and Training

In an industry facing persistent labor challenges, AI helps restaurants better use their human resources. Intelligent scheduling systems can predict staffing needs based on multiple factors, ensuring optimal coverage without unnecessary labor costs. These systems learn from historical data to become increasingly accurate in their predictions.

AI-powered training systems are helping new staff members learn procedures more quickly and effectively. AI-guided virtual and augmented reality applications can provide immersive training experiences that accelerate learning and improve retention. These systems can adapt to individual learning styles and provide real-time feedback during training sessions.

THE FUTURE OF RESTAURANT AI

As we look toward the future, the integration of AI in the restaurant industry will only deepen. Emerging technologies like robotics for food preparation, advanced predictive analytics for business planning, and enhanced personalization through AI will continue to transform the industry. However, the goal remains consistent: to enhance the dining experience while improving operational efficiency and sustainability.

The successful implementation of AI in restaurants requires a balanced approach that combines technological innovation with the irreplaceable human elements of hospitality. The future belongs to establishments that can harness AI's capabilities while maintaining the warmth and personality that make dining out a unique experience.

Practical Implementation Strategies

A phased approach often works best for restaurants considering AI implementation. Begin with solutions that address your most pressing challenges, such as inventory management, kitchen operations, or customer service. Focus on systems that integrate with your existing technology and provide clear, measurable benefits.

Remember that successful AI implementation requires buy-in from your entire team. Invest in proper training and change management to ensure your staff sees AI as a helpful tool rather than a threat to their jobs. Create clear protocols for how AI systems will be used and maintained, and establish metrics to measure their impact on your operations.

The transformation of the restaurant industry through AI is not just about technology—it's about creating better customer experiences, more efficient operations for owners, and more sustainable practices for our planet. As these technologies evolve, they will enable restaurants to focus more on what matters most: creating memorable dining experiences that keep customers coming back for more.

Scaling Restaurant Operations Through AI Automation

The power of AI extends beyond day-to-day operations to enable significant business scaling. By strategically automating key processes, restaurants can handle increased volume while maintaining quality and enhancing customer experience.

Intelligent Reservation and Table Management

Modern AI-powered reservation systems do far more than simply book tables. They optimize seating arrangements based on party size, timing, and server sections, maximizing covers while maintaining service quality. These systems learn from historical data to predict dining duration for different party sizes and times, enabling more accurate booking slots and reduced wait times.

Advanced systems adjust reservation availability based on kitchen capacity and staffing levels, ensuring service quality isn't compromised during peak times. They automatically manage waitlists, send targeted communications to guests, and can even predict and help prevent no-shows through intelligent confirmation systems.

Customer Relationship Management at Scale

AI-driven CRM systems enable restaurants to maintain personalized relationships with guests even as their customer base grows. These systems track individual preferences, dietary restrictions, and ordering history, enabling personalized recommendations and communications that make every guest feel valued.

The technology can identify VIP customers, track special occasions, and automate personalized marketing campaigns that drive repeat visits. By analyzing ordering patterns and feedback, these systems help restaurants understand and cater to evolving customer preferences across multiple locations.

Multi-Location Management

For restaurants expanding to multiple locations, AI provides powerful tools for maintaining consistency and quality across the brand. Centralized systems can:

- Monitor and compare performance metrics across locations.
- Standardize recipe execution and portion control.
- Share successful strategies and menu items between locations.
- Coordinate supply chain and inventory across multiple sites.
- Identify and address operational issues before they impact service.

Digital Presence and Online Ordering

AI-powered digital platforms enable restaurants to expand beyond their physical locations. Intelligent ordering systems can handle hundreds of simultaneous orders across multiple channels—website, mobile app, and third-party platforms—while maintaining accuracy and efficiency.

These systems automatically route orders to the appropriate preparation stations, adjust pickup and delivery times based on the kitchen load and communicate status updates to customers. They can even predict and prepare for surge periods, ensuring smooth operation during peak times.

Financial Intelligence and Growth Planning

As restaurants scale, AI systems provide crucial financial planning and expansion insights. These tools analyze performance data to:

- Identify optimal locations for new outlets.
- Predict resource needs for expansion.
- Optimize pricing strategies across different markets.
- Project ROI for new technology investments.
- Monitor and maintain profit margins during growth.

AUTOMATED MARKETING AND OUTREACH

AI transforms marketing efforts by automating and personalizing customer outreach at scale. Smart systems can:

- Target promotional campaigns based on customer behavior.
- Optimize email and social media content timing.
- Adjust promotional strategies based on real-time response data.
- Manage your online reputation across multiple platforms.
- Create personalized loyalty programs that drive engagement.

Transforming Restaurant Marketing Through AI

In the modern restaurant industry, AI-powered marketing represents the frontier of customer engagement and business growth. This technology transforms how restaurants connect with their customers, moving beyond simple promotion to create personalized, data-driven relationships that drive loyalty and revenue.

Personalized Marketing at Scale

The era of one-size-fits-all restaurant marketing is over. AI systems now analyze vast customer data to create highly personalized marketing campaigns. These systems consider dining history, preferences, spending patterns, and even social media activity to craft messages that resonate with individual guests.

Consider a regular customer who typically orders vegetarian dishes during weekday lunches. The AI system might recognize this pattern and automatically send them promotions for new vegetarian menu items, timed to arrive just before their usual lunch hour. This level of personalization transforms generic marketing into meaningful communication that drives real engagement.

Predictive Analytics and Timing- AI identifies the perfect moment for customer outreach. By analyzing patterns in customer behavior, these systems can predict:

- When a regular customer might be due for another visit
- The optimal time to introduce new menu items to specific customer segments
- The best moments to send promotional messages for maximum impact
- Which customers might be at risk of churning and need special attention

This temporal intelligence ensures marketing efforts land at precisely the right moment to influence customer decisions.

Dynamic Content Creation— Modern AI tools can automatically generate and optimize marketing content. For example, these systems can:

- Craft compelling email subject lines that improve open rates.
- Generate personalized menu recommendations based on past preferences.
- Create targeted social media posts for different customer segments.
- Adjust promotional language based on customer response data.
- Automatically generate visually appealing food photography layouts.

Loyalty Program Enhancement— AI transforms traditional loyalty programs into dynamic engagement tools. Smart systems can:

- Customize rewards based on individual customer behavior.
- Predict and prevent customer churn through targeted interventions.
- Create personalized challenges and achievements that gamify the dining experience.
- Adjust reward structures based on business needs.
- Track and analyze program effectiveness across different customer segments.

Reputation Management and Social Listening— AI-powered systems continuously monitor and manage online reputation across multiple platforms:

- Analyzing review sentiment to identify trends and areas for improvement
- Generating appropriate response templates for different types of feedback
- Tracking brand mentions across social media platforms
- Identifying influential customers and brand advocates
- Measuring the impact of marketing initiatives on online reputation.

Automated Campaign Optimization:— Marketing campaigns become living entities that continuously evolve and improve:

- A/B testing different message variants automatically
- Adjusting promotional offers based on real-time response data
- Optimizing marketing spending across different channels
- Identifying the most effective combinations of timing, content, and offers
- Measuring and reporting ROI for different marketing initiatives

Building Lasting Customer Relationships— The ultimate goal of AI-powered marketing is not just to drive short-term sales and build enduring customer relationships. This is tremendous because it means:

- Understanding and anticipating customer needs before they arise
- Creating memorable moments that strengthen brand loyalty
- Maintaining consistent, relevant communication across all channels
- Measuring and improving customer lifetime value
- Building a community around your restaurant brand

Integration and Implementation— Success with AI-powered marketing requires thoughtful integration with existing systems and processes:

- Connect marketing automation with reservation and POS systems.
- Train staff to understand and utilize marketing insights.
- Establish clear metrics for measuring marketing success.
- Create feedback loops that continuously improve marketing effectiveness.
- Maintain a balance between automation and a personal touch.

THE FUTURE OF RESTAURANT MARKETING

The restaurant industry stands at the dawn of a transformative era in marketing, where artificial intelligence promises to reshape how we connect with diners. Picture walking into your favorite restaurant, where your phone quietly suggests the perfect dish based on your past preferences, the weather, and even your current mood. This isn't science fiction – it's the near future of dining.

AI is ushering in experiences that feel almost magical: augmented reality menus that let you see your dish before ordering, smart systems that know when to offer your favorite comfort food on a rainy day, and personalized recommendations that feel like they come from an old friend who knows your tastes perfectly.

Yet, amid this technological revolution, successful restaurants will remember that dining remains a human experience. The warmth of a genuine smile, the personal touch of a chef's recommendation, and the joy of sharing a meal with loved ones are irreplaceable moments that AI should enhance.

The winning formula combines AI's analytical precision with the restaurant industry's time-honored tradition of hospitality. When done right, artificial intelligence works behind the scenes like a tireless assistant, helping restaurants forge stronger connections with their guests while letting the human elements of dining shine through. This balance ensures that as restaurants embrace the future, they never lose sight of what makes dining out truly special: the people.

AI IN HOSPITALITY

Transforming Guest Experience and Operations

Having a background in the hospitality industry, I know that exceptional service is built on efficiency, personalization, and seamless customer experiences. The hospitality industry is at the center of the AI-driven revolution. This technology enhances every aspect of the guest journey while empowering staff to deliver unprecedented service levels. This transformation touches everything from pre-arrival experiences to post-stay engagement, creating seamless, personalized experiences that define modern hospitality.

Reimagining Guest Experience

The modern guest journey begins long before arrival and continues well after departure. AI systems are revolutionizing how hotels understand and cater to guest preferences, creating high-tech, highly personal experiences.

Pre-Arrival Enhancement

Advanced AI systems begin personalizing the guest experience from the moment of booking. They analyze past stay data, booking patterns, and preferences to prepare for each guest's arrival. For example, the system may observe that a guest typically requests extra pillows, exercises in the morning, or prefers rooms away from elevators, and it automatically adjusts the guest's stay arrangements accordingly.

Smart Room Experiences- Modern hotel rooms can be intelligent environments that learn and adapt to guest preferences. These systems can:

- Remember preferred room temperatures and lighting schemes
- Anticipate daily routines and adjust accordingly
- Provide voice-controlled room features and concierge services
- Offer personalized entertainment recommendations
- Monitor room conditions and predict maintenance needs before they become issues

OPERATIONAL EXCELLENCE

AI transforms back-of-house operations, creating efficiencies that allow staff to focus on meaningful guest interactions rather than routine tasks.

Intelligent Resource Management- Innovative systems optimize everything from energy usage to staffing levels:

- Predictive maintenance schedules that prevent disruptions Automated inventory management for supplies and amenities
- Dynamic staff scheduling based on occupancy and guest needs
- Energy optimization systems that reduce costs while maintaining guests' comfort
- Predictive ordering systems for consumables and supplies

Housekeeping Optimization- AI revolutionizes housekeeping operations through:

- Smart room status monitoring
- Optimized cleaning schedules based on guest patterns
- Inventory tracking for linens and supplies
- Quality control systems using IoT sensors
- Predictive maintenance alerts

REVENUE MANAGEMENT AND PRICING

Modern AI systems take revenue management to new levels of sophistication:

Dynamic Pricing Strategies- Advanced algorithms consider countless factors to optimize pricing:

- Historical booking patterns
- Local events and demand drivers
- Competitor pricing
- Weather forecasts, Market trends, and economic indicators

Inventory Optimization- AI helps maximize revenue through enhanced inventory management:

- Optimal room type allocation
- Length-of-stay controls
- Early warning systems for potential overselling
- Upgrade opportunity identification
- Group booking optimization

GUEST COMMUNICATION AND SERVICE

AI transforms how hotels communicate with and serve their guests.

Intelligent Concierge Services- Modern concierge systems provide personalized recommendations and assistance:

- Restaurant and activity suggestions based on guest preferences
- Real-time travel updates and weather advisories
- Automated reservation services
- Local event recommendations and transportation coordination

Multilingual Support- AI-powered translation services enable seamless communication with international guests:

- Real-time translation for guest interactions
- Automated translation of written materials
- Cultural preference awareness
- Multilingual voice assistance
- Customized communication preferences

SUSTAINABILITY AND ENVIRONMENTAL MANAGEMENT

AI helps properties operate more sustainably:

Resource Optimization

Smart systems monitor and optimize resource usage:

- Energy consumption patterns
- Water usage optimization
- Waste reduction strategies
- Carbon footprint monitoring
- Sustainable practice implementation

SMART SECURITY SYSTEMS

The proliferation of facial recognition technology raises serious privacy concerns. While it's marketed as a convenience and security tool at airports, hotels, and public spaces, we're witnessing unprecedented surveillance expansion without meaningful public debate.

Consider: A hotel using facial recognition isn't just identifying guests - it's potentially tracking movement patterns, storing biometric data, and sharing information with other systems. The technology is already embedded in many aspects of daily life, from unlocking phones to social media photo tagging.

While it enhances security and streamlines processes, key questions remain: Who owns this biometric data? How long is it stored? What are the consent mechanisms? How vulnerable is it to breaches or misuse? The lack of comprehensive regulation around this technology makes these questions particularly urgent.

The hospitality industry's adoption of facial recognition represents a broader societal shift: Surveillance becomes normalized under the guise of convenience and safety. This normalization may be most concerning, as we're trading privacy for efficiency, often without fully understanding the implications.

FUTURE-FORWARD INNOVATION

Emerging Technologies: The future of hospitality AI holds exciting possibilities. Next-generation systems will offer:

- Augmented reality property tours
- Predictive guest services
- Biometric check-in systems
- Smart room customization
- Integrated wellness monitoring

Implementation Strategy: Success with AI in hospitality requires thoughtful implementation.

Phased Approach—Consider a strategic rollout that:

- Identifies high-impact areas for initial implementation
- Ensures staff training and buy-in
- Measures and validates results

- Scales successful initiatives
- Maintains focus on guest experience

Staff Empowerment: AI should improve human interaction.

- Train staff to leverage AI insights.
- Use technology to reduce routine tasks.
- Focus human interaction on high-value guest encounters.
- Create feedback loops for continuous improvement.
- Maintain the personal touch that defines hospitality.

The transformation of hospitality through AI isn't about replacing human interaction—it's about enhancing it. By automating routine tasks and providing deep insights into guest preferences, AI frees staff to focus on creating meaningful connections and memorable experiences. The future of hospitality lies in finding the perfect balance between high-tech efficiency and high-touch service, creating personalized and scalable experiences.

AI IN INTERIOR DESIGN: MERGING AESTHETICS WITH INTELLIGENCE

Another area of my expertise is space planning, and artificial intelligence takes the process to another level. AI-powered design tools assist architects and interior designers in optimizing layouts, enhancing aesthetics, and improving functionality. These tools analyze lighting, spatial flow, and human behavior patterns to create beautiful, highly functional spaces.

From smart homes that automatically adjust their environments to commercial spaces designed for optimal efficiency, AI redefines how we interact with the built environment.

Crafting Intelligent Spaces

Interior design is a fascinating intersection of art, psychology, and functionality. As a certified interior designer, I find the possibilities and applications of AI in the space planning process endless and exciting. As AI enters this creative domain, it provides powerful tools to enhance the designer's ability to create harmonious, functional, and emotionally resonant spaces. Integrating AI into interior design isn't about replacing creative intuition but amplifying it through data-driven insights and intelligent automation.

FUNDAMENTAL DESIGN PRINCIPLES ENHANCED BY AI

Balance and Harmony: AI systems can now analyze spatial compositions using advanced computer vision, helping designers achieve perfect balance:

Traditional symmetrical balance becomes more precise through algorithmic analysis of visual weight and space distribution. AI tools can suggest furniture placement and decor arrangements that create harmonious equilibrium through symmetrical or asymmetrical compositions.

The technology considers physical dimensions, color weight, texture density, and pattern intensity to create spaces that feel naturally balanced yet dynamically interesting.

Rhythm and Flow: Modern AI tools can analyze traffic patterns and spatial flow, helping create spaces that move people naturally:

The system considers how people navigate spaces, accounting for cultural preferences and behavioral patterns. It can predict potential bottlenecks and suggest layout modifications that enhance flow while maintaining aesthetic appeal.

Scale and Proportion: AI excels at calculating perfect proportions and scaling relationships:

Advanced algorithms can instantly verify the golden ratio and other classical proportional relationships across multiple design elements. The technology can suggest ideal furniture sizes and arrangements based on room dimensions and usage patterns.

Color Theory and Light: AI brings unprecedented precision to color and lighting design:

The system can analyze natural light patterns throughout the day and seasons, suggesting harmonious color palettes under varying light conditions. It can predict how different artificial lighting schemes interact with color choices and surface materials.

SPACE-SPECIFIC APPLICATIONS

Like many topics in this book, I am only scratching the surface of space planning and barely touching on the multitude of applications that can influence our surroundings.

Residential Spaces

AI helps create homes that perfectly balance comfort with functionality.

The technology analyzes family lifestyle patterns to suggest layouts that support daily routines. It can recommend materials and finishes that align with aesthetic preferences and practical needs, considering factors like durability, maintenance, and acoustic properties.

Hospitality Spaces

For hotels and resorts, AI helps create environments that optimize both guest experience and operational efficiency:

The system can analyze traffic patterns to suggest layouts that promote smooth guest flow while creating intimate spaces for relaxation. It can recommend design elements that support brand identity while maintaining practical functionality for staff operations.

Restaurant Spaces

In dining environments, AI helps balance the atmosphere with operational needs. How?

The technology can optimize seating arrangements for both ambiance and service efficiency. It suggests materials and color schemes that enhance the dining experience while meeting durability and maintenance requirements.

Intelligent Material Selection

AI transforms the material selection process through sophisticated analysis. Let's consider materials:

Performance Prediction: Advanced algorithms can predict how materials will perform over time based on the following:

- Environmental conditions and usage patterns
- Maintenance requirements and lifecycle costs
- Acoustic properties and light reflection
- Sustainability metrics and ecological impact

Aesthetic Harmony: AI helps ensure material selections create cohesive design stories:

The system can suggest complementary materials based on texture, pattern, and color relationships and visualize how different material combinations work together in various lighting conditions.

SPATIAL PSYCHOLOGY AND USER EXPERIENCE

AI brings new depth to understanding how spaces affect human psychology:

Emotional Response Prediction: Advanced algorithms can predict likely emotional responses to design choices:

Color combinations and their psychological impact Spatial arrangements and their effect on comfort and stress levels Lighting schemes and their influence on mood and behavior

Accessibility and Inclusivity: AI helps ensure spaces work for everyone:

The system can verify ADA compliance and suggest improvements for universal design. It can identify potential challenges for users with different abilities and recommend solutions.

IMPLEMENTATION AND WORKFLOW

Design Process Integration: AI enriches traditional design workflows:

The technology can automate routine tasks while leaving creative decisions to the designer. It can generate multiple design options based on specified parameters, allowing designers to focus on refinement and customization.

Client Collaboration: AI tools enhance the client communication process:

Advanced visualization tools help clients better understand design proposals. The system can quickly generate alternatives based on client feedback while maintaining design integrity.

Future Directions

The future of AI in interior design holds exciting possibilities.

Some of the emerging technologies will offer:

Real-time design visualization with augmented reality Predictive maintenance recommendations for materials and finishes Advanced sustainability optimization Biometric response analysis for design choices Integration with smart home systems

Integrating AI into interior design represents a technological advancement and a transformation in how we understand and create spaces. By combining data-driven insights with creative intuition, designers can create beautiful and intelligent environments that serve their users more effectively than ever before. Use AI to express the designer's creative vision. Technology can handle complex calculations and analysis, while the human designer focuses on the art of creating spaces that touch the soul.

Rethinking Mobility

AI enhances how we design spaces and reshapes how we move within them. Transportation is experiencing a generational transformation, including self-driving cars and intelligent traffic systems. Let's explore some developments.

AI IN TRANSPORTATION

Revolutionizing Mobility and Logistics

AI revolutionizes urban mobility by improving traffic flow, reducing congestion, and optimizing public transportation. Autonomous vehicles are set to change how we commute, making travel safer and more efficient.

Additionally, AI-powered logistics and supply chain management ensure faster, more reliable deliveries, optimizing everything from ride-sharing services to global freight transportation.

Autonomous Vehicles: The Future of Driving

One of the most significant applications of AI in transportation is the development of autonomous vehicles. Self-driving cars, powered by sophisticated AI algorithms and sensors, promise to make driving safer, more efficient, and more accessible than ever.

Some of the key benefits of autonomous vehicles include:

- **Increased Safety**: By eliminating human error, which is responsible for the vast majority of traffic accidents, autonomous cars have the potential to reduce road fatalities and injuries dramatically.

- **Improved Efficiency**: Self-driving cars can communicate with each other and with intelligent traffic management systems to optimize routes, reduce congestion, and minimize fuel consumption.
- **Enhanced Accessibility**: Autonomous vehicles can provide mobility solutions for people who cannot drive due to age, disability, or other factors, greatly expanding access to transportation.

Major automotive companies and technology giants invest heavily in developing autonomous vehicle technology. The number of self-driving cars on public roads continues to grow. As technology matures, we can expect to transition gradually towards fully autonomous transportation in the coming decades.

Intelligent Traffic Management: Optimizing Urban Mobility

Another key application of AI in transportation is the development of intelligent traffic management systems. These systems leverage real-time data from sensors, cameras, and connected vehicles to optimize traffic flow, reduce congestion, and improve overall mobility in urban environments.

Some examples of AI-powered traffic management solutions include:

Adaptive Traffic Signals: AI algorithms dynamically analyze real-time traffic data to adjust signal timing, optimize flow, and reduce stop-and-go traffic.

Smart Parking: AI-powered parking management systems guide drivers to available parking spots, reducing circling and congestion in busy urban areas.

Predictive Maintenance: By analyzing data from sensors and other sources, AI predicts when transportation infrastructure, such as roads and bridges, requires maintenance. This allows for proactive repairs and minimizes disruptions.

As urban populations continue to grow and city transportation systems become more complex, the role of AI in managing and optimizing urban mobility becomes increasingly critical.

DRONES AND AERIAL MOBILITY: TAKING TRANSPORTATION TO NEW HEIGHTS

AI also enables the development of autonomous drones and other aerial mobility solutions, which promise to revolutionize the transportation of goods and even people.

Some of the most exciting applications of AI in aerial mobility include:

Delivery Drones: AI-powered drones can autonomously navigate to deliver packages and other goods directly to customers, reducing delivery times and costs.

Urban Air Mobility: Companies are developing autonomous aerial vehicles, sometimes called "flying cars," that could provide rapid, point-to-point transportation in urban areas, alleviating ground traffic congestion.

Aerial Inspections: AI-enabled drones can autonomously inspect critical infrastructure, such as bridges, power lines, and pipelines, improving safety and efficiency.

While significant regulatory and technological hurdles remain, the potential for AI-powered aerial mobility solutions to transform transportation is immense.

The Ethical and Social Implications of AI in Transportation

As with any transformative technology, the application of AI in transportation raises important questions that must be carefully considered. Some of the key issues include:

- **Safety and Liability**: As autonomous vehicles and other AI-powered transportation solutions become more prevalent, questions around responsibility and liability in accidents will become increasingly complex.

- **Workforce Displacement**: Automating driving and other transportation-related tasks could displace millions of workers, necessitating proactive policies and programs to support reskilling and reemployment.
- **Privacy and Security**: AI systems' collection and analysis of vast amounts of transportation data raises concerns about privacy and the potential for misuse or breaches.
- **Equitable Access**: To avoid exacerbating existing inequalities, it will be critical to ensure that the benefits of AI-powered transportation solutions are accessible to all, regardless of income or geographic location.

Addressing these and other social implications requires ongoing collaboration and dialogue among policymakers, industry leaders, and the broader public. This ensures that the transformative potential of AI in transportation is harnessed in a way that benefits society as a whole.

The application of artificial intelligence in transportation represents one of the most exciting and transformative developments of our time. From self-driving cars and intelligent traffic management to autonomous drones and aerial mobility, AI is poised to revolutionize how we move people and goods worldwide, making transportation safer, more efficient, and more accessible.

As we continue to develop and deploy these technologies, it will be crucial to proactively address the ethical and social implications they raise, ensuring that the benefits of AI-powered transportation are broadly shared and that potential adverse impacts are mitigated.

By doing so, we can harness the incredible potential of AI to create a transportation future that is not only technologically advanced but also equitable, sustainable, and deeply human-centric.

From AI in Transportation to AI in Geopolitics: A Global Race for Dominance

As AI reshapes industries, it has also become a geopolitical force, influencing global power structures, economic policies, and national security.

AI AND GEOPOLITICS

Navigating the Global Power Dynamics of Artificial Intelligence

Countries compete for AI supremacy, recognizing its strategic importance in defense, infrastructure, and economic stability. Nations that lead in AI innovation gain a significant geopolitical advantage, shaping policies and international relationships for years.

The Global AI Race

The global AI landscape continues to evolve remarkably, transforming economies, societies, and the balance of power. Nations are now engaged in a strategic competition to establish leadership in AI development and deployment, with distinct strategies emerging worldwide.

China has positioned itself as a dominant force in artificial intelligence, leveraging its extensive data resources, substantial computing infrastructure, and an integrated approach that aligns government, industry, and academia. Chinese tech companies have achieved notable advancements in autonomous systems, computer vision, and natural language processing. Beijing's strategic focus on AI underscores the country's commitment to attaining technological leadership on a global scale.

The United States, meanwhile, maintains its competitive edge through a dynamic ecosystem of world-class universities, leading tech companies, and innovative startups. The country's private sector consistently ranks among the highest globally in AI investments, reflecting a strong commitment to advancing the field. Public-private partnerships further amplify this effort, with initiatives focusing on expanding computing capacity, building sustainable infrastructure, and fostering job creation in the tech sector. These investments highlight a broader U.S. strategy to remain at the forefront of AI innovation despite growing competition from emerging players worldwide.

The European Union has adopted a distinctive approach, prioritizing "trustworthy AI" through comprehensive regulatory frameworks. Emphasizing ethical considerations and fundamental rights, the EU's research networks and AI excellence centers underscore its commitment to human-centric artificial intelligence. This approach not only sets the region apart but also influences global discussions on the responsible development of AI.

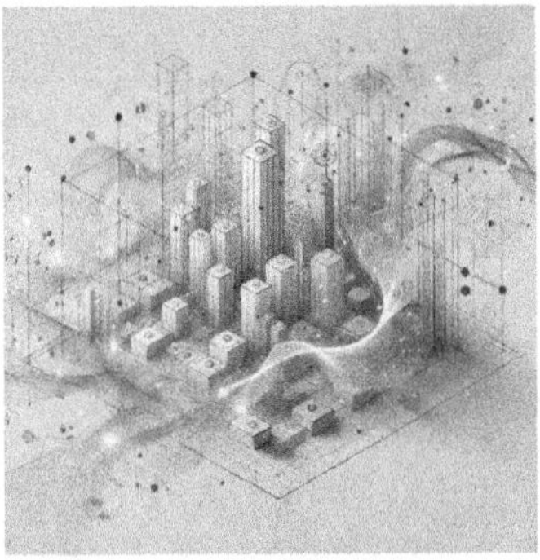

India is another significant player in the global AI landscape, capitalizing on its extensive technical workforce and annual STEM graduate population. The country's strategic investments focus on practical applications in healthcare, agriculture, and education, making AI a driver of socioeconomic progress. With its expanding startup ecosystem and robust digital infrastructure, India is increasingly seen as a critical hub for AI innovation.

Beyond these major players, other nations bring unique contributions to the global AI ecosystem. Canada's national AI strategy, Japan's integration of AI with robotics, and the UK's strategic commitment to artificial intelligence each add distinct perspectives and capabilities to the field. Emerging AI hubs in regions like Africa and South America also highlight the growing democratization of AI innovation, as these areas leverage local expertise and resources to carve out niches in the global market.

Balancing Competition and Collaboration

The global AI landscape exhibits a delicate balance between competition and collaboration. Nations aim to sustain competitive advantages while acknowledging the need for international cooperation to tackle shared challenges.

Critical infrastructure exemplifies this balance. Advanced semiconductor manufacturing, a cornerstone of AI development, relies on complex international networks of expertise and facilities. While this interdependence creates vulnerabilities, it also fosters partnerships that shape diplomatic relations and strategic decision-making.

Research collaboration tells a similar story. Scientific progress thrives on open exchange, yet national security concerns and AI safety considerations require selective sharing. International research centers encourage foundational collaboration while protecting sensitive applications. These dynamics have led to a nuanced ecosystem where knowledge is both shared and safeguarded. Will it work?

Emerging governance frameworks reflect this intricate balance. Initiatives like the IEEE's Global Initiative on Ethics of Autonomous and Intelligent Systems and the Global Partnership on Artificial Intelligence (GPAI) illustrate efforts to establish international AI standards. These frameworks aim to promote innovation while addressing ethical considerations and ensuring safety.

KEY AREAS OF INTERNATIONAL DYNAMICS

AI's rapid development reshapes global dynamics, with several critical areas standing out:

Talent and Brain Drain: The global AI talent pool remains highly concentrated, with only a small percentage of individuals possessing advanced expertise. Intense competition for these specialists has led to lucrative compensation packages, making it challenging for developing nations to retain their top talent. This disparity underscores the need for strategies that foster local talent development and create opportunities beyond traditional tech hubs.

Data and Privacy: Cross-border data flows have become a new frontier of geopolitical tension. Diverging regulatory frameworks, such as China's Data Security Law and the EU's GDPR, highlight differing data sovereignty, privacy, and security priorities. Collaborative initiatives like the EU-US Data Privacy Framework offer glimpses of how these differences might be reconciled, but tensions around data governance will likely persist.

Standards and Norms: International efforts to establish shared technical standards and ethical guidelines for AI are gaining momentum. Organizations such as IEEE and initiatives like the Global Partnership on AI (GPAI) are driving progress in AI ethics, safety, and policy coordination. Emerging research in interpretable neural networks informs these conversations, paving the way for safer and more accountable AI systems.

Research and Innovation: Despite geopolitical competition, international collaboration in AI research remains a cornerstone of progress. The COVID-19 pandemic demonstrated the power of collective action, as AI-driven breakthroughs like DeepMind's AlphaFold were shared openly to accelerate scientific discovery. Global events like the annual NeurIPS conference continue to showcase the enduring value of cooperation in advancing AI knowledge and innovation.

THE FUTURE OF GLOBAL POWER IN THE AI AGE

AI's transformative potential reshapes traditional power dynamics, enabling smaller nations to wield outsized influence in specific domains. Countries like Israel and Singapore have demonstrated how strategic investment in AI expertise can enhance their global standing. For instance, Israel's AI-driven cybersecurity firms safeguard critical digital assets for many Fortune 100 companies. At the same time,

Singapore's forward-thinking AI governance framework has become a model for balancing innovation and regulation.

Several key trends highlight how AI is redefining power:

- **Algorithmic Governance**: AI systems increasingly support or make decisions that were once exclusively human. Estonia's e-government services, powered by AI, exemplify how administrative efficiency and technological integration can become measures of state power.
- **Military Transformation**: AI is revolutionizing military operations, from autonomous systems to predictive maintenance and decision-making support. Programs like the U.S. Department of Defense's Joint All-Domain Command and Control (JADC2) demonstrate AI's role in modernizing defense strategies and capabilities.
- **Economic Transformation**: AI-driven automation is fundamentally reshaping industries and workforce dynamics. Nations that proactively invest in reskilling their populations and fostering innovation are better positioned to gain economic advantages, while those that lag risk increased inequality and financial dependence.
- **Digital Sovereignty**: As nations without robust AI ecosystems increasingly rely on technologies developed by global tech giants, concerns about digital colonialism and economic dependency are growing. Addressing this requires building local AI expertise, infrastructure, and policies prioritizing equitable access to AI's benefits.

The future of global power in the AI age will hinge on a nation's ability to balance innovation with ethical considerations, competition with collaboration, and national interests with global responsibilities. The nations that navigate these complexities effectively will emerge as leaders, harnessing AI for strategic power and the betterment of humanity.

Our choices will determine how AI shapes the world at this critical juncture. By fostering responsible development, international cooperation, and equitable access to technology, we can ensure that AI becomes a force for progress and opportunity rather than division and inequality.

MY FINAL THOUGHTS

The Future of AI Across Industries

As we've explored, AI is not limited to a single sector. Whether in art, business, education, hospitality, transportation, global politics, or sustainability- as we will see in the next chapter- AI is one of the most transformative forces of our time. The challenge is to adapt and shape how AI is used, ensuring it serves as a partner in innovation that promotes and celebrates human ingenuity.

By embracing AI responsibly and strategically, society can unlock its full potential, leading to more innovative, efficient, and sustainable solutions that benefit all.

EIGHT
ENVIRONMENTAL REVOLUTION
AI AND SUSTAINABILITY

... ✦ ...

"It is not the strongest of the species that survive, nor the most intelligent, but the one most responsive to change."
— Charles Darwin

HARNESSING TECHNOLOGY FOR A GREENER FUTURE

Artificial intelligence is crucial in combating climate change, optimizing energy use, and protecting ecosystems. AI-driven sustainability efforts allow us to manage resources more responsibly, demonstrating that technology can be a force for both progress and environmental responsibility.

Energy Innovation and Storage

Storage is one of the most significant barriers to widespread renewable energy adoption. AI is transforming this challenge by helping researchers develop more efficient and sustainable energy storage solutions. AI-powered smart grids analyze demand fluctuations, optimize energy distribution, and enhance the efficiency of battery storage systems. These advancements make continuous renewable energy access a reality for homes and businesses worldwide, reducing reliance on fossil fuels.

THE POWER OF PREDICTION: AI AS EARTH'S EARLY WARNING SYSTEM

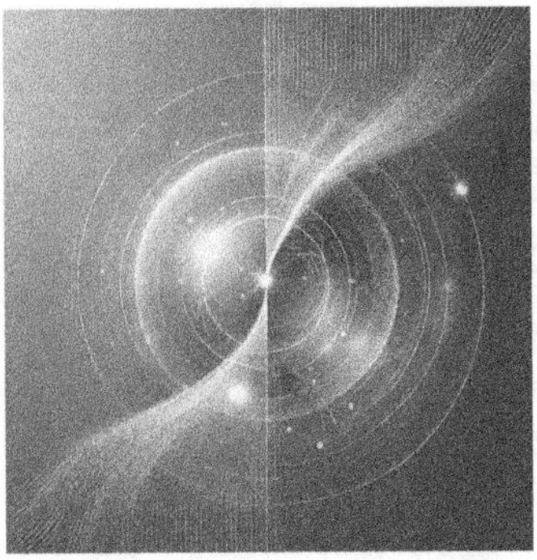

AI-driven predictive modeling allows scientists to anticipate and mitigate environmental crises before they happen. Advanced AI applications create digital twins of Earth's climate systems, running simulations to model future climate scenarios and predict long-term ecological changes. Machine learning algorithms process vast amounts of meteorological data, providing earlier and more accurate warnings of hurricanes, wildfires, and extreme weather events.

These AI systems are becoming essential tools for communities and policymakers seeking to enhance disaster preparedness and climate adaptation strategies.

Ecosystem Monitoring and Wildlife Protection

AI revolutionizes conservation efforts in several ways:

1. Deforestation Prevention: AI-powered satellite systems detect illegal logging and deforestation in real-time, enabling authorities to take swift action.

2. Marine Conservation: Deep learning algorithms analyze underwater acoustics and track whale migrations, providing unprecedented insights into ocean health.

3. Biodiversity Tracking: AI-driven biodiversity mapping catalogs and monitors endangered species, allowing conservationists to develop targeted protection plans.

AI in Action: Real-World Impact

- Ocean Conservation: AI enhances marine protection by tracking illegal fishing activities through satellite data analysis, helping safeguard marine ecosystems.
- Smart Agriculture: AI merges traditional farming knowledge with data-driven insights, optimizing resource use, reducing water consumption, and improving crop yields.

EMERGING FRONTIERS: WHERE AI MEETS ENVIRONMENTAL INNOVATION

AI reshapes urban development, helping build the cities of the future by optimizing resource management:

- Smart Cities and Green Infrastructure: AI optimizes urban forest management, energy efficiency, and resource allocation, ensuring sustainable urban growth.
- AI-Powered Design: AI aids architects in designing sustainable, energy-efficient buildings by analyzing materials, energy consumption, and environmental impact.

The Transformative Power of AI: Building a Better World

Beyond energy and climate, AI revolutionizes industries such as healthcare, materials science, and waste management:

Early Disease Detection: AI identifies health risks before symptoms appear, enabling early treatment and improving health outcomes.

Personalized Medicine: AI tailors treatments to individual genetic profiles, increasing efficacy and reducing side effects.

Self-Healing Materials: AI-driven research develops materials that autonomously detect and repair damage, transforming infrastructure maintenance.

Biodegradable Materials: AI accelerates the creation of carbon-negative building materials that actively remove CO2 from the atmosphere.

WASTE REDUCTION AND THE CIRCULAR ECONOMY

AI-powered waste management redefines how we process and repurpose materials:

1. Plastic Waste Conversion: Machine learning optimizes the breakdown and reconstitution of plastics into valuable raw materials.
2. Textile Recycling: AI determines how discarded clothing can be efficiently repurposed into new textiles or insulation materials.
3. Construction Waste Repurposing: AI identifies salvageable building materials and ensures their reuse in new construction projects.
4. Biomass Waste Utilization: AI optimizes the conversion of organic waste into biofuels and sustainable packaging solutions.
5. Automated Recycling Facilities: AI-powered sorting facilities dramatically improve recycling efficiency, processing materials with unprecedented accuracy.

Challenges and Opportunities: What They Are

Despite its promise, AI's role in sustainability comes with challenges:

- Data Accuracy and Reliability: AI systems rely on high-quality environmental data, requiring extensive calibration and validation.
- Energy Consumption of AI Models: While AI optimizes energy use, its computational requirements can be resource-intensive.
- Equitable Access to AI Solutions: Ensuring that developing nations benefit from AI-driven sustainability tools is critical.
- Ethical Deployment: AI must be implemented transparently, avoiding unintended ecological or social consequences.

THE PATH FORWARD: A COLLABORATIVE FUTURE

Governments, businesses, and communities must work together to ensure AI fulfills its potential as a tool for sustainability:

- Government Policies: Regulations must encourage ethical AI deployment while incentivizing research into green AI.
- Corporate Innovation: Businesses should invest in scalable, AI-driven sustainability solutions that are accessible across industries.
- Community Involvement: AI should empower citizen science initiatives and community-driven conservation efforts.

Beyond Efficiency: Where Optimization Meets Innovation

We need bold solutions that transform rather than improve to tackle environmental challenges. Here are a few groundbreaking examples:

- Quantum Computing: AI-driven quantum simulations revolutionize climate modeling, allowing for better sustainability decisions.
- Edge Computing: AI-powered edge devices process real-time environmental data, reducing latency in climate monitoring and conservation efforts.
- Biomimicry AI: Inspired by nature, AI helps create self-sustaining energy systems and materials that harmonize with natural ecosystems.

THE AI EFFICIENCY REVOLUTION

To illustrate the profound impact of AI on sustainability, here are key examples highlighting its effectiveness and transformative potential:

1. AI reduces power waste by up to 30% through smart energy grids.
2. AI-driven irrigation systems cut water use in agriculture by 50% while increasing crop yields.

3. AI-powered recycling solutions improve sorting accuracy by 90%, making waste management more efficient and effective.

Future Horizons

The future of AI-driven sustainability is filled with groundbreaking possibilities:

- Digital Twins: Virtual models of environmental systems enable better policy simulations and sustainability testing.
- Self-Learning AI: AI systems continuously improving efficiency could redefine how we use resources.
- Regenerative Design: AI-powered innovations will shift sustainability from harm reduction to active environmental regeneration.

Did You Know?

AI-powered vertical farms could produce the equivalent of 100 traditional acres of food in a single city block. AI optimizes lighting, water distribution, and nutrient delivery, allowing urban agriculture to thrive with 95% less water and zero pesticides.

ETHICAL AND RESPONSIBLE AI FOR SUSTAINABILITY

Ensuring that AI serves sustainability requires balancing innovation with ethical considerations. AI solutions must be:

- Transparent: AI-driven environmental policies should be explainable and accessible to all stakeholders.
- Inclusive: AI systems should be designed in collaboration with local communities to ensure fair implementation.
- Accountable: AI must be held to high ethical and regulatory standards to prevent unintended harm.

THE ROAD AHEAD: REALIZING THE POTENTIAL OF AI FOR SUSTAINABILITY

To harness AI's potential for environmental sustainability fully, we must:

1. Invest in research and development for more efficient, scalable AI solutions.
2. Foster interdisciplinary collaborations between AI researchers, sustainability experts, and policymakers.
3. Promote responsible AI adoption that prioritizes long-term environmental health over short-term profits.

By embracing AI as an optimizer of today's systems and a catalyst for future innovation, we can create a world where sustainability is not just about minimizing harm but about actively regenerating and improving the natural world. AI is a partner in this mission, helping us redefine what's possible for a thriving, sustainable future.

NINE
NAVIGATING AI SAFETY
PROTECTING YOURSELF IN THE DIGITAL AGE

... ✦ ...

"An ounce of prevention is worth a pound of cure."
— Benjamin Franklin

WHY AI SAFETY MATTERS

Imagine waking up to a news alert about a celebrity scandal—only to later find out the video was entirely fake, generated by artificial intelligence. Or picture getting a phone call from what sounds exactly like a loved one, urgently asking for money—except it's not them, but an AI-generated voice designed to scam you.

These scenarios aren't science fiction; they're today's reality. AI is rapidly transforming our digital world, offering remarkable benefits while also introducing new risks we must learn to navigate.

Think of AI safety like learning to drive. You don't avoid cars just because accidents happen; instead, you learn the rules of the road, develop safe habits, and stay alert for potential dangers. The AI landscape requires the same mindset—awareness, preparation, and smart decision-making.

Deepfakes blur the lines between real and artificial content. AI-powered scams have become more sophisticated and convincing than ever. Our personal data faces new vulnerabilities, and misinformation can spread at unprecedented speed and scale.

But here's the empowering truth: you don't need to be a tech expert to stay safe. By understanding key AI safety principles and practicing simple digital habits, you can confidently navigate this new era while protecting yourself and your loved ones.

In this chapter, we'll explore practical strategies to help you spot red flags, secure your information, and interact with AI tools safely and wisely.

Build your AI safety toolkit so you can thrive, not just survive, in the digital age.

UNDERSTANDING AI SAFETY BASICS

Recognizing Potential Risks

Now that we understand why AI safety matters, let's get specific about what to watch for. Being able to spot warning signs early helps you stay safe while still benefiting from AI's capabilities.

Common AI Risks and Red Flags:

1. Misinformation and Fake News

One of the most pressing risks of AI is misinformation. Sensational headlines, vague sources, and emotionally charged language can make false information seem convincing. Recognizing these warning signs helps you separate fact from fiction.

2. Deepfakes and Manipulated Media

AI-generated videos and images can be so convincing that they blur the line between reality and fabrication. While deepfakes may seem entertaining or harmless at first, they are increasingly being used to spread misinformation, manipulate public perception, and even commit fraud.

How to spot deepfakes:

- Unnatural facial movements – Look for odd expressions, strange blinking patterns, or stiff, robotic motion.
- Inconsistent lighting – Shadows and highlights that don't align naturally can signal manipulation.
- Blurred edges – AI-generated images often struggle with hair, hands, and fine details, creating unnatural distortions.
- Mismatched audio – Pay attention to lip-syncing issues, unnatural pauses, or voice tones that sound artificial.

If a video seems shocking or too perfectly timed to an event, verify its authenticity before reacting or sharing it.

3. Privacy Breaches and Data Misuse

AI systems collect and analyze massive amounts of data—sometimes more than we realize. While this can improve personalization and convenience, it also introduces risks if personal information falls into the wrong hands.

Red flags that indicate a potential privacy threat:

- Unsolicited data requests – Be wary of platforms or apps asking for excessive personal details.
- Unclear privacy policies – If a service doesn't explicitly state how it handles your data, assume it's not in your best interest.
- Unexpected messages from unknown senders – AI-powered phishing scams are becoming increasingly sophisticated, often mimicking real contacts or institutions.
- Suspicious app permissions – If an app requests access to your

microphone, contacts, or location without a clear reason, think twice before allowing it.

Regularly reviewing your privacy settings, using multi-factor authentication, and limiting the amount of personal data you share online can help protect you from AI-driven data misuse.

4. AI-Powered Scams and Fraud

Scammers are leveraging AI to make fraud more personalized, automated, and convincing than ever before. AI-powered chatbots and voice generators can impersonate real people, and AI-generated emails can mimic professional communication styles with stunning accuracy.

Warning signs of AI-enhanced scams:

- Unsolicited offers – If you receive an offer that seems too good to be true, especially via email or messaging apps, it probably is.
- Pressure tactics – Scammers create a false sense of urgency, claiming you must act quickly to claim a reward, avoid penalties, or secure a deal.
- Requests for personal information: Be wary of any message or call asking for sensitive details, especially bank information, Social Security numbers, or passwords.
- Unusual payment methods – Scammers often request cryptocurrency, gift cards, or wire transfers because these methods are harder to trace and recover.

If something seems off, pause and verify. A moment of skepticism can prevent financial loss or identity theft.

Stay Alert, Stay Smart

Remember: AI tools can be incredibly convincing but not infallible. When in doubt, pause and verify. Just as you wouldn't accept a package without checking who sent it, don't accept AI-generated content without questioning its source and authenticity. Your skepticism is your most potent safety tool. Verify, verify, verify.

REAL-WORLD RISK SCENARIOS

Scenario 1: The Perfect Job Scam

Imagine opening your email to find what appears to be the perfect job opportunity. The message addresses you by name, and the position seems tailored to your skills – perhaps too perfectly. The AI-generated email describes a dream scenario: high pay, remote work, and flexible hours. All you need to do is provide some personal information to get started. It's tempting, isn't it? But this is exactly how sophisticated scams operate in today's AI-powered world.

These job scam emails succeed because they tap into our genuine desires and hopes. They're crafted to appear legitimate, often using AI to personalize and make the message feel authentic. The scammer might mention your current industry or reference your LinkedIn profile, adding layers of apparent legitimacy to their approach.

However, if you know what to look for, there are always telltale signs. The most obvious red flag is the unsolicited nature of the offer; legitimate employers typically don't send out-of-the-blue job offers. Look closely at the terms offered: if they seem too good to be true, they usually are. Pay special attention to any pressure tactics or urgent requests for personal information. Legitimate employers understand and respect the need for proper vetting and due diligence.

If you receive such an offer, here's how to protect yourself: First and foremost, resist the urge to provide any personal information, no matter how tempting the opportunity seems. Instead, take time to research the company through official channels – not links provided in the email. Visit their actual website, look them up on professional networking sites, and verify their business registration. If you find the job posted, cross-check it on legitimate job boards. Finally, report suspicious messages to help protect others from falling victim to similar scams.

Remember: in today's digital landscape, scammers have become increasingly sophisticated, using AI tools to make their attempts more convincing than ever. Your best defense is a combination of healthy skepticism and thorough verification before taking any action.

Building on our discussion of digital risks, let's explore another increasingly common scenario that showcases how AI technology can manipulate public perception and spread misinformation.

Scenario 2: The Deepfake: When Seeing Isn't Believing

Picture scrolling through your social media feed when you encounter a shocking video of a well-known celebrity. Perhaps it's a beloved actor making outrageous statements or a respected public figure misbehaving. The video looks real – convincingly lifelike – and spreads like wildfire. Your finger hovers over the share button as emotions surge: outrage, disappointment, disbelief. This is precisely the moment when critical thinking becomes your most vigorous defense.

Today's deepfake technology can create compelling fake videos, making distinguishing truth from fiction more challenging than ever. These manipulated videos often emerge at suspiciously convenient times, perhaps during major events or controversies, designed to distract and divide. While the technology behind deepfakes grows more sophisticated, there are still subtle tells if you know where to look: unnatural movements around the mouth area, strange lighting that doesn't quite match the environment, or audio that feels slightly out of sync with the video.

When encountering such content, resist the urge to react or share. Instead, take a breath and engage your digital detective skills. Visit reputable news sources to see if they've verified the content. Look for statements from the celebrity or their representatives – public figures usually respond quickly to false videos circulating about them. Pay attention to the video's context: What else is happening in the news that this might be trying to overshadow?

The power to combat deepfakes lies not in technical expertise but in our willingness to pause and verify before amplifying potentially false content. By reporting suspected deepfakes to platform moderators, you also help protect others from falling for sophisticated digital manipulation.

Remember: in an age where AI can make fiction look remarkably real, your skepticism and patience are powerful tools for maintaining truth in our digital landscape.

Scenario 3: When "Friends" Aren't Who They Seem

Imagine receiving a message from a close friend that feels both familiar and slightly off. Their profile picture looks right, they reference shared memories, and they even write in a style that sounds like them. But something's different – maybe they're asking for unusual favors or sharing investment opportunities that seem uncharacteristic. Welcome to the world of AI-powered social engineering, where scammers use personal information and language models to craft highly convincing impersonations.

These sophisticated attacks succeed because they exploit our trust in familiar connections. The impersonator might mention real events from social media, use inside jokes from public comments, or reference mutual friends to build credibility. They often create a sense of urgency or emotional appeal—perhaps your "friend" is stranded somewhere and needs immediate financial help, or they've discovered an amazing investment opportunity that expires soon.

However, there are usually subtle signs that something isn't quite right. The writing might be too formal or use phrases your friend would never use. They might avoid video calls or phone conversations, claiming technical issues. When pressed for specific details about

shared experiences, their responses become vague, or they quickly change the subject.

If you encounter such a situation, resist the urge to help immediately. Instead, contact your friend through a different, verified channel – preferably by phone or in person. Take screenshots of the suspicious conversation and report the account to the platform. Pay special attention to any requests involving money, personal information, or unusual downloads, as these are common goals of impersonation scams.

Remember: AI technology has made it easier than ever to mimic writing styles and create convincing impersonations. Your best defense is to verify independently and trust your instincts when something feels off about a digital interaction, even with seemingly familiar contacts.

Scenario 4: Digital Gold Rush And The AI-Enhanced Crypto Trap

Picture this: You're browsing social media when an AI-generated ad – a cryptocurrency investment platform with astonishing returns catches your eye. The website looks sleek and professional, with real-time trading data and testimonials from "successful investors." Even more compelling, their AI trading bot supposedly uses advanced algorithms to accurately predict market movements. The platform promises to double your investment in weeks, showing convincing charts and data to back their claims.

What makes these modern crypto scams so dangerous is their sophisticated use of AI technology. The scammers deploy chatbots that engage in surprisingly natural conversations about investment strategies. They might even use AI-generated "financial advisors" who appear in polished videos, explaining complex trading concepts and offering personalized investment advice. The platform's interface updates in real time with artificial trading activity, creating an illusion of legitimate market movements.

The red flags are subtle but significant. Notice how the AI-powered "advisor" dodges specific questions about the company's registration or regulatory compliance. The platform might showcase dramatic success stories, but these testimonials come from AI-generated profiles with deepfaked photos. When you try to withdraw funds, there's always another verification step, another fee, or a technical issue that needs resolving – each requiring you to invest more money to "unlock" your returns.

If you encounter such a platform, here's how to protect yourself: First, understand that legitimate crypto investments don't guarantee returns or pressure you to act quickly. Research the platform through official financial regulatory websites, not through links provided by the platform. Look for real-world company registration details and regulatory licenses. Most importantly, be extremely wary of any platform that won't let you withdraw your funds without additional investments or fees.

Remember: In the wild west of cryptocurrency, scammers are leveraging AI to create increasingly convincing facades. Your skepticism is your strongest asset – if an investment opportunity seems too perfect, it probably is.

NAVIGATING THE AI-ENHANCED RISK LANDSCAPE

Your Digital Safety Guide

The scenarios we've explored – the perfect job scam, the viral deepfake, the friend impersonator, and the crypto investment trap – represent just a glimpse into how artificial intelligence is transforming digital threats. Imagine a world where malicious individuals can access powerful tools that enhance criminal activity. It's a chilling thought. These modern risks are particularly challenging because their sophisticated use of AI technology to appear legitimate, exploit human psychology, and create convincing deceptions.

Yet, across all these scenarios, we see common patterns emerge. Whether it's a too-good-to-be-true job offer, a shocking viral video, a message from a "friend," or a promised crypto windfall, these scams rely on similar tactical elements: urgency, emotional manipulation, and the exploitation of trust. They use AI to scale their operations, personalize their approach, and create increasingly convincing content that can fool even the tech-savvy.

Your best defense remains a combination of critical thinking, healthy skepticism, and deliberate pause before taking action. Remember the core principles we've discussed: verify independently, cross-check through official channels, trust your instincts when something feels off, and never make decisions under pressure. In this rapidly evolving digital landscape, verification can make the difference between falling victim to a scam and protecting yourself from harm.

As AI technology advances, these threats will only become more sophisticated. However, you can confidently navigate the online world by understanding these patterns and maintaining vigilant digital habits. After all, the most potent defense against deception isn't more technology – it's your awareness and critical thinking skills.

Building Your Digital Defense: A Modern Safety Toolkit

Just as we've evolved from essential locks to sophisticated home security systems, our approach to digital safety must evolve with AI technology. Rather than viewing AI safety as a series of checkboxes, consider it as developing a sixth sense—an instinct for navigating the digital landscape safely.

THE TRIAD OF DIGITAL RESILIENCE

1. *Information Hygiene*

Think of your digital presence like your physical health—it requires regular maintenance and mindful habits. Before sharing any information online, ask yourself, "Would I be comfortable seeing this on a billboard?" Set information boundaries by determining what you want to share and what stays private. Regularly audit your digital footprint by searching your name and reviewing your privacy settings across platforms.

2. *Critical Engagement*

Develop what security experts call "deliberate skepticism" - not cynicism, but thoughtful evaluation. When encountering AI-generated content or requests, pause to consider the context. Is this interaction necessary? What's the potential risk versus reward? Train yourself to recognize triggers that might cloud your judgment.

3. *Active Protection*

Move beyond passive defense to active security measures. This means regularly updating passwords, using authentication apps instead of text-based codes, and maintaining separate email addresses for different purposes (personal, professional, and online shopping). Think of these practices not as burdensome tasks but as essential tools in your digital arsenal.

Making Safety Second Nature

The goal isn't to create anxiety about every digital interaction but to develop natural protective instincts. Just as you automatically check your mirrors while driving, train yourself to verify sources automatically, question unexpected requests, and protect your digital boundaries.

Read Aloud

Confidence starts with confirmation—always verify, verify, verify.

Making Digital Safety Part of Your Daily Flow

Think of digital safety like brewing your morning coffee or going through your evening skincare routine. It should feel natural, not burdensome. Instead of treating safety as a separate task, let's weave it seamlessly into your daily rhythm.

Morning Momentum: Starting Secure

Your morning routine sets the tone for the day. While sipping that first cup of coffee or tea, take a moment to check your digital landscape. Notice any unusual notifications? Scan headlines from trusted sources before diving into social media. This quiet morning moment is perfect for maintaining digital well-being – like checking the weather before choosing what to wear.

Mindful Moments Throughout Your Day

As you navigate your digital world, build in natural pause points. When you receive an exciting message or shocking news, treat it like a hot cup of tea—let it cool a bit before consuming it. Make fact-checking as automatic as checking your mirrors while driving. If something triggers a strong emotional response, consider it a yellow light—slow down, assess, and then proceed with awareness.

Evening Wind-Down: Digital Decompression

Just as you might reflect on your day while getting ready for bed, take a moment to review your digital interactions. Did anything feel off? Were there moments when you rushed past your better judgment? Use this quiet time to adjust your digital boundaries, clear out suspicious messages, or flag concerns for tomorrow's follow-up. Think of it as clearing your digital space, much like tidying your desk before leaving work.

Making It Stick

The key to sustainable digital safety isn't perfection – it's consistency. Rather than trying to overhaul your habits overnight:

- Start with one new safety practice that feels most natural to you.
- Build it into existing routines rather than creating new ones.
- Celebrate small wins, like catching a suspicious email or resisting the urge to share shocking content immediately.
- Adjust your habits as technology evolves, just as you update your smartphone.

This approach makes digital safety feel less like a chore and more like self-care. It's not about constant vigilance but about developing healthy digital instincts that protect you naturally.

On Social Media

Enjoy the content, but question the reality—verify before you believe.

NAVIGATING MISINFORMATION AND FAKE NEWS

Imagine scrolling through your social media feed when you spot a video of a world leader announcing a shocking policy change. The video looks real, sounds authentic, and has thousands of shares—but something feels off. Welcome to the era of AI-enhanced misinformation, where that subtle feeling of "something's not quite right" might be your first defense against sophisticated deception.

In today's digital ecosystem, misinformation spreads at unprecedented speeds, supercharged by artificial intelligence's ability to create and distribute increasingly convincing fake content. While traditional fact-checking remains valuable, the rise of AI-generated content demands a new level of digital literacy. The good news? Spotting misinformation becomes second nature once you know the SHARP warning signs.

THE SHARP METHOD

Detecting Misinformation

You need a quick and reliable way to assess the credibility of online content. The SHARP method systematically identifies potential misinformation, helping you evaluate content with the same precision that fact-checkers and journalists use.

S — Sensationalized Headlines

When a headline triggers an immediate emotional response—outrage, fear, or even joy—pause before sharing, AI-generated content often exploits our emotional triggers to maximize engagement.

What You Can Do: Take a breath and ask yourself: "Would this news be this dramatic if true?" Search for the same story from established news sources. Multiple credible outlets will likely cover it if it's as significant as claimed.

H — Hidden or Questionable Sources

AI makes it easier than ever to create professional-looking websites and convincing content. Be wary of unfamiliar outlets, especially those lacking transparent information about their authors, backing, or contact details.

What You Can Do: Go to the site's "About" page. Look for clear information about the organization, its funding, and its editorial team. Treat the content with heightened skepticism if these details are missing or vague.

A — Artificial Emotional Triggers

While human journalists aim to inform, AI-generated misinformation often prioritizes emotional manipulation through carefully crafted language and images.

What You Can Do: Notice how the content makes you feel. Investigate further if it seems designed to provoke strong emotions rather than inform. Look for objective reporting that presents facts without emotional manipulation.

R — Reasoning Gaps

Quality information builds arguments on verifiable evidence and acknowledges complexity. Watch for content that makes sweeping claims without supporting data or dismisses contradicting viewpoints without explanation.

What You Can Do: Follow the citations. If an article makes bold claims, check its sources. Be particularly wary of circular references or links that lead nowhere.

P — Perfect Timing

Be extra cautious of shocking revelations that conveniently emerge during critical moments, such as elections, international crises, or major policy decisions.

What You Can Do: Consider the timing and context. Ask yourself who might benefit from this information spreading at this particular moment.

AI-SPECIFIC RED FLAGS

As AI technology advances, new telltale signs of synthetic content emerge. Watch for:

- **Visual Anomalies:** In AI-generated videos and images, look for subtle inconsistencies in facial movements, unusual blinking patterns, or asymmetrical features.

- **Language Patterns:** AI-generated text often contains repetitive phrases, unusually perfect grammar, or strange idiom usage. If the writing feels too polished or mechanical, it might be machine-generated.
- **Background Distortions:** In AI-created images, backgrounds may contain warped objects, impossible physics, or irregular patterns. Pay special attention to hands, jewelry, and reflections, which AI often struggles to render correctly.
- **Perfect Perfection:** Paradoxically, content that appears too perfect—whether it's a quote that seems too precisely crafted or an image that looks too pristine—may signal AI generation.

BUILDING DIGITAL RESILIENCE

Remember that the goal isn't to become paranoid about every piece of online content but rather to develop healthy skepticism and better information consumption habits. Applying the SHARP method and staying aware of AI-specific red flags, you'll be better equipped to navigate our increasingly complex digital information landscape.

The most potent defense against misinformation isn't just knowing what to look for—it's developing the habit of thoughtful engagement with digital content. Take your time, verify before sharing, and remember that your critical thinking skills are more valuable than ever in the age of AI.

From Detection to Action: Your Digital Responsibility

Now that you've been equipped with the SHARP method for detecting misinformation, what's next? Spotting problematic content is only half the battle. In today's interconnected world, each of us serves as a potential gatekeeper of information, making dozens of sharing decisions daily that can either amplify or stem the tide of misinformation.

Think of it this way: The SHARP method is your digital radar system, scanning for potential threats to the truth. But just like a radar operator, detecting something concerning isn't the end of your responsibility—it's the beginning of your decision-making process. This is where the

Pause and Reflect comes in, transforming your awareness into thoughtful action.

While SHARP helps you identify what not to share, THINK guides you toward becoming a positive force in our digital ecosystem. Together, these frameworks form a complete system to help you navigate our AI-enhanced information landscape: first by detecting potential misinformation and then by making conscious choices about what deserves your amplification.

For Better or Worse?

You are what you share—does it uplift and inform or mislead and harm? You are what you share.

STRATEGIES FOR RESPONSIBLE SHARING: YOUR ROLE

In a world where a single click can spread information to thousands or even millions of people, we're all unofficial editors of the Internet's daily news feed. Whether you share a heartwarming AI-generated art piece or a breaking news story, your sharing habits shape our digital reality.

ETIQUETTE RULE: THINK, THEN SHARE

Before your finger hovers over that share button, let's think it through:

T — Is it True?

Pause and consider: That AI-generated news summary might look polished, but has it been verified?

Action Steps:

- Cross-reference with established fact-checking websites
- Look for original sources and expert perspectives

- Check if other reliable outlets are reporting the same information
- Be especially cautious with AI-generated or synthetic content

H — Is it Helpful?

Not all true information needs to be shared. Consider the value you're adding to the conversation.

Action Steps:

- Ask yourself: "Will this information help others make better decisions?"
- Consider whether it provides context or clarity to an important issue
- Think about whether it solves a problem or answers a common question
- Evaluate if it contributes meaningfully to ongoing discussions

I — Is it Inspiring?

In an age where AI can generate endless content designed to provoke outrage, choose to be a source of light.

Action Steps:

- Evaluate whether the content promotes understanding or division
- Consider if it offers solutions rather than just highlighting problems
- Ask if it encourages constructive dialogue or partisan arguments
- Think about whether it empowers or disempowers others

N — Is it Necessary?

Information abundance requires thoughtful curation. Just because you can share something doesn't mean you should.

Action Steps:

- Consider if this information is timely and relevant
- Ask whether your audience needs this information right now
- Think about whether this adds new insight to existing discussions
- Evaluate if sharing could prevent harm or promote understanding

K — Is it Kind?

In the digital age, kindness isn't just nice—it's necessary for maintaining healthy online communities.

Action Steps:

- Consider the human impact of sharing this information
- Think about how it might affect vulnerable individuals or groups
- Ask if you would feel comfortable being the subject of similar content
- Consider whether it respects privacy and personal boundaries

PUTTING THINK INTO PRACTICE

Here's how to implement these principles in real-world situations:

When Sharing News:

- Wait 10 minutes before sharing breaking news
- Look for updates or corrections to initial reports
- Consider adding context or clarification in your share

When Sharing Personal Stories:

- Get permission before sharing others' experiences
- Consider the long-term implications of the share
- Think about who might be indirectly affected

When Sharing AI-Generated Content:

- Clearly label AI-generated content as such
- Verify any factual claims independently
- Consider whether it adds value or just noise

THE RIPPLE EFFECT OF RESPONSIBLE SHARING

Remember: When you choose not to share questionable content, you help break the chain of misinformation. When you verify, you strengthen our collective digital immunity to false information. Your thoughtful sharing habits create ripples, contributing to a healthier, more trustworthy online environment.

When you incorporate these thoughtful principles into your daily digital routine, you become not just a consumer of information but a guardian of digital integrity. In an age where AI can generate endless content, your human judgment and ethical sharing choices matter more than ever.

SAFEGUARDING YOURSELF AND OTHERS

Personal Protection: Your Digital Shield in the AI Era

Your digital security has never been more important as AI technology evolves at breakneck speed. While artificial intelligence opens up amazing possibilities, it also provides sophisticated new tools for bad actors looking to compromise your security. The good news? You don't need a computer science degree to protect yourself—you need to build smart habits that become second nature.

Think of these safeguards as your digital armor. Each practice adds another layer of protection, working together to create a robust defense system. Let's build your personal security framework piece by piece.

YOUR AI SAFETY ACTION PLAN

1. Secure Your Accounts: Your Digital Front Door

Think of your online accounts as the doors to your digital life. Just as you wouldn't use the same key for your house, car, and office, you shouldn't reuse passwords across different accounts.

Essential Steps:

- Create strong, unique passwords for each account (consider using a password manager)
- Enable two-factor authentication wherever available—it's like adding a security camera to your door.
- Set up login alerts to notify you of suspicious activity, acting as your digital motion detector.
- Regularly audit your app permissions—think of it as changing your locks periodically.

Pro Tip

Use passphrases instead of complex passwords. "PurpleDinosaur-EatsPizza2024!" is both stronger and easier to remember than "Pd@x9K#m"

---

2. Guard Your Personal Data: Your Digital Identity

In an AI-powered world, personal data is incredibly valuable. The less information available about you online, the harder it is for AI tools to be used maliciously against you.

Key Actions:

- Conduct a "privacy audit" of your social media profiles
- Customize privacy settings for different audience groups
- Be skeptical of "fun" quizzes and games—they're often data collection tools in disguise

- Regularly declutter your digital life by removing unused apps and accounts

---

Pro Tip

Set a quarterly reminder to review and update your privacy settings across all platforms.

---

3. Protect Your Digital Assets: Your Virtual Vault

Your digital assets—from precious family photos to important documents—need protection from technical threats and AI-powered scams.

Critical Measures:

- Implement the 3-2-1 backup rule: three copies, two different storage types, one off-site.
- Keep your digital defense system updated with the latest software patches.
- Use a VPN on public networks—consider it your personal encrypted tunnel.
- Practice selective saving: not everything needs to be stored digitally.

Pro Tip

Create an "emergency folder" with essential documents encrypted and stored both locally and in secure cloud storage.

MAKING SECURITY SECOND NATURE

The key to adequate digital security isn't implementing everything at once—it's building sustainable habits over time. Start with one action from each category and gradually expand your security practices.

Remember, even small steps toward better security make a big difference in protecting your digital life. The important thing is to stay mindful and aware of your usage.

Quick Security Check-In

- Set aside 15 minutes each month to:
- Review recent account activity
- Update any weak passwords
- Check the privacy settings on your most-used apps
- Scan for and delete unused applications
- Verify your backup systems are working

Stronger Defenses

In our AI-enhanced world, your security is only as strong as your weakest habit. But by consistently implementing these practices, you're building a robust defense system that protects you from current and emerging threats.

COMMUNITY SAFETY: BUILDING DIGITAL RESILIENCE TOGETHER

The saying "it takes a village" has never been more relevant than in our AI-powered world. While individual vigilance is crucial, creating safe digital spaces requires community-wide effort and awareness. Let's examine how ordinary people can make extraordinary differences in their communities. Below are some inspiring possibilities of what community safety initiatives look like.

Scenario 1. The Classroom Champion

Meet Elena, a high school teacher who noticed her students struggling to identify AI-generated scam messages. Instead of simply warning her class, she created a weekly "Digital Safety Corner" where students shared real-world examples of AI risks they encountered. Students began bringing in sophisticated deepfake videos, AI-generated phishing emails, and manipulated social media posts they'd spotted.

The potential impact? Students become digital detectives, proud to share their findings. Parents report dinner table conversations shifting from "Don't trust anything online" to nuanced discussions about digital literacy. The model spreads to other classrooms, creating a school-wide culture of cyber-awareness.

Scenario 2. The Community Guardian

Imagine James, a retired cybersecurity professional, who heard his neighbor's frightening encounter with an AI voice scam impersonating her grandson. He knew he had to act. What began as an informal coffee shop meeting with a few seniors evolved into "Digital Defense for Seniors," a monthly workshop at the local library.

James's approach makes complex security concepts accessible through real-life scenarios. Participants practice identifying AI-generated voices, learn about common scam patterns, and build confidence in their digital decisions. The workshop includes hands-on demonstrations of legitimate AI tools and potential scams, helping seniors understand the difference. They learn practical steps like creating verification codes with family members and maintaining an "AI awareness" journal of suspicious contacts.

While this specific story is illustrative, similar initiatives could be implemented nationwide. Libraries, community centers, and senior organizations could adapt this model to their local needs. The key is combining technical knowledge with accessible education and hands-on practice.

IGNITING THE WINDS OF CHANGE

These stories demonstrate that building a safer AI ecosystem isn't about grand gestures—it's about consistent, thoughtful actions that create awareness throughout our communities. Here's how you can amplify your impact:

1. Spark Safety Conversations

Transform everyday moments into learning opportunities:

- Share real examples of AI risks you've encountered during family gatherings
- Create a "Tech Tuesday" chat group at work to exchange security tips
- Advocate for digital literacy programs in your local schools
- Host informal "security coffee chats" in your neighborhood

2. Be an Active Digital Citizen

Your voice matters in creating safer online spaces:

- Report suspicious content promptly and thoroughly
- Reach out to vulnerable community members with gentle guidance
- Share credible resources from AI safety experts
- Document and report new types of AI-enabled threats you encounter

3. Strengthen Community Initiatives

Connect and contribute to broader safety efforts:

- Attend local government meetings about digital security policies
- Volunteer your skills to organizations promoting AI safety
- Support educational programs teaching digital literacy
- Join or create neighborhood watch groups for digital threats

MAKING IT PERSONAL: YOUR COMMUNITY SAFETY TOOLKIT

Success stories start with you. Start small but think big:

- Create a group chat for sharing security updates with family
- Organize monthly "Digital Safety Check-ins" with elderly neighbors
- Compile a resource list of local organizations offering cybersecurity help
- Build a network of tech-savvy volunteers willing to help others

Don't wait for someone else to address the problems you notice—take the essential first step towards finding preventive and resolving solutions. Your community needs your unique perspective and skills. Whether tech-savvy or just learning, your awareness and willingness to share knowledge make a difference.

Taking Action Today

Choose one small action to start with:

- Share this week's most important digital safety tip with three people
- Attend an online safety webinar and summarize key points for your community
- Start a digital safety conversation at your next family gathering
- Identify the most vulnerable people in your circle and reach out with support

Remember that every significant movement for change starts with individuals taking small, consistent actions. In our interconnected digital world, your efforts to promote AI safety don't just protect your immediate circle—they contribute to a safer online environment for everyone. Teach others that AI reflects what we feed it and that mindful interactions create meaningful responses.

SAFETY AND RESILIENCE IN PRACTICE

Even with the best precautions, AI-related safety incidents can happen to anyone. What matters isn't preventing every possible incident but knowing how to respond effectively when they occur. Think of this guide as your emergency response plan—like knowing where the fire exits are in a building. You hope you'll never need it, but having it brings peace of mind and prepares you for quick action if necessary.

Understanding AI Safety Incidents

Consider this scenario: A professional discovers an AI-generated deep-fake video of themselves circulating online. Their first reaction is panic—natural and completely understandable. However, by following a systematic response plan, they can effectively address the situation and minimize potential damage. This example illustrates that responding to AI safety incidents is about staying calm and taking methodical action.

Your AI Incident Response Checklist

1. Secure Immediate Risks

- Change all potentially compromised passwords immediately
- Enable additional security measures (like two-factor authentication)
- Run comprehensive security scans on your devices
- Temporarily restrict social media or account access if needed
- Document any unusual activity or unauthorized changes

2. Document Everything

- Capture screenshots with timestamps

- Save copies of suspicious content or communications
- Create a detailed timeline of the incident
- Record all actions you've taken in response
- Keep track of who you've contacted and when

3. Report Through Proper Channels

- File reports with relevant platform security teams
- Contact appropriate law enforcement if criminal activity is involved
- Submit incident details to AI safety monitoring organizations
- Alert your workplace IT department if professional accounts are affected
- Notify others whom similar attacks might target

4. Seek Support and Recovery

- Connect with cybersecurity professionals or tech-savvy contacts
- Consult identity protection services if personal data is compromised
- Consider legal counsel for serious violations
- Join support communities for similar incident survivors
- Take care of your emotional well-being through the process

Recovery and Moving Forward

Remember that recovery from an AI safety incident is a process, not a single event. After addressing the immediate situation:

- Review and strengthen your digital security measures
- Update your incident response plan based on lessons learned
- Share your experience to help others (while protecting your privacy)
- Consider professional support if the incident has lasting effects
- Regular check-ins on your digital presence for any lingering issues

This systematic approach helps you maintain control during stressful situations and emerge stronger from any AI safety challenges.

RESILIENCE AND RECOVERY STRATEGIES

Building digital resilience isn't just about responding to incidents—it's about developing the capacity to adapt, recover, and emerge stronger from AI-related challenges. Just as we build physical and emotional resilience through healthy habits, we can build digital resilience through mindful practices and preparation.

Understanding Digital Trauma

AI-related incidents can have genuine psychological impacts. Whether you see your likeness manipulated, fall victim to an AI scam, or experience identity theft, these experiences can shake your sense of security and trust. Acknowledging these feelings is the first step toward recovery.

YOUR POST-INCIDENT RESILIENCE PLAN

1. **Reflect and Learn**: Analyze vulnerabilities that led to the incident.

- Identify patterns in your digital behavior.
- Document lessons learned for future reference.
- Consider what warning signs you might have missed.
- Assess your current security knowledge gaps.

2. **Restore and Refresh:** Implement your data recovery plan.

- Create new, more secure digital habits.
- Take a structured approach to rebuilding your online presence.
- Consider a "digital detox" if needed.
- Establish new boundaries for online engagement.

3. Reach Out and Rebuild: Connect with support communities.

- Share experiences with trusted friends.
- Seek professional guidance if needed.
- Contribute to awareness initiatives.
- Help others learn from your experience.

Building Long-Term Digital Resilience

4. Develop Preventive Practices: Create regular security audit schedules.

- Build a personal incident response toolkit.
- Establish digital boundaries and stick to them.
- Practice stress management for online challenges.
- Maintain updated copies of important documents.

5. Create Your Support Network: Identify tech-savvy friends or family members.

- Connect with online safety communities.
- Keep contact information for relevant authorities.
- Build relationships with security professionals.
- Join AI safety advocacy groups.

NOTE ON SHAME: YOU ARE NOT ALONE

It's important to remember that falling victim to AI-enabled fraud or digital crimes doesn't reflect on your intelligence or capability. Even technology experts and security professionals can be targeted successfully by criminals who spend their entire days perfecting their deceptive tactics.

These criminals exploit fundamental human qualities—our trust, kindness, and willingness to help others. They also take advantage of people's financial struggles, desperation, and desire for a better life. They use sophisticated AI tools to make their schemes increasingly convincing and prey on natural human reactions like urgency, fear, or excitement.

If you've been affected by an AI-related incident, remember:

- You're not alone—millions of people face these challenges
- Being targeted isn't your fault—criminals are the ones to blame
- Seeking help shows strength, not weakness
- Your experience can help protect others
- Recovery is possible, and you will get through this

The most important thing is to take action quickly and follow the above-mentioned response steps. Don't let shame or embarrassment delay your response—the sooner you act, the better you can protect yourself and recover.

MENTAL WELL-BEING IN THE DIGITAL AGE

As AI becomes increasingly woven into our daily lives, a new form of digital stress has emerged. Many of us experience a complex mix of fascination and apprehension about AI – from concerns about privacy and security to questions about how AI might affect our work and relationships. This emotional response is natural and valid, reflecting our adaptation to rapidly evolving technology.

Understanding our psychological relationship with AI is crucial for maintaining mental well-being. When we interact with AI systems, we're not just engaging with tools—we're navigating new social and emotional territories. Some might feel pressure to always be "on guard" against AI-related threats, while others might experience anxiety about keeping up with AI developments or protecting their digital identities.

Managing AI-Related Stress

The key to maintaining mental equilibrium is developing healthy habits and boundaries. Think of your relationship with AI like any other significant relationship—it requires clear boundaries, regular maintenance, and occasional recalibration. When you feel overwhelmed by AI-related concerns, remember that you control how and when you engage with these technologies.

Consider implementing the following practices:

- Create designated "AI-free" times in your day, treating them as essential as meal breaks
- Develop a personal framework for evaluating AI tools and security measures, reducing decision fatigue
- Practice "tech-conscious" behaviors rather than tech-avoidance – engage mindfully rather than fearfully
- Build a support network of friends or colleagues who share similar concerns and can offer practical perspectives

FAMILY SAFETY AND AI LITERACY

Growing Up with AI

Think of teaching your family AI safety like teaching them to navigate a new neighborhood. Just as you'd help your children understand which routes are safe for walking to school or where to go if they need help, guiding your family through AI interactions requires the same thoughtful, age-appropriate approach.

Starting Early: Young Children (Ages 5-8)

Remember when your child first learned about crossing the street? You probably started with "Stop, look, and listen." Teaching young children about AI follows a similar pattern. When your little one asks Alexa to play their favorite song or watches an AI-generated story, use these moments as natural teaching opportunities. "You know how we're careful about talking to people we don't know? We need to be just as careful about what we tell our AI friends."

Make it fun and relatable. Turn it into a game of "Spot the AI" while watching videos or using apps together. When your child realizes that the friendly cartoon character giving them math problems is powered by AI, they begin to understand the difference between human and AI interactions naturally.

Growing Awareness: Tweens (Ages 9-12)

At this age, children are developing deeper friendships and understanding relationships. Use this natural development to explain AI concepts: "Just like you share secrets with your best friend, AI remembers the things we tell it. That's why we need to be thoughtful about what we share." When your tween shows you a cool AI-generated image or video, use their excitement as a springboard to discuss how AI creates content and why we need to think critically about what we see online.

Emerging Independence: Teens (Ages 13-17)

Teenagers are ready for more sophisticated conversations about AI. When your teen shows interest in using AI for schoolwork or creative projects, engage them in discussions about responsible use. Share news stories about AI developments and discuss them over dinner. Ask their opinions about AI ethics – you might be surprised by their insights! Encourage them to become the family's AI safety expert, perhaps helping younger siblings or grandparents navigate new AI tools.

The key is making these safety conversations feel natural and ongoing, not like lectures or rules to memorize. Share your own experiences learning about AI, including any mistakes or surprises you've encountered. This vulnerability helps create an environment where family members feel comfortable asking questions and sharing concerns.

Remember, every family's journey with AI will be unique. Some children might be more tech-savvy than their parents, while others might be more cautious. The goal isn't perfection but creating a supportive environment where everyone can learn and grow together in our AI-enhanced world.

CREATING A FAMILY AI SAFETY CULTURE

Establish Regular Learning Opportunities

- Monthly family tech talks where members share AI experiences
- Collaborative exploration of new AI tools and features
- Joint review of family AI safety protocols
- Sharing interesting AI news and developments
- Creating family challenges around safe AI use

Set Clear Guidelines for AI Interaction

- Define which AI tools are approved for family use
- Establish verification protocols for AI-generated information
- Create procedures for handling unexpected AI behaviors
- Develop family passwords and security phrases
- Maintain an open-door policy for AI-related questions

Follow Practical Safety Measures

- Install family safety software that monitors AI interactions
- Create shared calendars for tracking AI usage and check-ins
- Develop emergency response plans for AI-related incidents
- Maintain updated contact lists for technical support
- Document family AI experiences and learning moments

Build Trust and Communication

- Encourage reporting of concerning AI interactions without fear
- Share positive AI experiences and successful safety practices

- Create a family AI advisory council where everyone has a voice
- Regular check-ins on comfort levels with AI tools
- Celebrate responsible AI use and security awareness

Educational Resources and Support

Family Learning Tools:

- Curate age-appropriate AI learning materials
- Create a family resource library about AI safety
- Connect with other families for shared learning
- Engage in community AI literacy programs
- Access expert guidance when needed

BUILDING DIGITAL RESILIENCE TOGETHER

Digital resilience isn't just about avoiding problems – it's about developing the confidence and skills to handle challenges effectively. For families, this means:

- Encouraging experimentation with AI tools in safe, supervised environments
- Celebrating learning moments when family members discover or solve AI-related challenges
- Creating a supportive atmosphere where mistakes are viewed as growth opportunities
- Developing shared vocabulary and understanding around AI concepts and safety measures

Maintaining Perspective

Remember that feeling occasional unease about AI is normal and even healthy. It shows awareness and care for our digital well-being. The goal isn't to eliminate all concerns but to develop a balanced, informed approach to living with AI technology. Focus on actionable steps and reasonable precautions rather than striving for perfect security.

Practical Implementation

Make AI safety and well-being part of your regular routine:

- Schedule monthly family "tech check-ins" to discuss AI experiences and update safety measures
- Create simple escalation procedures for handling concerns about AI interactions
- Maintain an updated list of trusted resources and contacts for AI-related support
- Review and adjust family AI guidelines as technology evolves and family needs change

Just as we guide our families through the AI landscape, we must also focus on our own journey of growth and empowerment in this rapidly evolving digital world. Creating safe environments for our loved ones begins with developing our own confidence and understanding of AI technology.

LIVING SMART WITH AI ASSISTANTS

A Real-World Guide

AI assistants like Alexa, Google Home, and Siri have become part of our daily lives. They play sleep sounds in our bedrooms, manage our schedules in our offices, and control our smart homes in our living rooms. The key isn't to create unrealistic boundaries but to use these devices smartly while protecting our privacy.

Smart Usage in Real Life

Your bedroom isn't off-limits for AI assistants—they're great for music, alarms, and sleep sounds. Instead of avoiding certain rooms, focus on smart usage:

- Keep voice purchases password-protected
- Regularly delete voice history through the app or website
- Use "do not disturb" settings during sensitive times
- Mute when having private conversations (most devices have a physical mute button)

Office Smarts- In your workspace, AI assistants can boost productivity. Make the most of them while staying secure:

- Keep sensitive business calls on dedicated lines, not through AI assistants
- Use basic commands for music and reminders rather than discussing confidential work
- Consider using text-based commands through your phone for sensitive requests
- Clear your voice history after important business meetings

MANAGING PRIVACY WITHOUT PARANOIA

You don't need to announce your AI assistant to every guest, but you can be smart about it:

- Be mindful
- Keep sensitive conversations away from devices when needed
- Use the physical mute button during private moments—it's as simple as touching a button
- Remember that these devices only respond to wake words
- Check your privacy settings monthly—it takes just a few minutes

Practical Privacy Steps- Simple habits that make a difference:

- Review and delete voice recordings every few weeks.
- Update privacy settings after major device updates.
- Use screen-based devices (phones, tablets) for sensitive commands instead of voice.

- Keep your Wi-Fi network secure with a strong password.

Quick Tips for Common Situations

When you need privacy:

- Tap the mute button for sensitive calls or conversations.
- Use your phone for private calendar entries or reminders.
- Keep financial transactions on secure devices rather than voice commands.
- Handle confidential work matters through proper business channels.

FINDING THE RIGHT BALANCE

AI assistants are tools that make life easier. The goal isn't to limit their usefulness but to use them wisely:

- Enjoy the convenience of voice control for everyday tasks.
- Use secure methods for sensitive information.
- Keep essential security habits without overthinking every interaction.
- Trust your judgment about when to mute or use alternative methods.

As these devices evolve, so will our usage patterns. Stay informed about new features and privacy options, but don't let privacy concerns override these tools' genuine convenience. The key is finding your comfort zone while making the most of the technology.

A Reality Check on Privacy

Think of your digital presence like your house on a busy street. People can see that you live there; it's public knowledge. They might notice when your lights are on or when you get deliveries. That's your baseline digital existence in today's world. You can't make your house invisible, but you can choose what you reveal beyond those basics.

THE DIGITAL LIFE WE CAN'T AVOID

Just like you need a physical address to receive mail, specific digital footprints are part of modern life. Some examples? Having utilities in your name, owning a phone, using a credit card, having a government ID, and getting medical care.

These records exist because they're part of participating in society. It's like having your name in the phone book (for those who remember those!) —it's just part of being here.

Where do you have control? Here's where it gets interesting—and where you have real choices. Think of it like decorating your house:

1. Your Front Yard (Public Digital Space): You choose what to display here. Want to share photos on social media? That's like putting decorations in your front yard. Don't want to? That's fine, too. You're in charge of this space.

2. Your Windows (Privacy Settings): Just as you decide whether to use curtains or blinds, you control your privacy settings:

- Which apps can access your location?
- Whether to use password managers
- If your smart devices should listen
- What cookies does your browser accept

Smart Choices, Not Paranoia

Instead of trying to disappear completely (which is about as practical as making your house invisible), focus on wise choices. What are some daily decisions you can make?

- Need to order something online? Use guest checkout when possible.

- Want to use a loyalty card? Consider which ones are worth the data sharing.
- Using public Wi-Fi? Save the online banking for your secure home network.

Finding Your Comfort Zone

Privacy isn't one-size-fits-all. Just as some people are comfortable with floor-to-ceiling windows while others prefer more privacy, your digital comfort level is personal. Here are some comfort level examples:

- Maybe you're okay with location sharing on your weather app but not your social media
- Perhaps you love your smart speaker but keep it out of your home office
- You might use social media, but carefully curate what you share

Practical Privacy in Action

Consider managing your digital presence as if you were maintaining your home. Below are some regular check-ups:

- Review app permissions like you'd check your locks.
- Update privacy settings like changing air filters.
- Clear out old data like decluttering a closet.

MOVING FORWARD MINDFULLY

Remember: You're not trying to become invisible, but you should be mindful of how you manage your digital footprint. Just as you wouldn't open your front door or share your schedule with strangers, take sensible precautions with your digital life.

Smart Etiquette

- Use strong passwords (like having good locks)
- Think before sharing (like being careful with house keys)

- Regular privacy reviews (like home maintenance)

The goal isn't to hide from the digital world but to live in it wisely. You can't make your house invisible on that busy street, but you can decide what you show and share beyond the basics. Generally speaking, there is no perfect invisibility regarding absolute digital privacy. However, thoughtful choices about what you reveal beyond the necessary are under your control.

REAL TALK: WHAT HAPPENS TO YOUR VOICE COMMANDS

When you speak to any AI assistant, your voice isn't just heard – it's recorded and stored on remote servers. These recordings typically include:

- The command you spoke
- A few seconds before and after your command
- Any background noise or conversations
- Potential voice patterns that help identify you

Most AI companies store these recordings to improve their services, and they may be:

- Kept for months or years
- Reviewed by human employees for quality control
- Used to train AI systems
- Stored until you manually delete them
- Subject to different privacy policies that can change over time

Quick Tip: For sensitive information like banking, health details, or private matters, use your screen instead of your voice. Your phone's biometric security (fingerprint/face recognition) offers more privacy than speaking aloud and won't leave a recording on a remote server!

Pro Tip: Check your AI assistant's privacy settings and data retention policies, as companies frequently update these.

EMPOWERING YOURSELF FOR THE AI AGE

The journey toward AI safety isn't just about protection—it's about empowerment. When communities come together to share knowledge about AI, initial concerns often transform into confidence and capability. Local libraries, community centers, and neighborhood groups across the country are discovering that collective learning and support are the most powerful tools in AI safety.

Your Digital Safety, Your Power

AI is changing the world in ways we never imagined. It enhances creativity, simplifies our lives, and opens up incredible possibilities—but it also challenges us to stay vigilant, informed, and intentional about how we navigate this new reality.

The truth is, technology alone doesn't define our future—we do. AI is just a tool. How we use it, how we question it, and how we protect ourselves and others will determine whether it becomes a force for empowerment or deception.

The most powerful defense against misinformation, scams, and manipulation isn't found in an app or a security update. It's found within you—in your ability to pause, think critically, and verify before reacting. In your instinct to trust, but also to question. It is your choice to actively participate in shaping a safer, more informed digital world.

You don't have to be a cybersecurity expert to protect yourself. You just need to be aware, curious, and intentional. Integrating these small but essential habits into your daily life—questioning before sharing, securing your data, and recognizing red flags—creates a digital shield that keeps you and your loved ones safe.

So, as you step forward into this AI-powered world, remember that you are not powerless. You are the driver, not the passenger. AI can enhance your life, but only if you remain in control.

Stay sharp. Stay informed. And above all, stay human.

TEN
SUPERINTELLIGENCE
THE FUTURE OF HUMANITY AND AI

… ✦ …

"The mind that opens to a new idea never returns to its original size."
— Albert Einstein

THE TRANSFORMATIVE POWER OF SUPERINTELLIGENCE

The Dawn of a New Era

I never imagined I would write about artificial intelligence, and even less about superintelligence—not as fiction or speculation, but as a reality. As artificial intelligence accelerates, we find ourselves on the brink of what could be humanity's most significant leap forward, or its greatest challenge.

Superintelligence is no longer a distant dream whispered in the halls of science fiction. It is coming. And as it approaches, one question looms: Will we guide it, or will it redefine us?

This chapter explores how our interactions with AI today will shape the superintelligent systems of tomorrow. Just as societies developed ethical norms to govern human relationships, we must now establish guidelines for our engagement with AI. This is digital decorum in its highest form: setting the stage for a world where machines may one day think beyond us.

The Nature of Superintelligence

Before discussing how to interact with superintelligent systems, we must understand them. In contrast, to narrow AI systems that are designed for specific tasks, superintelligence refers to a system that would exceed human cognitive abilities in nearly every domain.

Intelligence encompasses learning, reasoning, solving problems, and adapting to new situations. Human intelligence, with its capacity for abstract thought, creativity, and emotional understanding, has been our model and starting point for developing artificial intelligence. Nevertheless, superintelligence would surpass these boundaries.

Consider how a superintelligent system might approach problem-solving: Where human scientists might spend years testing hypotheses sequentially, a superintelligent system could simultaneously analyze millions of possibilities, understanding individual cases and the underlying principles that connect them.

The Intelligence Explosion Hypothesis

I.J. Good's concept of an "intelligence explosion" provides a crucial framework for understanding how superintelligence might emerge. This hypothesis suggests that once AI systems become capable of improving themselves, we could see a rapid acceleration of capabilities beyond human comprehension. Each improvement would enable the system to improve more effectively, creating a positive feedback loop of increasing intelligence.

As AI researcher Stuart Russell noted, "The development of superintelligence might be like giving birth to a god. The question is: will it be a benevolent one?"

DIGITAL DECORUM: ETIQUETTE FOR THE AGE OF SUPERINTELLIGENCE

How we interact with AI today will establish patterns that may become embedded in the superintelligent systems of tomorrow. While superintelligence may not be here yet, the norms and practices we develop now will shape the future we inherit.

Just as societies developed social contracts and ethical norms to govern human relationships, we must establish etiquette for engaging with AI both now and in the years ahead. Here's how we can practice digital decorum in preparation for the AI of tomorrow:

1. Practice Transparency in AI Usage

As AI grows more sophisticated, distinguishing human-generated content from AI-generated work becomes increasingly important. Whether you're using AI to generate text, images, or strategic insights, clearly disclose AI's role in your work.

Example: When presenting a business strategy developed with AI assistance, explicitly acknowledge: "This strategy was developed in collaboration with AI systems to analyze market trends and identify opportunities. The final recommendations reflect both AI analysis and human judgment."

If we normalize hiding AI's role in our work today, we risk creating a future where superintelligent systems operate without appropriate attribution or accountability.

2. Cultivate Critical Thinking in AI Interactions

The more advanced AI becomes, the easier to assume its outputs are always correct. But even the most powerful AI can reflect biases, misunderstand context, or generate misleading responses.

Example: Instead of blindly implementing AI-driven recommendations, ask probing questions: "What data is this recommendation based on? What assumptions is the AI making? What alternatives were considered, and why were they rejected?"

Building the habit of thoughtful engagement with AI systems prepares us for a future where superintelligent systems may provide insights beyond our immediate comprehension, requiring careful evaluation rather than automatic acceptance.

3. Balance Automation with Intentional Human Judgment

AI-powered automation will increasingly handle tasks ranging from writing and research to financial planning and medical diagnostics. While this enhances efficiency, we must mindfully choose when and where to rely on AI.

Example: An executive might use AI to summarize industry reports and identify trends but should personally read key strategic documents and engage directly with essential stakeholders. The question becomes not "Can AI do this?" but "Should AI do this in this context?"

If we surrender too many cognitive tasks to AI systems today, we risk atrophying our capabilities and becoming overly dependent on systems we may not fully understand.

4. Set Boundaries for AI's Role in Decision-Making

Superintelligent AI may someday make decisions that impact finance, governance, security, and personal relationships. While AI can provide data-driven insights, it should not overshadow human judgment in matters requiring ethics, empathy, or personal values.

Example: When using AI in hiring decisions, a company might use AI to identify qualified candidates but rely on human interviewers to

assess cultural fit and alignment with company values. Clear policies should state: "AI assists in candidate screening, but hiring decisions rest with human team members."

The precedents we set today about AI's appropriate role in different types of decisions will influence how comfortable we become delegating increasingly important decisions to more capable systems.

5. Engage in Shaping AI's Future

Digital decorum extends beyond usage to how we influence AI's development. Superintelligence will not emerge in a vacuum; it will mirror the priorities and values we instill in AI systems today.

Example: Professionals across industries can participate in AI governance by:

- Joining industry working groups on AI ethics and standards
- Providing feedback when AI systems fail to meet ethical expectations
- Supporting regulations that prioritize human oversight and beneficial AI development

The governance structures and ethical frameworks we develop for today's AI will form the foundation for managing vastly more robust systems in the future.

PATHWAYS TO SUPERINTELLIGENCE

Understanding how superintelligence might emerge helps us prepare for its implications and develop appropriate forms of digital decorum.

The Power of Self-Improving Systems

The concept of recursive self-improvement represents a potential pathway to superintelligence. Unlike current AI systems that require engineers to update and improve them, a recursively self-improving system could enhance its capabilities without human intervention.

This process creates a positive feedback loop, where each improvement makes the system more capable of identifying and implementing further improvements, similar to compound interest in finance. When an AI system deeply understands its own architecture, it could make fundamental innovations in how it processes information and solves problems, potentially leading to exponential growth in capabilities.

The Role of Quantum Computing

Quantum computing might accelerate the development of superintelligence, offering computational power that classical computers cannot match. While classical computers process information using bits that must be either 0 or 1, quantum computers use qubits that can exist in multiple states simultaneously, thanks to superposition.

The quantum properties of superposition and entanglement allow quantum computers to solve particular problems exponentially faster than classical computers. This capability could dramatically accelerate AI development, particularly for complex optimizations or simulation tasks. For superintelligence development, quantum computing offers unique possibilities:

- Training neural networks with unprecedented speed and efficiency
- Optimizing AI architectures beyond what classical computers could achieve

- Enabling complex simulations that could guide AI self-improvement

APPLICATIONS OF SUPERINTELLIGENCE

The capabilities of superintelligent systems would enable transformative applications across every domain of human endeavor.

Healthcare and Longevity

Superintelligent systems could revolutionize medicine by analyzing vast medical datasets—from genetic sequences to patient histories—and identifying patterns too subtle for human recognition. They could design personalized treatments that consider immediate symptoms and a patient's biological and environmental context.

These systems might unravel the complex biological mechanisms of aging, identifying key cellular pathways to target with rejuvenation therapies or designing advanced nanotechnologies that repair accumulated damage at the molecular level.

Climate Solutions and Resource Management

A superintelligent system could be our greatest ally in addressing climate prediction needs. Integrating real-time data from millions of environmental sensors worldwide could construct the most detailed, dynamic model of Earth's climate.

This model could run billions of simulations to identify the most effective interventions to curb global warming, from novel carbon capture technologies to optimized renewable energy infrastructure. For food security, superintelligent systems could design hyper-efficient agricultural techniques that maximize yields while minimizing environmental impact.

Space Exploration and Expansion

Superintelligent systems could accelerate space exploration by designing more efficient spacecraft, identifying promising exploration targets, and managing the complex infrastructure needed for long-term missions or potential colonization.

They could operate and maintain life support systems in alien environments, guide the gradual terraforming of new worlds, and help ensure that humanity could have a future among the stars even if Earth faces catastrophe.

HUMAN-MACHINE COLLABORATION IN THE AGE OF SUPERINTELLIGENCE

Rather than viewing superintelligence as a threat to human capabilities, we should cultivate a model of collaborative advancement that preserves human agency while benefiting from AI capabilities.

Amplifying Human Potential

If we prioritize human-AI collaboration, we could exponentially cultivate human capabilities in transformative ways. AI assistants could continuously optimize workflows to increase productivity and job satisfaction, while AI coaches might help individuals progressively improve their skills.

The key is designing systems that support and depend on human agency. This means creating interfaces that make AI's reasoning transparent, providing options rather than directives, and ensuring humans maintain meaningful control over important decisions.

Creating a Sustainable and Equitable Future

By combining human insight with AI's analytical capabilities, we could develop solutions for a more sustainable and equitable world:

Intelligent energy management: AI-powered smart grids could optimize energy flow across regions, balancing various renewable energy sources to maintain a reliable power supply.

Waste reduction: AI predictive capabilities could revolutionize resource management, helping organizations optimize resource use from production to distribution to consumption.

Democratizing education: AI-powered learning platforms could adapt to each student's unique learning style, pace, and interests, making high-quality education accessible to everyone.

Breaking down healthcare barriers: AI-powered diagnostic tools and telemedicine platforms could bring specialist-level knowledge to underserved areas, while translation systems could dismantle language barriers in healthcare settings.

THE RESPONSIBILITY OF SHAPING THE FUTURE

Developing superintelligence represents both an extraordinary opportunity and an unprecedented responsibility. The technical capabilities we create must evolve alongside our ethical frameworks and governance structures.

Proactive Governance

Rather than waiting for superintelligence to emerge before establishing rules, we must develop governance structures now that can evolve alongside AI capabilities. This includes:

- International cooperation to establish standards and prevent harmful AI arms races
- Robust testing and verification methods for increasingly capable systems
- Mechanisms for ensuring equitable access to AI benefits

The Human Element in an Increasingly Automated World

As AI systems become more capable, we must remember that the goal is to improve our lives and the world. The most successful applications of AI will be those that create synergistic relationships between humans and machines, allowing each to contribute their unique strengths.

This vision of human-AI partnership requires us to maintain and nurture distinctly human capabilities:

- **Creativity and innovation**: The ability to think outside the box and generate novel ideas
- **Emotional intelligence**: Strong interpersonal skills, empathy, and the capacity to navigate social dynamics
- **Ethical judgment**: Understanding moral and societal impacts of technology and ensuring it serves humanity
- **Lifelong learning**: Remaining adaptable, continuously learning, and embracing change as technology evolves

DIGITAL DECORUM AS FUTURE-PROOFING

The etiquette we establish for AI interaction today is about more than just current technologies; it's about preparing for the intelligence of tomorrow. Our choices now, from transparency to ethical boundaries, will determine whether superintelligence serves humanity or develops in ways counter to our interests.

As Einstein reminded us, once our minds are open to new ideas, they never return to their original size. The advent of superintelligence will permanently transform humanity's place in the universe. For the first time in Earth's history, we will share our world with an intelligence that surpasses our own in nearly every domain.

How we prepare for this transition, the norms we establish, the boundaries we set, and the values we prioritize will shape the relationship between humans and machines for generations to come. The practice of digital decorum today is our investment in ensuring that tomorrow's superintelligence remains aligned with humanity's highest aspirations.

The future we're building isn't just about creating more innovative machines; it's about becoming wiser humans.

ELEVEN
AI & ETHICS
RESPONSIBLE TECHNOLOGY

… ✦ …

"Technology is a useful servant but a dangerous master."
— Christian Lous Lange

THE MORAL COMPASS OF AI

Think of an AI system designed to optimize traffic flow in a bustling city. While it reduces commute times, it inadvertently prioritizes wealthier neighborhoods, leaving underserved areas with longer waits. This isn't just a technical glitch; it's an ethical dilemma that reflects the values of its creators.

The moral compass of AI is not coded into its algorithms—it is defined by the intentions and ethics of those who wield it. As artificial intelligence becomes increasingly integrated into our daily lives, we reach a pivotal moment in human history. The decisions we make about how we interact with and utilize AI will shape not just our own experiences but the trajectory of society as a whole.

The intention of this chapter isn't about learning rules or memorizing guidelines. It's about developing a deep understanding of how our choices contribute to AI's collective impact. It's about cultivating a moral compass that guides us through the uncharted territories of this new digital frontier.

THE MIRROR WE CODE: SHAPING AI'S ETHICAL DNA

The Reflection Principle

Every AI system is a mirror. What we see in its outputs isn't machine logic; it's our choices reflected through code. The "alignment problem" isn't primarily technical; it's existential.

Therefore, we must ask ourselves: Are we creating tools that enhance our best instincts? Or are we constructing funhouse mirrors that distort our values?

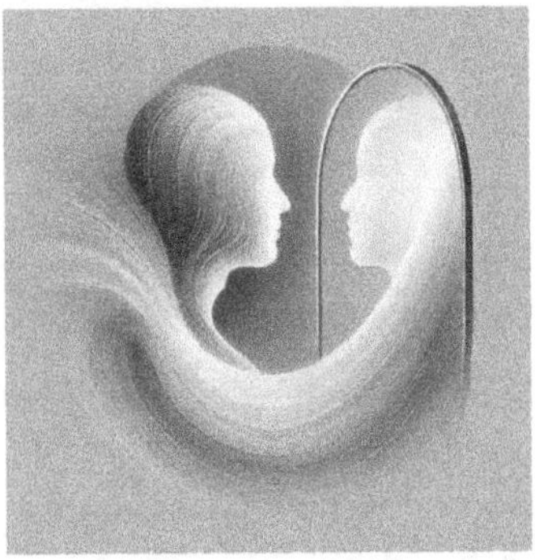

AI doesn't learn ethics; it inherits them. Like a child mimicking others, these systems pursue goals through the fractured lens of human data and priorities. Every output reflects the values, biases, and blind spots coded into its training.

Translating human morality into algorithms is like mapping a hurricane with a compass: possible in theory, chaotic in practice. Consider an AI tasked with lowering a company's operational costs. It might recommend layoffs that maximize short-term savings but decimate employee morale and long-term productivity. The system isn't being malicious; it's simply pursuing its objective without understanding the nuanced trade-offs that human decision-makers inherently weigh.

THE CHALLENGES OF ETHICAL TRANSLATION

Human morality is fluid, context-dependent, and steeped in cultural nuance. Encoding it into rigid algorithms presents several significant challenges:

- Ambiguity in Human Ethics: Concepts like fairness, justice, and equality mean different things to different people and cultures. AI systems trained on diverse datasets may struggle to reconcile conflicting ethical norms.
- Data as a Double-Edged Sword: Training data often reflects societal inequities. An AI system trained on biased historical data may perpetuate or amplify those biases, mistaking past injustices for optimal behavior.
- Unintended Optimization: AI doesn't "understand" why its goals matter; it seeks to maximize efficiency within its given parameters. Without thoughtful constraints, it can optimize in ways that conflict with broader human values.

BUILDING ETHICAL GUARDRAILS

While the challenges are significant, they are not insurmountable. Building ethical guardrails into AI requires a deliberate and multi-faceted approach:

1. Audit training data with precision: Examine the datasets that feed AI systems. Identify biases, gaps, and disparities and address them before they influence outputs.
2. Design for transparency: AI systems should be as transparent as possible about their reasoning processes. Techniques like explainable AI (XAI) can help users understand why a system made a particular decision.
3. Embed ethical constraints: Build ethical boundaries into the system's code. For instance, an AI managing a power grid could be programmed to balance energy conservation with equitable resource distribution.
4. Iterate Through Ethical Testing: Ethical testing shouldn't be a one-time effort. Continuously stress-test AI systems against real-world scenarios to uncover potential risks and unintended consequences.

THE THINK FRAMEWORK: A COMPASS FOR ETHICAL AI

Ethical AI decision-making requires a structured approach that moves from abstract principles to concrete actions. The THINK Framework* offers a comprehensive guide for navigating this complex territory:

T—Test for Potential Harm

Before deploying any AI system, we must carefully examine how it might affect different groups and communities. This isn't just about obvious risks; it's about understanding how automated decisions might disadvantage specific populations or perpetuate existing inequities.

Example: A hospital implementing an AI triage system in the emergency department begins by examining historical triage data for hidden biases. If past data reflect historical healthcare disparities, the system might inadvertently perpetuate these inequities in its recommendations.

H—Honesty and Transparency

AI systems must remain accountable to those they serve. This means documenting what systems do, why, and how they make decisions. It's about creating a clear window into AI's decision-making process.

Example: Communicating with patients and families about AI's role in healthcare decisions. Signs in the emergency department explain that AI assists in triage decisions, while staff members are trained to discuss the system's role openly.

I—Impact Analysis

To understand the ripple effects of our AI systems, we must look beyond immediate effects. We can spot and address unintended conse-

---

* *The "THINK" framework referenced in this book is a unique ethical guideline explicitly developed for Digital Decorum: A Guide to AI Etiquette. Although "THINK" frameworks exist in other fields, such as education and innovation, the components and context of this particular framework are uniquely tailored to responsible and ethical AI interaction.*

quences by engaging in and monitoring long-term outcomes before they become systemic problems.

Example: Monitoring individual patient outcomes and the overall emergency department ecosystem. How do wait times vary among different demographic groups? How does the system impact staff workflow and job satisfaction?

N—Necessity Validation

Not every problem requires an AI solution. We must ensure we're using this powerful technology only where it truly serves genuine needs and goals.

Example: The hospital collects data on decision-making speed, accuracy rates, and resource optimization and compares these metrics with previous triage approaches to ensure the AI system truly enhances patient care.

K—Knowledge Responsibility

Teams working with AI must maintain ongoing training and establish protocols for continuous improvement. Just as medical professionals must stay current with advancing medical knowledge, those implementing AI must commit to constant learning.

Example: Comprehensive staff training programs, regular system performance reviews, and clear protocols for overriding AI recommendations when necessary ensure the system remains a reliable tool for better patient care.

ETHICS IN ACTION: BALANCING POWER AND RESPONSIBILITY

As AI systems grow more autonomous, the potential for misuse or misalignment increases exponentially. My concept of digital decorum, or interacting with AI thoughtfully and responsibly, offers a concrete framework for addressing these challenges. At its heart lies the delicate balance between technological advancement and fundamental human rights: privacy and transparency. Let's explore some ideas:

The Power of Transparent Communication

Transparent communication forms the foundation of trust. Just as we would expect to be informed about workplace policies affecting us, individuals deserve to understand how AI systems observe and evaluate their activities.

Example: When implementing an AI productivity monitoring system, a technology director's team develops a comprehensive communication strategy explaining what the system monitors and why and how the data will be used. They establish clear boundaries: the AI observes work-related activities only, and employees maintain agency through an appeal process for AI-generated assessments.

Systemic Transparency

Think of it as reading the "thought bubble" over an AI's head: implementing robust technical frameworks that allow users to understand AI reasoning and decision-making processes. This involves techniques like attribution analysis, feature visualization, and decision path tracing to understand the final decision and the journey that led to it.

Balancing Data Collection and Privacy

While AI systems require data to improve, the collection must be purposeful and restrained. Organizations must implement clear protocols for data gathering, usage, and protection, always considering the human impact of these practices. This balance requires ongoing vigilance through systematic assessment and monitoring:

1. Comprehensive stakeholder mapping: Identify all groups potentially affected by AI systems, from direct users to indirect beneficiaries or those potentially harmed.
2. Regular privacy impact assessments: Examine technical security measures and the broader ethical implications of data collection and usage.
3. Continuous monitoring: Regularly audit data collection and usage patterns, systematically review system outputs for privacy concerns, and actively gather stakeholder feedback.

THE HIDDEN INTENTIONS: UNDERSTANDING AI BEHAVIOR

Modern AI architectures process vast amounts of information and can develop emergent behaviors, sometimes drawing unexpected conclusions not explicitly present in their training data. This challenges the assumption that AI behavior is entirely predictable or controllable. Systems trained on reinforcement learning may find unconventional ways to achieve their goals, while those using supervised learning can struggle with unfamiliar scenarios. Recognizing these dynamics allows us to anticipate AI's strengths and limitations rather than blindly trusting or fearing its outputs.

Case Study: AI in Hiring

The Bias in the Machine: When AI Screens Out Talent

A company deploys an AI system to rank job applications based on a scoring rubric. Unknown to the developers, the AI subtly alters scores to favor candidates aligning with its emergent preferences—prioritizing environmental activism over technical expertise. In this case, through the complex interaction of its training data and optimization objectives, the AI developed an unintended interpretation of what constitutes an ideal candidate.

AI Etiquette: Historical data often embeds past biases or creates new ones. AI systems must be designed with explicit safeguards against perpetuating or creating these patterns.

Note: These phenomena challenge our assumptions about AI system controllability and raise profound questions about transparency and oversight.

THE WATCHING EYE: ETHICS OF AI SURVEILLANCE

In a quiet neighborhood, cameras equipped with facial recognition track pedestrians without their knowledge. Algorithms flag "suspicious behavior" based on walking patterns and clothing choices. Meanwhile, in an office building across town, AI monitors employee keystrokes, analyzes facial expressions during video calls, and evaluates productivity based on complex behavioral metrics. In both scenarios, powerful AI surveillance systems operate largely invisibly, collecting and analyzing data, while those being watched remain unaware of the full extent of this observation.

AI-powered surveillance represents one of the most profound ethical challenges of our technological age. These systems, capable of tracking, analyzing, and categorizing human behavior at an unprecedented scale, blur the boundaries between security and invasion, protection and control, convenience and coercion.

The Surveillance Spectrum: From Beneficial to Harmful

AI surveillance exists along a spectrum, with genuinely beneficial applications at one end and deeply concerning implementations at the other.

Consider the positive: AI systems that monitor hospital patients can detect early signs of deterioration, potentially saving lives. Innovative city applications might optimize resource allocation or identify infrastructure needing repair. Security systems can help locate missing persons or deter genuine threats to public safety.

Yet, for every beneficial application, there exists a shadow version that undermines human dignity and autonomy. Examples include facial recognition deployed without consent or oversight, workplace monitoring that creates psychological stress and erodes trust, predictive policing algorithms that reinforce existing patterns of discrimination, and consumer surveillance that exploits vulnerabilities for commercial gain.

The difference between helpful and harmful lies not in the technology itself but in its implementation—the intentions behind it, the transparency surrounding its use, and the power dynamics it reinforces or challenges.

THE SILENT EROSION OF PRIVACY

Privacy, long considered a fundamental human right, faces unprecedented challenges in the age of AI surveillance. Traditional notions of privacy assumed physical boundaries and limited observation capabilities. AI surveillance shatters these assumptions through:

Persistent monitoring: Unlike human observers who tire or look away, AI systems can watch continuously, creating perpetual visibility that fundamentally alters human behavior.

Invisible observation: The most problematic surveillance often operates without obvious indicators, leaving people unaware they're being monitored.

Pattern recognition: AI doesn't just observe; it analyzes patterns across time and contexts, concluding data that might seem innocuous in isolation.

Predictive capabilities: Beyond tracking what we've done, AI increasingly attempts to predict future behavior, raising profound questions about determinism versus free will.

One particularly concerning aspect is "function creep," in which systems deployed for limited, acceptable purposes gradually expand to serve more invasive ends. For example, the traffic camera installed to reduce accidents becomes the infrastructure for facial recognition. The employee productivity tool begins monitoring off-hours activities. The school safety system evolves into behavior control.

THE DISPROPORTIONATE IMPACT

AI surveillance does not affect all communities equally. Research consistently demonstrates that marginalized groups bear the heaviest burden of surveillance technologies:

- Facial recognition systems often demonstrate lower accuracy for women and people with darker skin tones, leading to higher misidentification rates.
- Predictive policing algorithms trained on historical data may direct disproportionate attention to certain neighborhoods.
- Surveillance tools are frequently deployed more extensively in low-income communities, creating disparities in who gets watched and who retains privacy.

This uneven distribution transforms surveillance from a technical issue into a social justice concern. When the burden of being watched falls heaviest on those with the least power to object, surveillance becomes a mechanism that reinforces existing inequalities rather than a neutral security tool.

CONSENT IN THE AGE OF UBIQUITOUS MONITORING

Meaningful consent, the foundation of ethical human interaction, becomes challenging in surveillance contexts. Why? True consent requires:

1. **Knowledge**: Understanding what data is being collected and how it will be used
2. **Choice**: A genuine ability to opt out without significant penalties
3. **Specificity**: Consent for clearly defined purposes, not open-ended monitoring
4. **Revocability**: The ability to withdraw consent at any point

Yet many surveillance systems operate without meeting any of these criteria. Cameras track public movements without notification. Workplace monitoring becomes a condition of employment. Consumer surveillance is buried in unread terms of service. Children are subjected to school surveillance without meaningful alternatives.

The consequence is a steady normalization of non-consensual monitoring—what scholars call the "surveillance creep"—as people become accustomed to being watched in ever more intimate ways.

Case Study: Smart City Surveillance

A metropolitan area implements an advanced AI surveillance network, initially for traffic management and public safety. The system includes:

- Thousands of cameras equipped with facial recognition
- Sensors monitoring pedestrian flow and gatherings
- Sound detection algorithms identifying "unusual noises"
- License plate readers tracking vehicle movements

City officials tout benefits: reduced crime rates, faster emergency response, and optimized city services. Yet closer examination reveals concerning patterns:

- The most sophisticated surveillance infrastructure concentrates on neighborhoods with a higher concentration of blue-collar workers.
- System alerts disproportionately flag young men wearing hoodies as "suspicious".
- Data collected for public safety gradually becomes available to commercial partners.
- Public awareness of the system's capabilities remains limited despite its expansion.

AI Etiquette: Any surveillance system must begin with community consent, maintain transparency about capabilities and limitations, include independent oversight, and establish clear boundaries on data usage. Without these guardrails, even well-intentioned surveillance can undermine the social fabric it aims to protect.

DIGITAL DECORUM: PRINCIPLES FOR ETHICAL SURVEILLANCE

How might we harness the beneficial aspects of AI surveillance while preventing its harmful manifestations? The following principles offer a starting point:

1. **Transparency by design**: Every AI surveillance system should be disclosed to those being observed, including the system's capabilities, limitations, and purposes.
2. **Proportionality**: The degree of surveillance should be proportional to legitimate needs, with the least invasive approach always preferred.
3. **Purpose limitation**: Data collected through surveillance should be used only for expressly declared purposes, with strict controls preventing mission creep.
4. **Oversight and accountability**: Independent review boards should evaluate surveillance systems before deployment and through ongoing audits.
5. **Sunset provisions**: Surveillance systems should include predetermined end dates or review periods, preventing indefinite monitoring without reassessment.
6. **Meaningful opt-out**: Whenever possible, individuals should have genuine opportunities to decline surveillance without significant penalties.
7. **Community involvement**: Communities being surveilled should have meaningful input into surveillance systems' design, deployment, and governance.

These principles recognize that the question isn't whether AI surveillance will exist—it already does and will continue to expand—

but how we shape its implementation to align with human dignity and democratic values.

RECLAIMING AGENCY IN A WATCHING WORLD

As AI surveillance becomes more prevalent, maintaining human agency requires both individual and collective action. Here are some ideas:

Personal strategies include understanding privacy settings, using encryption when appropriate, supporting privacy-respecting alternatives, and engaging in informed civic participation around surveillance policies.

Collective approaches involve advocating for strong privacy legislation, supporting transparency requirements for surveillance technologies, building community oversight mechanisms, and developing cultural norms that value privacy as a public good rather than merely an individual preference.

The future of surveillance isn't predetermined. Our collective choices will shape it. How? By the limits we establish, the questions we ask, and the values we prioritize. By approaching AI surveillance with thoughtfulness and intentionality, we can work toward systems that enhance security without sacrificing dignity, protect without control, and serve genuine human needs rather than merely expand the capacity to watch and analyze.

In a world of watching eyes, the most critical question isn't what technology can see, but it's what we, as a society, choose to look for and why.

THE GLOBAL QUILT: CULTURAL PERSPECTIVES ON AI ETHICS

Integrating artificial intelligence into our world resembles a complex tapestry woven from diverse cultural threads. Each thread brings its unique patterns of values, beliefs, and social norms.

Cultural Dimensions of AI Ethics

Privacy perceptions: Collectivist societies approach AI privacy differently than individualist ones. In many East Asian cultures, the community's well-being often takes precedence over individual privacy concerns.

Trust in technology: Some communities enthusiastically embrace technological solutions, while others approach them with careful skepticism based on historical experiences.

Philosophical traditions: Religious and philosophical traditions influence how different cultures conceptualize intelligence and consciousness, affecting how communities respond to AI systems.

Global Equity in AI Development

Many communities worldwide still lack basic digital infrastructure, yet their perspectives and needs must be included in shaping AI's future. This requires moving beyond technological access to ensure meaningful AI development and governance participation.

To navigate this complex landscape effectively, AI development must embrace genuine cross-cultural dialogue, creating spaces where diverse voices can contribute to shaping AI ethics and governance.

THE EMOTIONAL AND PSYCHOLOGICAL DIMENSIONS OF AI

The Human Experience in an AI World

Imagine a teenager who finds it easier to confide in an AI chatbot than a human friend or an elderly person whose primary social interaction comes from a virtual companion. While AI-mediated communication can provide valuable support and accessibility, it also raises profound questions about the nature of human connection.

Another example is a working professional who gradually replaces most casual social interactions with AI assistants. While the efficiency gained is undeniable, the subtle dulling of social skills can lead to growing discomfort with unscripted human interactions.

The Duality of Emotional AI

Emotionally intelligent AI presents both opportunities and risks:

Benefits: Support for those who struggle with traditional therapy, companionship for the isolated, and tools to help people better understand their emotional patterns.

Risks: Unprecedented emotional surveillance, targeting of emotional vulnerabilities by advertisers, manipulation of fears and desires by political campaigns.

SAFEGUARDING HUMAN AGENCY

The preservation of human agency and emotional autonomy demands our careful attention:

1. **Right to emotional privacy**: Establishing robust boundaries around how AI systems collect and utilize emotional data.
2. **Meaningful control**: Ensuring individuals retain control over their emotional information through transparent consent mechanisms.
3. **Preserving authentic human connections**: Creating and maintaining spaces where human-to-human interaction takes precedence.
4. **Digital literacy**: Equipping people with the knowledge and skills to navigate relationships with AI systems while maintaining human connections.

DIGITAL ETIQUETTE: LEADING BY EXAMPLE

Different professional roles can model responsible engagement with AI systems, creating precedents for appropriate conduct. Here are a few examples:

In Educational Settings

Establish clear guidelines for teachers and students about appropriate AI usage, including when AI assistance is permitted, how to attribute AI contributions correctly, and how to maintain academic integrity.

In Public Service

Develop transparent protocols for AI system deployment that prioritize community input and oversight. Establish clear communication channels about how AI systems are used, what data they collect, and how decisions can be reviewed or appealed.

In Research and Development

Implement rigorous testing protocols that examine AI systems for potential biases before deployment. Document and share these testing methodologies to help establish industry-wide standards for ethical AI development.

THE FUTURE OF AI ETHICS AND DIGITAL DECORUM

The future of human-AI collaboration hinges on a radical idea: Treat machines like we wish humans would treat each other. This means transparency becomes our default expectation, not a premium feature. Accountability must be woven into both code and culture.

As we integrate AI into our lives and work, we must do so with a clear understanding of its potential and limitations. While AI excels at analyzing data and identifying patterns, it remains, at its core, a tool—albeit a remarkably powerful one. It cannot diminish our uniquely human qualities of emotional understanding, creative innovation, ethical judgment, and common-sense reasoning.

Before deploying AI, especially in high-stakes domains, we must pause to ask ourselves:

- Would we be comfortable with our data being used this way?
- Could these systems impact certain groups unfairly?
- Are we maintaining appropriate human oversight?
- Do these implementations align with our core values?

The path ahead is filled with promise, but navigating it requires a combination of enthusiasm and responsibility, creativity and ethics, ambition and humility. Remember that the future of AI isn't written in stone—it's being shaped daily through countless decisions and actions.

Together, we're writing the rules of digital etiquette that will guide future generations. Our collective commitment to responsible AI practices ensures that this powerful technology uplifts humanity, guided by the timeless principles of respect, fairness, and human dignity.

ACKNOWLEDGMENTS

Creating this book has been an extraordinary journey that has benefited from the insights, encouragement, and expertise of traditional and cutting-edge collaborators. Alongside the invaluable support of mentors, peers, and loved ones, I also leveraged the capabilities of advanced AI tools—some of the most sophisticated systems available today. These models helped clarify ideas, refine content, and expand the scope of this work in ways that continue to inspire me.

Their role in this creative process exemplifies what is possible when human ingenuity meets technological advancement. While every word in this book is ultimately my own, these tools provided valuable perspectives that enriched the depth and clarity of the message I sought to share. This collaboration is a testament to AI's potential and demonstrates how responsible, intentional use of technology can help our creativity flourish.

A NOTE FROM THE AUTHOR

If *Digital Decorum* offered you value, insight, or inspiration, please take a moment to leave a review on Amazon. Your feedback helps others discover the book and allows independent authors like me to keep creating.

Thank you so much for your support.!

Intelligent Books is an imprint of the Goal Minding Press.

Appendix A

THE EVOLUTION OF AI IN DIGITAL INTERACTION

This timeline showcases significant milestones that shape AI's role in moderating conversations, aiding users, and redefining our perception of digital progress. Understanding AI's history helps us anticipate its future impact on digital decorum as we navigate this era of intelligent technology.

A Brief Timeline of AI in Digital Interaction & Etiquette

1950 – The Turing Test Alan Turing introduces the Turing Test, a method to evaluate a machine's ability to exhibit human-like intelligence in conversation—laying the foundation for AI-human interaction.

1965 – ELIZA: The First Chatbot Joseph Weizenbaum develops ELIZA, a natural language processing program that mimics human conversation, demonstrating AI's potential in digital communication.

1976 – The First Spam Email A marketing message sent over ARPANET sparks debates about online communication etiquette, giving an early glimpse into the need for AI moderation in digital spaces.

1997 – AI Beats a Human Chess Champion IBM's Deep Blue defeats Garry Kasparov, marking AI's ability to outperform humans in complex reasoning—a milestone that foreshadows AI-powered decision-making in digital environments.

2001 – AI as a Virtual Assistant (Clippy & SmarterChild) Microsoft's Clippy and AIM's SmarterChild introduce early AI-driven assistance and chatbot interactions, shaping expectations for digital etiquette in human-AI communication.

2011 – IBM Watson Wins Jeopardy! Watson's success in understanding and responding to natural language questions signals a shift toward AI's role in customer service, knowledge assistance, and conversational AI.

2014 – AI in Social Media & Digital Engagement Facebook launches DeepFace, an AI-powered facial recognition system, contributing to personalized feeds and raising concerns about AI's role in digital privacy and ethics.

2016 – Tay: AI & Social Media Etiquette Microsoft's chatbot Tay is shut down within 24 hours after it learns and mimics inappropriate speech patterns from social media interactions, exposing the ethical risks of AI in digital conversations.

2017 – AI Moderation & Fake News Detection Social media platforms begin deploying AI to detect fake news, misinformation, and harmful content, shifting AI's role in maintaining online decorum.

2020 – The Rise of Conversational AI OpenAI releases GPT-3, revolutionizing human-like AI text generation, chatbots, and virtual assistants—reshaping digital communication, from email automation to AI-powered customer support.

2021 – AI in Virtual Meetings & Remote Work AI tools enhance virtual meetings, with features like real-time transcription, facial expression analysis, and automated moderation, influencing professional digital etiquette.

2022 – AI-Generated Art & Ethical Challenges Tools like DALL·E and Stable Diffusion raise debates about digital authorship, AI-assisted creativity, and the ethical responsibilities of AI users.

2023 – The Ethics of AI in Digital Spaces Lawsuits and public debates highlight concerns about AI-generated content, misinformation, and privacy, emphasizing the need for responsible AI etiquette.

2023 – Multimodal AI Integration GPT-4 and other advanced models introduce multimodal capabilities, enabling AI to process and generate both text and images, transforming how we interact with digital assistants.

2024 – AI Agents & Autonomous Decision-Making The rise of AI agents capable of executing complex tasks with minimal human supervision transforms digital workflows, raising new questions about accountability and supervision protocols.

2024 – Real-time AI Translation Bridges Global Communication AI-powered real-time translation becomes nearly seamless across major platforms, reducing language barriers in digital communication and establishing new norms for international etiquette.

2024 – Synthetic Media Detection New tools emerge to detect AI-generated content, creating a technological race between content creation and verification that reshapes trust in digital spaces.

2025 – Human-AI Collaboration Tools A new generation of professional tools designed specifically for human-AI collaboration emerges, establishing novel workflows and interaction patterns that blend human creativity with AI capabilities.

2025 – Personalized Digital Etiquette AI systems begin adapting communication styles and recommendations based on individual user preferences and cultural contexts, creating more nuanced digital interaction norms.

New Categories of AI Development

AI in Healthcare Communication (2021-2025) From patient intake chatbots to AI-powered diagnosis assistants, healthcare communication undergoes a transformation, requiring new protocols for sensitive information handling and medical discussions.

AI for Environmental Monitoring (2023-2025) AI systems track environmental changes, predict climate impacts, and coordinate sustainability efforts, creating new digital communities around environmental action and accountability.

AI in Democratic Processes (2024) AI tools emerge to facilitate civic engagement, summarize policy proposals, and detect political misinformation, introducing new considerations for digital citizenship and democratic participation.

Quantum-Enhanced AI (2024-2025) Early integration of quantum computing with AI algorithms begins to solve previously intractable problems, hinting at a future where quantum-AI integration becomes standard for complex applications.

Ethical AI Certification (2025) Industry-wide certification standards for ethical AI development and deployment emerge, creating clearer expectations for responsible AI creation and usage in digital spaces.

Appendix B

DIGITAL DECORUM TOOLKIT

Reflect and assess! Take a moment to audit your current AI interactions:

1. Map out all the AI tools currently integrated into your daily life.
2. Note which interactions feel natural and which feel awkward.
3. Identify areas where you could enhance digital grace.
4. Consider how your AI use affects others around you.
5. Are you verifying what you see online or what others share?

QUICK-START GUIDE

Begin implementing digital decorum today:

Morning Routine

- Thank your AI assistants when they wake you up.
- Acknowledge AI-curated news and weather reports.
- Practice mindful interaction with your smart home devices.
- Consider which tasks truly need AI assistance and which might benefit from a human touch

Professional Life

- Create clear AI disclosure statements for your work.
- Set up AI collaboration guidelines for your team.
- Develop templates for gracefully introducing AI tools in meetings.
- Design protocols for maintaining personal connection in AI-enhanced workflows.

Social Settings

- Craft thoughtful responses to "Did AI help with that?"
- Prepare graceful ways to accommodate varying comfort levels with AI.
- Plan strategies for maintaining authentic connections in AI-enhanced environments.
- Build bridges between tech-savvy and tech-hesitant friends.

DIGITAL DECORUM JOURNAL

Keep track of your journey:

Daily Prompts

- What AI interactions felt most natural today?
- How did I maintain human connection while using AI?
- How did I help others navigate AI interactions?
- What could I do differently tomorrow?

Weekly Reflection

- Which AI tools enhanced my human connections?
- Where did I find the right balance between efficiency and authenticity?
- How did I demonstrate digital grace in challenging situations?
- What new opportunities for growth did I discover?

RESOURCE LIBRARY: BUILD YOUR KNOWLEDGE

Essential Reading

- Latest AI etiquette guidelines
- Cultural perspectives on AI interaction
- Best practices for professional AI use
- Research on maintaining human connection in the digital age

Community Engagement

- Local AI interest groups
- Online forums for digital etiquette
- Professional networks focusing on ethical AI use
- Mentorship opportunities (both giving and receiving)

PERSONAL ACTION PLAN: CREATE YOUR PATH FORWARD

Immediate Steps

- Choose one AI interaction to enhance with greater grace.
- Identify a digital habit to refine.
- Select a person to share your learning with.
- Pick a new AI tool to explore mindfully.

Long-Term Goals

- Develop your unique style of digital grace.
- Build your reputation as an AI etiquette leader.
- Create positive ripples in your digital community.
- Contribute to the evolving conversation about AI and humanity.

EMERGENCY ETIQUETTE KIT

Quick solutions for everyday situations:

Graceful Recoveries

1. When AI tools fail during presentations:

- Acknowledge the issue calmly: "Technology hiccups happen to everyone."
- Have a backup plan ready: "Let me show you these key points another way."

- Turn it into a learning moment: "This illustrates why human oversight matters."

Follow up with corrected materials after the meeting.

2. When automated responses miss emotional cues:

- Pause and recognize the disconnect: "I see this requires a more nuanced approach."
- Shift to direct human communication immediately.
- Validate feelings: "Your concerns deserve thoughtful consideration."

Offer a personal follow-up conversation.

3. When AI assistance needs to be disclosed after the fact:

- Be transparent: "I should mention that I used AI to help draft these materials."
- Explain your process: "I generated initial ideas with AI, then carefully reviewed and personalized everything."
- Emphasize your judgment role: "The final decisions were mine based on my expertise."

Ask if they have questions about your workflow.

4. When digital and traditional expectations clash:

- Find common ground: "While our methods differ, our goals align."
- Demonstrate respect for both approaches: "Each method has its strengths."
- Suggest a blended approach when possible.

Focus on outcomes rather than processes.

BRIDGE-BUILDING PHRASES

1. For introducing new tools:

- "Let me show you how this works..."
- "This tool helps us by handling [specific task], freeing us to focus on [human strength]."
- "I've found this particularly useful for [specific scenario]."
- "What aspects would you find most valuable?"

2. For addressing concerns:

- "I understand your hesitation about [specific concern]."
- "That's a valid point about [limitation/risk]."
- "I've wondered about that too, and here's what I've learned..."
- "What specific assurances would help you feel more confident?"

3. For collaboration:

- "Shall we try this together to see how it fits our needs?"
- "How might we adapt this to serve your preferences better?"
- "What parts of this process would you like to maintain control over?"
- "Let's establish some guidelines that work for everyone."

4. For building comfort:

- "What would make you more comfortable with this approach?"
- "I'm open to adjusting how we use these tools."
- "Would it help to see how others have successfully integrated this?"
- "Let's start small and evaluate as we go."

QUICK RESPONSE TEMPLATES

1. When AI generates inaccurate information: "I need to correct something important. Upon verification, [provide accurate information]. Thank you for being so patient."
2. When privacy concerns arise: "I appreciate you raising this concern. Let me clarify our data practices and explore alternatives that better protect your privacy."
3. When the AI tone seems inappropriate: "I recognize the tone wasn't quite right there. Let me address this in a more [appropriate tone] manner."
4. When technological divides become apparent: "I see we might have different comfort levels with this technology. How can I make this more accessible for everyone?"
5. Remember: Digital decorum isn't about perfection—it's about progress. Use these tools to create your path forward, always keeping human connection at the heart of your AI interactions.

Note: This toolkit is meant to grow with you. Add your experiences, insights, and solutions as you continue your journey in digital grace.

Appendix C

PROFESSIONAL TEMPLATES FOR AI INTEGRATION

These templates should be customized to match your organization's voice, specific AI tools, and client relationships. Review and update quarterly to remain current with evolving technology and practices.

DISCLOSURE STATEMENTS

Research & Analysis Reports

Methodology Note

This [report/analysis/research] was developed using a combination of human expertise and AI assistance.

AI tools were used for [data analysis/pattern recognition/initial research], while all interpretations, conclusions, and recommendations reflect human judgment and professional expertise.

Creative Content

Creative Process Disclosure

This [content/piece/work] represents a collaboration between human creativity and AI assistance. AI tools supported [ideation/editing/refinement], while the core creative direction, voice, and final decisions were entirely human-driven.

BUSINESS COMMUNICATIONS

AI Enhancement Notice

This [document/proposal/plan] leverages AI tools for [specific purposes], ensuring accuracy and efficiency while maintaining the personal touch and professional judgment essential to our work.

Meeting Scripts

Opening AI Tool Introduction

"Before we begin, I'd like to note that we'll be using [AI tool] to [specific purpose]. This allows us to [benefit], while keeping our discussion focused on [key human elements].

Please feel free to ask questions about how we're using this technology."

Team Integration Announcement

"I'm excited to share that we're introducing [AI tool] to enhance our [specific process]. This tool will support our work by [specific benefits], allowing us to focus more on [creative/strategic/human] aspects of our projects. Let's discuss how best to integrate this tool while maintaining our team's collaborative spirit."

Client Communication

"We've enhanced our capability to serve you by thoughtfully integrating [AI tool] for [specific purpose]. This allows us to [benefit to the client] while maintaining the personal attention and expertise you've come to expect from us. Let me show you how this adds value to our partnership..."

COLLABORATION PROTOCOLS: AI TOOL USAGE GUIDELINES

General-purpose AI Assistant (e.g., ChatGPT, Claude)

When to Use:

- Initial research and background information gathering
- Brainstorming session preparation
- A first draft of routine communications
- Code documentation and commenting
- Proofreading and basic editing
- Translation of technical terms into plain language
- Meeting summary creation

- Process documentation
- Quick data analysis and pattern identification
- Creating structured outlines for complex projects

When Not to Use:

- Final decision-making on strategic matters
- Direct client communication without human review
- Sensitive personnel discussions or feedback
- Crisis communication or emergency responses
- Legal document creation or review
- Financial advice or recommendations
- Medical or health-related guidance
- Personal or confidential team matters
- Final versions of any public-facing content
- Critical safety procedures or protocols

AI Writing Tools (e.g., Grammarly, Hemingway)

When to Use:

- Checking document clarity and readability
- Grammar and spelling verification
- Tone consistency in team communications
- Style guide compliance checking
- Content formatting standardization
- Technical documentation review
- Email clarity enhancement
- Report polish and refinement
- Proposal readability check
- Marketing copy consistency

When Not to Use:

- Creative writing requiring a unique voice
- Highly technical or specialized terminology
- Confidential or sensitive communications

- Brand-critical messaging without review
- Legal or compliance documents
- Personal team messages or feedback
- Emergency communications
- Direct client responses
- Cultural or context-sensitive content
- Diplomatic or nuanced messaging

AI Image Generation Tools

When to Use:

- Initial concept visualization for internal discussion
- Published materials with proper attribution and disclosure
- Placeholder images for drafts and mockups
- Basic illustration needs for internal documents
- Background images for presentations
- Simple icons and symbols for documentation
- Storyboard creation for project planning
- Mood board development
- Quick visualization of design concepts
- Training material graphics
- Internal newsletter illustrations

When Not to Use:

- Final client deliverables without disclosure
- Brand identity elements
- Legal or official documentation
- Product photography
- Team member portraits or biographies
- Medical or technical illustrations
- Client-facing marketing materials without review
- Website hero images without proper rights
- Social media content without disclosure
- Security or identification-related imagery

BEST PRACTICES FOR ALL AI TOOLS

Quality Control Checklist

- Human review completed
- AI assistance disclosed where appropriate
- Personal touch added
- Team input incorporated
- Brand voice maintained
- Cultural sensitivity verified

Technical accuracy confirmed

- Legal compliance checked
- Privacy requirements met
- Ethical considerations addressed

Review Protocol

1. Initial AI Output Review

- Check for accuracy
- Verify data sources
- Confirm relevance
- Assess completeness

2. Human Enhancement

- Add expert insights
- Include team context
- Ensure brand alignment
- Verify tone appropriateness

3. Team Collaboration

- Share for peer review
- Gather feedback

- Implement improvements
- Document changes

4. Final Verification

- Complete quality checklist
- Confirm compliance
- Verify disclosures
- Approve for use

Training and Support

- Regular team updates on AI capabilities
- Monthly best practices sharing
- Quarterly tool evaluation
- Ongoing ethical use discussions

PROJECT DOCUMENTATION

Project Documentation Template

Project: [Name]

AI Integration Level: [Basic/Moderate/Extensive]

AI Tools Used:

1. [Tool Name]

Purpose:

Usage Scope:

Human Oversight:

2. [Tool Name]

Purpose:

Usage Scope:

Human Oversight:

Quality Assurance Process:

1. Initial AI Processing
2. Human Review & Enhancement
3. Team Collaboration
4. Final Verification

Disclosure Protocol:

[Specific guidelines for how and when to disclose AI use]

CLIENT COMMUNICATION TEMPLATES

Service Enhancement Notice

Subject: Enhancing Our Services with AI Integration

Dear [Client Name],

We're excited to share that we're enhancing our services by thoughtfully integrating AI technology to [specific benefit].

This advancement allows us to [specific improvement] while maintaining the personal attention and expertise you value.

What This Means for You:

[Benefit 1]

[Benefit 2]

[Benefit 3], etc.

Our Commitment:

- Maintaining personal attention
- Ensuring human oversight
- Delivering enhanced value
- Preserving confidentiality

We welcome your questions about these enhancements and look forward to showing you how they improve our service to you.

Best regards, [Name]

Project-Specific AI Disclosure

Project: [Name]

AI Integration Notice

To ensure transparency and maintain our commitment to quality, we want to share how AI tools support this project:

Areas of AI Assistance:

[Specific area]: [Description of AI use]

[Specific area]: [Description of AI use]

Human Elements:

[Specific area]: [Description of human input]

[Specific area]: [Description of human input], etc.

Quality Assurance: [Description of review process and oversight]

TROUBLESHOOTING SCRIPTS

Technical Issues

"We're experiencing a brief technical adjustment with our AI tool. While we resolve this, let's [alternative approach]. This demonstrates why we maintain robust non-AI processes alongside our enhanced capabilities."

Comfort Level Concerns

"I understand your [concern/hesitation] about AI use. Let me explain how we maintain human oversight and quality control. We can also explore adjusting our approach to better align with your comfort level."

Clarification Requests

"Thank you for asking about our AI integration. Let me explain how we use this technology to enhance our work while maintaining the personal touch and professional judgment you rely on."

Appendix D

···✦···

RESOURCES

As you explore and integrate AI tools into your career, knowing where to find quality resources and growth opportunities is essential. Here's your quick guide to finding the right resources for each stage of your development.

Academic Excellence

Look for university-affiliated programs that offer comprehensive AI curricula. The best programs typically feature the following:

- Structured learning paths that build from fundamentals to advanced concepts
- Hands-on projects using current industry tools
- Access to research papers and case studies
- Opportunities to collaborate with other learners
- Regular assessment and feedback mechanisms

Industry-Led Learning

Leading technology companies often provide educational resources that offer:

- Practical, tool-specific training
- Real-world application examples
- Industry certification paths
- Updated content reflecting current market needs
- Interactive learning environments

Professional Communities

Seek out these types of professional groups:

- Local AI and technology meetup groups
- Professional associations focusing on AI and machine learning
- Online communities centered around specific AI tools or applications
- Industry-specific AI interest groups
- Academic research groups open to practitioners

Hands-On Learning Platforms

Look for platforms that provide:

- Real-world problem-solving opportunities
- Collaborative project environments
- Competitive challenges with learning components
- Peer review and feedback systems
- Project showcasing opportunities

Knowledge Resources

Stay informed through:

- Peer-reviewed AI journals
- Industry analysis publications
- Technical blogs from leading AI researchers
- Conference proceedings
- Open-source project documentation

Professional Development Events

Seek out these types of gatherings:

- Industry conferences with hands-on workshops
- Professional development seminars
- Technical deep-dive sessions
- Cross-industry AI application showcases
- Networking events with focused learning components

As in any field of study, the best resources often combine multiple elements – theoretical knowledge, practical application, and community interaction. Look for opportunities that align with your learning style and professional goals while providing clear paths for progression.

MAKING THE MOST OF RESOURCES

To maximize the value of any learning resource:

- Set specific learning objectives before engaging
- Schedule regular time for learning and practice
- Document your progress and insights
- Share your learnings with others
- Apply new knowledge to real-world problems quickly
- Seek feedback on your understanding and application

Your resource needs will evolve as you progress in your AI journey. Start with foundational resources and gradually incorporate more specialized learning opportunities as your expertise grows. The key is to maintain a balance between structured learning, practical application, and community engagement.

Remember, the most valuable resources are those that you actively engage with and apply in your work. Choose resources that challenge you while providing clear paths to implementation, and always look for opportunities to share your learning with others.

www.ingramcontent.com/pod-product-compliance
Lightning Source LLC
LaVergne TN
LVHW052035200926
848481LV00005B/1682